W9-BDV-102

Your Complete Guide to

Green Card Lottery

(Diversity Visa)

Do-It-Yourself Immigration Books - Green Card

WITHDRAWN

2nd Edition

Schaumburg Township District Library
130 South Roselle Road
Schaumburg, IL 60193

342.083
FARO,M

3 1257 02394 3722

342.083
FARO,M

FIRST EDITION	SEPTEMBER 2010
SECOND EDITION	JULY 2011
Author	Michael Faro and Kevin M Walton
Cover Design	Qingsong Ju
Editor	Michael Journey and Carol Ketel
Indexing	Kevin M. Walton
Production	Lily Faro
Proofreader	Maryam Rowghani
Printing	Emily Johnson

Library of Congress Control Number: 2010937451

ISBN-13: 978-0984454303
ISBN-10: 0984454306

Copyright © 2011 by UNorth LLC.
ALL RIGHTS RESERVED. PRINTED IN THE U.S.A

No part of this publication may be reproduced, stored in a retrieval system, or transmitted in any form or by any means, electronic, mechanical, digitalized, photocopying, recording, or otherwise without prior written permission. requests to the publisher for permission should be addressed to: UNorth, LLC – Legal Department, PO Box 1116, Campbell, CA 95009 or via email at info@unorth.com

Quantity Sales: For information on bulk purchases or corporate premium sales, please contact the Special Sales Department at (888) 324-2787, via or website at http://www.greencard123.com or email info@greencard123.com , or write to PO Box 1116, Campbell, CA 95009

THE INFORMATION CONTAINED ON THIS PRODUCT IS DESIGNED TO PROVIDE ACCURATE INFORMATION WITH REGARD TO THE SUBJECT MATTER COVERED. IT IS OFFERED WITH THE UNDERSTANDING THAT THE PUBLISHER(S) IS(ARE) NOT ENGAGED IN RENDERING LEGAL, ACCOUNTING, OR OTHER PROFESSIONAL SERVICES. IF LEGAL ADVICE OR OTHER EXPERT ADVICE IS REQUIRED, THE SERVICES OF A COMPETENT PROFESSIONAL SHOULD BE SOUGHT.
(Adapted from a Declaration of Principles jointly adopted by a committee of the American Bar Association and a Committee of Publishers and Associations)

DISCLAIMER: THE PUBLISHER AND AUTHOR HAVE MADE REASONABLE EFFORTS TO VERIFY THE ACCURACY OF THE FACTS AND INFORMATION CONTAINED IN THIS WORK, BUT THEY MAKE NO REPRESENTATIONS OR WARRANTIES WITH RESPECT TO THE ACCURACY OR COMPLETENESS OF THE CONTENTS OF THIS WORK AND SPECIFICALLY DISCLAIM ALL WARRANTIES, INCLUDING WITHOUT LIMITATION WARRANTIES OF FITNESS FOR A PARTICULAR PURPOSE.

NO WARRANTY MAY BE CREATED OR EXTENDED BY SALES OR PROMOTIONAL MATERIALS. THE ADVICE AND STRATEGIES CONTAINED HEREIN MAY NOT BE SUITABLE FOR EVERY SITUATION. NEITHER THE PUBLISHER NOR THE AUTHOR SHALL BE LIABLE FOR DAMAGES ARISING HEREFROM.

THE FACT THAT AN ORGANIZATION OR WEBSITE IS REFERRED TO IN THIS BOOK AS A CITATION AND / OR A POTENTIAL SOURCE OF FURTHER INFORMATION DOES NOT MEAN THE AUTHOR OR PUBLISHER ENDORSES THE INFORMATION THE ORGANIZATION OR WEBSITE MAY PROVIDE OR RECOMMENDATIONS IT MAY MAKE. FURTHER, READERS SHOULD BE AWARE THAT INTERNET WEBSITES LISTED IN THIS WORK MAY HAVE CHANGED OR DISAPPEARED BETWEEN WHEN THIS WORK WAS WRITTEN AND WHEN IT IS READ.

ANY AND ALL FORWARD LOOKING STATEMENTS HERE OR ON ANY OF OUR SALES MATERIAL ARE INTENDED TO EXPRESS OUR OPINION OF THE PARTICULAR SUBJECT. MANY FACTORS WILL BE IMPORTANT IN DETERMINING THE RESULTS OF YOUR CASE AND NO GUARANTEES ARE MADE THAT YOU WILL ACHIEVE RESULTS SIMILAR TO THE INFORMATION PROVIDED IN THIS BOOK, EXAMPLES, IN FACT NO GUARANTEES ARE MADE THAT YOU WILL ACHIEVE ANY RESULTS FROM OUR IDEAS AND TECHNIQUES IN OUR MATERIAL.

Introduction

The 1960s-1990s saw an astronomical rise in the number of immigrants entering the United States and with it the United States Government encountered a considerable increase of immigrants of certain races and ethnicities compared to the rest of the population in the United States. Notable were immigrants from Mexico, Asia (China, Philippines, Vietnam, and India) and from South American countries such as Brazil.

The primary reason for this biased increase in ratio was a gap in the immigration laws of the United States which allowed permanent residents and citizens to request visas for their close relatives. For instance, a US citizen could request an immigrant visa for his/her parents, children, spouse, brother(s) and sister(s) and each one of these immigrants would in turn sponsor their own relative(s) and over time, the number of people from certain ethnicities grew significantly. Because America has been built on diversity, the government's focus has been to increase diversity among population and remove the visa 'monopoly 'by certain countries.

One solution has been a visa cap and quotas for certain countries.. In other words, if there are 50,000 Visas available for a certain category during a calendar year, the quota-holding-countries can consume only so many of these visas and the remaining will be available for all other countries without quota. This quota is still in place for China, Mexico, Philippines, and India.

The other solution was the introduction of the Diversity Visa program, also known as Visa Lottery or Green Card Lottery for the countries without a high number of immigrants (e.g. holders of quota and some other countries) to promote migration to the United States for those without a relative in the country. The bill was introduced in 1960 and finally in 1990 became effective into law.

Obviously such a law would receive strong opposition; the latest being in 2006, which called this visa program unfair and unjustified and discriminating to the excluded population. The opposition stems from the fact that the Diversity Visa requires minimum education requirement unlike other visas (e.g. high school Diploma compared to Bachelor, Master, or PhD in some visa categories) and thus the priority should be given to those with higher education or better financial resources.

In addition, due to September 2001 attacks on New York and the security implementations that followed across the world, there have been concerns that Diversity Visa recipients have higher probability of originating from perceived terrorist supporting countries, and thus the calls for the exclusion of certain countries from the program.

At this time, none of these restrictions have been placed.

Copyright © 2011 - GreenCard123.Com by UNorth® - All Rights Reserved

This book, will provide you with the most complete information about the Diversity Visa Lottery; from the very basic information in Chapter 1,'What is visa Lottery', to Chapter 7,'Getting Technical'. You can quickly go through each step of the process with full examples, sample forms, notes, and recommendations to benefit beginner to advanced readers, and even attorneys.

The Diversity Visa lottery is one of the visa categories that attracts a high number of fraudulent applications. Every year, millions of people get disqualified due to duplicate or falsified information in their applications. Thousands of agencies (although not all agencies) charge applicants and provide them with false hope that they could increase their chances in the Visa Lottery by paying a higher cost. Please be reminded that participation in the Diversity Visa Lottery involves absolutely no cost. In this book you'll be walked through a few simple steps showing how you can submit your own application at no cost.

This book unlike others is focused on providing sufficient information on the program in the shortest amount of time to get you going, or if interested use it as reference. The Book explains how to increase your chances in the Diversity Visa Lottery in a legal and mathematical way, how to be your own attorney, and full examples of how to perform each step. Whether you're a cautious person who likes to do everything right or a go-getter, or perhaps an attorney, this book can serve as a great reference for the Diversity Visa Lottery program.

Copyright © 2011 - GreenCard123.Com by UNorth® - All Rights Reserved

Table of Contents

Copyright © 2011 - GreenCard123.Com by UNorth® - All Rights Reserved

Copyright © 2011 - GreenCard123.Com by UNorth® - All Rights Reserved

Copyright © 2011 - GreenCard123.Com by UNorth® - All Rights Reserved

Copyright © 2011 - GreenCard123.Com by UNorth® - All Rights Reserved

1. LET'S GO TO THE UNITED STATES!

WHY GO TO UNITED STATES OF AMERICA?

The answer varies widely as every person has a different perspective and goal in life, some of which would become a reality in a nation like the United States. What appeals to most people's mind is that the United States is a free nation with numerous opportunities including education, money making, job, business, higher quality of life, investment, and many others things. All these are good, but as we all know, good things don't come easily. What is the price to pay? Would you be willing to sacrifice for these benefits above at the price of leaving your families and friends behind or work hard, long hours for little pay until you reach your goal?

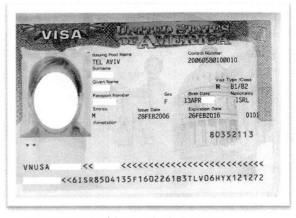

Figure 1-1 United States Visa in Passport

These are just some of the realities that face immigrants coming to the United States. Regardless of the reason, I'm sure you agree with me that we need a plan for any change in life and should consider advantages and disadvantages before making a decision. Here is our plan:

A. THE PLAN TO GO TO UNITED STATES:

Ok. We assume you have made up your mind up your mind, or you are just exploring the possibilities.. Whatever the reason, you want to know how. The short answer is-unless through the Green Card Lottery, if you want to go to US, you must have a valid reason proving that you will not overstay in the US.. You can't just go there without a reason. This reason can be, visiting your ill family member, studying, working, living with your fiancé, wife/husband, or a meeting, etc. For each of these 'valid' reasons, you need to complete certain requirements and steps so that you can open the gates one by one until you reach the golden gate. Don't get scared yet! You have plenty of opportunities to get scared later in the book!

One thing to keep in mind is that these steps are designed for ALL COUNTRIES, and all nationalities in the world. Whether you want to invite your fiancé from France or South Africa, or Canada, or China, the process is the same for everyone so don't think that they purposely made it hard for Iranians to get visa. No, it's hard for **EVERYONE**.

REAL FACTS

- Bribery is a NO NO in United States.
- Immigration is one place that you do not want to falsify your documents or lie in ANYWAY possible.
- If you don't get your visa this time, you can always try later. Of course, except if you don't listen to the recommendation above and get banned for years
- Don't just go and get any immigration attorney blindly and hope that you'll get a visa. (Read the section "Do I need an attorney?")

Once you have gone through the facts above and they all look okay to you, check the following list of visas. They are listed according to possible scenarios that you may or may not fall under. If you do fall under any of the visas above, you can read the corresponding chapter for more detailed instruction.

Copyright © 2011 - GreenCard123.Com by UNorth® - All Rights Reserved

B. WHAT IS A VISA?

Contrary to what most people think, a visa is permission for you to <u>request an entry</u> to United States of America at the border.

While the definition above is correct, normally by the time you get to the border with a valid Visa, you'll be permitted to enter United States. This is of course if you haven't disqualified yourself since the time the visa was issued (e.g. committing crime, etc.).

Foreign nationals from qualifying countries below do not need to go through the travel visa process (i.e. getting a visa prior to traveling to the US)*:

> Citizens of the Visa Waiver Program Countries* (VWP) Citizens of Canada or Bermuda Mexican and Canadian NAFTA Professional Workers *There are other options available for Mexican citizens.

USCIS Definition of Visa

A U.S. visa allows the bearer to apply for entry to the U.S. in a certain classification (e.g. student (F), visitor (B), temporary worker (H)). A visa does not grant the bearer the right to enter the United States. The Department of State (DOS) is responsible for visa adjudication at U.S. Embassies and Consulates outside of the U.S. The Department of Homeland Security (DHS), Bureau of Customs and Border Protection (BCBP) immigration inspectors determine admission into, length of stay and conditions of stay in, the U.S. at a port of entry. The information on a nonimmigrant visa only relates to when an individual may apply for entry into the U.S. DHS immigration inspectors will record the terms of your admission on your Arrival/Departure Record (I-94 white or I-94W green) and in your passport.

Resource: http://www.uscis.gov

Note: There are many different ways that an individual may enter United States on Temporary Visas which are not considered Migration. Don't confuse the term "Migration - Permanent Resident" with "Temporary Visa."

List of Visa Waiver Program Countries as of 2011:

Asia and Oceania	
• Brunei	• Singapore
• Japan	• Australia
• South Korea	• New Zealand

Europe	
• Andorra	• Liechtenstein
• Austria	• Lithuania
• Belgium	• Luxembourg
• Czech Republic	• Malta
• Denmark (inc. Greenland and Faroe Islands)	• Monaco
	• Netherlands (incl. Aruba and Netherlands Antilles)
• Estonia	
• Finland	• Norway
• France	• Portugal
• Germany	• San Marino
• Greece	• Slovakia
• Hungary	• Slovenia
• Iceland	• Spain
• Ireland	• Sweden
• Italy	• Switzerland
• Latvia	• United Kingdom (full British citizens only)

Table 1-1 List of Visa Waiver Programs as of 2011

C. VISA TYPES

There are two basic types of U.S. visas:

Non-immigrant Visas: For temporary visits such as studying, tourism, visiting family and friends, business, and work

Immigrant Visas: For persons interested to become permanent residents of the United States

Copyright © 2011 – GreenCard123.Com by UNorth® - All Rights Reserved

without any time limitation (e.g. can exit and re-enter United States repeatedly without needing to get permission again). An individual who possesses an Immigrant Visa is called "Lawful Permanent Resident" or commonly called a "Green Card Holder".

D. NON IMMIGRANT VISAS

As mentioned above, the only purpose of getting a non-immigrant visa is to visit the United States on a short-term, temporary basis. Unfortunately, there has been a considerable number of visitors overstaying the duration of their visa and/or use the non-immigrant visa as an easy way to enter the United States.

As a result, the presumption in law is that every non-immigrant visa applicant (except certain employment-based applicants) is an intending immigrant, unless otherwise proven!

Therefore, applicants for non-immigrant visas must overcome this presumption by demonstrating that they are not intending to migrate to the United States. This is primarily accomplished by providing:

- The purpose of the trip to the United States (e.g. business, pleasure, or medical treatment), and related documentation if applicable
- The travel plan (e.g. the time period, entrance and exit date, etc.)
- Establish a residency outside of the United States and other binding ties which would ensure their return to their country
- Establish financial independence, or employment
- Not having a previous history of overstaying visas or be inadmissible *(see to be Admissible or Not to be section below)*

E. NON-IMMIGRANT VISA CLASSIFICATION

Each visa in the USCIS system follows a Classification Code; a letter followed by a number. For example, a visitor visa is classified as B-1 or B-2 and student visa is classified as F-1 and F-2.

Copyright © 2011 - GreenCard123.Com by UNorth® - All Rights Reserved

	Visa Classification	Description	Publicly Available?
B Class	B-1	Temporary visitor for business	
	B-2	Temporary visitor for business and pleasure	YES
	BCC, BCV	Temporary visitor and Border Crossing Card and Mexican Lincoln	
C Class	C-1	Person in transit	
	C1/D	Combination transit/crew member	
	C2	Person in transit to United Nations Headquarters	NO
	C3	Foreign government official, immediate family, attendant, servant, or personal employee in transit	
E Class	E-1	Treaty trader, spouse and children	
	E-2	Treaty investor, spouse and children	
	E-3	Australian specialty occupation professional	YES
	E-3D	Spouse or child of Australian specialty occupation professional	
	E-3R	Returning Australian specialty occupation professional	
F Class	F-1	Student (academic or language training program)	
	F-2	Spouse or child of student	YES
	F-3	Border commuter academic or language student	
H Class	H-1A	Temporary worker performing services as a registered nurse	
	H-2B	Temporary worker of distinguished merit and ability performing services other than as a registered nurse	
	H-1B1	Free trade agreement professional	
	H-1C	Shortage area nurse	YES
	H-2A/B/R	Temporary worker performing agricultural services	
	H-3	Trainee	
	H-4	Spouse or child of H1A/B/B1/C, H2A/B/R, or H3	
J	J-1	Exchange Visitor	
	J-2	Spouse or child of exchange visitor	YES
K Class	K-1	Fiancé(e) of U.S. citizen	
	K-2	Child of K1	
	K-3	Certain spouse of U.S. citizen	YES
	K-4	Child of K3	
M Class	M-1	Vocational and other non-academic student	
	M-2	Spouse or child of vocational student	YES
	M-3	Border commuter vocational or non-academic student	
V Class	V-1	Certain Spouse of Legal Permanent Resident	
	V-2	Certain Child of Legal Permanent Resident	YES
	V-3	Child of V-1 or V-2	

Table 1-2 – List of Immigrant Visa Categories

Non Immigrant Visas below are available strictly to certain groups:

Copyright © 2011 – GreenCard123.Com by UNorth® – All Rights Reserved

	Visa Classification	Description	Publicly Available?
A Class	A-1	Ambassador, public minister, career diplomat, consul, and immediate family	
	A-2	Other foreign government official or employee, and immediate family	NO
	A-3	Attendant, servant, or personal employee of A1 and A2, and immediate family	
D	D-1	Crew member (sea or air)	NO
	D-CREW	Crew list visas	
G Class	G-1	Principal resident representative of recognized foreign member government to international organization, staff, and immediate family	
	G-2	Other representative of recognized foreign member government to international organization, and immediate family	
	G-3	Representative of non-recognized or nonmember foreign government to international organization, and immediate family	NO
	G-4	International organization officer or employee, and immediate family	
	G-5	Attendant, servant, or personal employee of G1 through G4, and immediate family	
I	I	Representative of foreign information media, spouse and children	YES
L Class	L-1	Intra-company transferee (executive, managerial, and specialized Personnel continuing employment with international firm or corporation)	YES
	L-2	Spouse or child of intra-company transferee	
N	N-8	Parent of SK3 special immigrant	NO
	N-9	Child of N8 or of SK1, SK2 or SK4 special immigrant	
NATO Class	NATO-1	Principal permanent representative of member state to NATO resident in the U.S., and resident members of official staff; principal NATO officers; and immediate family	
	NATO-2	Other representatives of member states to NATO	
	NATO-3	Official clerical staff accompanying a representative of member state to NATO	
	NATO-4	Officials of NATO	NO
	NATO-5	Experts, other than NATO4 officials, employed in missions on behalf of NATO, and their dependents	
	NATO-6	Members of a civilian component accompanying a force entering in accordance with the provisions of NATO agreements, and their dependents	
	NATO-7	Attendant, servant, or personal employee of NATO1 through NATO6, and immediate family	
O Class	O-1	Person with extraordinary ability in the sciences, arts, education, business, or athletics	
	O-2	Person accompanying and assisting in the artistic or athletic performance by O-1	YES
	O-3	Spouse or child of O-1 or O-2	
P Class	P-1	Internationally recognized athlete or member of an internationally recognized entertainment group	
	P-2	Artist or entertainer in a reciprocal exchange program	YES
	P-3	Artist or entertainer in a culturally unique program	
	P-4	Spouse or child of P1, P2, or P3	
Q	Q-1	Participant in an International Cultural Exchange Program	
	Q-2	Irish Peace Process trainee	YES
	Q-3	Spouse or child of Q2	

Copyright © 2011 - GreenCard123.Com by UNorth® - All Rights Reserved

R	R-1	Person in a religious occupation	NO
	R-2	Spouse or child of R1	
S Class	S-5 / S-6	Informant possessing critical reliable information concerning criminal organization or enterprise, terrorist organization, enterprise, or operation	NO
	S-7	Spouse, married or unmarried son or daughter, or parent of S5 or S6	
T Class	T-1,	Victim of a severe form of trafficking in persons	YES
	T-2 / T-3 / T-4	Spouse or Child or Parent of T-1	
	T-5	Unmarried sibling under 18 years of age on date T-1 applied	
TN/TD	TD	NAFTA professional	YES
	TN	Spouse or child of TN	
U	U-1	Victim of criminal activity	NO
	U-2/U-3/U-4	Spouse or Child or Parent of U-1	

Table 1-3 Non Immigrant Special Category Visas

F. IMMIGRANT VISAS

Immigrant visas are for those who intend to stay in the United States permanently, in other words migrate to the United States. In general, to be eligible to apply for an immigration visa and be issued a Green Card (Permanent Resident Card), you must fall into one of the following categories:
Family immigration
Employment Immigration (including investment)
Special immigration
Diversity Visa program immigration

The above four are the primary ways through which a foreigner can migrate to the United States of America. For family and employment visas, a foreign citizen must be sponsored by a relative(s) who is a U.S. Citizen, U.S. lawful permanent resident, or by a prospective employer, and be the beneficiary of an approved petition filed with USCIS and special immigration is for certain type of workers such as religious workers or certain interpreters.
If Petitioner is an Employer in the United States:

VISA CATEGORY	DESCRIPTION
E1	Priority workers
E2	Professionals with advanced degrees
E3*	Skilled workers and professionals
E3W*	Other workers
E4	Special immigrants

If Petitioner is a legal permanent resident:

VISA CATEGORY	DESCRIPTION
F2A*	Applicant is spouse and/or minor child of a legal permanent resident*
F2B*	Applicant is unmarried son or daughter of a legal permanent resident (21 years or older, single, widowed or divorced)*

If Petitioner is a US Citizen:

VISA CATEGORY	DESCRIPTION
IR1	Applicant is spouse of a U.S. citizen
IR2	Applicant is minor child of a U.S. citizen
CR1	Applicant is spouse of a U.S. citizen for less than two years

Copyright © 2011 - GreenCard123.Com by UNorth® - All Rights Reserved

CR2	Applicant is minor child of a U.S. citizen for less than two years
IR3	Applicant is orphan adopted abroad by a U.S. citizen
IR4	Applicant is orphan to be adopted in the United States by a U.S. citizen
IR5	Applicant is parent of a U.S. citizen
IW	Applicant is widow of a U.S. citizen who died less than two years ago and to whom the applicant was married at least two years
K1	Applicant is fiancée of a U.S. citizen who will travel to get married in the U.S
K3	Applicant is spouse of a U.S. citizen who has an immigrant visa petition filed but not yet approved
F1*	Applicant is unmarried son or daughter of a U.S. citizen (21 years or older, single, widowed or divorced)*
F3*	Applicant is married son or daughter of a U.S. citizen*
F4*	Applicant is brother or sister of a U.S. citizen*

Special categories:

VISA CATEGORY	DESCRIPTION
SB1	Applicant is former legal permanent resident who lost his/her residency for reasons beyond their control

Diversity Visa category

VISA CATEGORY	DESCRIPTION
DV	Diversity Visa Lottery that provides permanent residency through random drawing to all countries, except those that have had high number of immigrants in the past five years

Each of the Visa categories requires in-depth explanation of the process and thus does not fit in the subject of this book.

G. DO I NEED AN ATTORNEY?

The answer can be yes, no and maybe. Attorneys are usually helpful - no doubt; they will do the paperwork for you, and they tell you what to do, and they also may share some of their past experiences with you. They may have learnt from their previous mistakes. Yes, these are all good things, but first of all there are some rules of the thumb:

Specifically for the Diversity Visa Lottery, deciding whether or not to hire an attorney is more of a personal choice (with some exceptions for complex cases and type of visas which are discussed later). Most of the visa applications are designed and explained in plain English and they are easy to read and understand. At the same time, there may be some subjects not explained on the form. For example, "how much evidence is enough?" Take a look at the cases below for example:

> **Diversity Visa is by far the easiest way to get into the United States, especially if you do not have a sponsor in the United States (e.g. relative or spouse) to send a petition for you and this was the primary reason behind the creation of the Diversity Visa program in the first place (and to promote migrant diversity in the United States)**

Example: The United States provides for a fiancé visa for United States citizens. This type of visa requires you to submit evidence showing that you and your fiancé have met in-person and you intend to marry. You'll need to submit this evidence to USCIS as part of your initial petition. On the USICS form it explains in general that you'll need to submit evidence. Many will think that a picture or two will suffice. Don't be surprised when your application gets delayed or rejected due to lack of evidence. However, if you had an attorney do the homework for you, he/she would have asked you to bring other things beside a picture of you and your fiancé, such

Copyright © 2011 - GreenCard123.Com by UNorth® - All Rights Reserved

as copy of your phone bills, chats, emails, airline ticket, etc. This is basically where an attorney's previous experience would help you expedite your case. Of course, you could easily do the research yourself and figure these out; t depends on your time, flexibility, and diligence

If your immigration plans are important to you, it is worthwhile to have an experienced immigration attorney to guide you through the complex and always-changing process. An attorney (or at least consulting with one) will greatly improve your chances of success, and help you avoid obvious mistakes, and possibly save you tons of time that you would normally spend to research the requirements, etc.

Every immigration class has its own set of rules, regulations, and procedures. Many of them are complex and time-consuming. Especially after the September 11, 2001 incident, many cases are being scrutinized thoroughly and a small mistake that USCIS agent might have overlooked in the past would most likely trigger a problem (e.g. minor changes in the name, misspellings, etc.)

Beware of
- People, consultants, agencies, service bureaus, travel agents, other others who promise quick, easy solutions to immigration problems and try to convince you that an agent or consultant can be as effective as an attorney
- Anyone or any company who guarantees to get a visa for a certain fee
- Lawyers from other countries who are not familiar with US laws and are not licensed to practice in the US
- People who say they "Know Someone" who has a friend or relative inside the US Government or anyone who wants money to influence or bribe government personnel
- And of course, unlicensed operators. Pay special attention to this one as there have been many cases where unlicensed operators have sold clients' legitimate documents to other parties or

try to send people with bad records in your place.

No matter who recommended the attorney, do your own research. There are many fraudulent attorneys (mostly unlicensed); this is especially important for nationals from poorer countries who want to migrate.

If...	Then...
• You are filing within the United States	Attorneys and accredited representatives may communicate with USCIS on your behalf and receive information from USCIS regarding your application or petition.
• You are filing an application or petition at an office outside the United States	Attorneys and accredited representatives may communicate with USCIS on your behalf and receive information from USCIS regarding your application or petition. You may also be represented by an attorney admitted to the practice of law in the country where you file the application or petition. An attorney admitted to the practice of law in a country other than the United States must ask the USCIS official to permit him or her to represent you.
• You need legal advice about an immigration matter but cannot afford to hire an attorney	You may be able to ask an attorney, an association of immigration lawyers, a state bar association, or a specially-accredited organization about the availability of free or reduced-cost legal services on immigration issues.

1-4 Table – Determining Need for Attorney Source: USCIS.gov

Continue to Figure 1-2 for an example of attorney misconduct:

Copyright © 2011 - GreenCard123.Com by UNorth® - All Rights Reserved

Department of Justice Press Release
White spacer
For Immediate Release
March 22, 2010   United States Attorney's Office
Northern District of Georgia
Contact: (478) 752-3511
Attorney Sentenced to Federal Prison for Filing False Immigration Documents
Lawyer Must Also Forfeit Fees Obtained for Assisting Clients in Committing Fraud

ATLANTA, GA—SAI HYUN LEE, 63, of Duluth, Georgia, was sentenced today by United States District Judge Thomas W. Thrash, Jr., to federal prison on charges of filing false documents with the United States Department of Labor and with Citizenship and Immigration Services, in an effort to assist clients in obtaining legal status in the United States by fraudulent means.

"The investigation established that on 17 occasions, SAI HYUN LEE filed false documents to help clients fraudulently obtain lawful status through their employment," said United States Attorney Sally Quillian Yates. "We expect lawyers to uphold and defend the rule of law, not assist clients in breaking the law. As part of her plea agreement, LEE has given up her license to practice law in the state of Georgia and $100,000 which represents the fees LEE charged for assisting her clients to commit immigration fraud. Not only is LEE going to federal prison for her crimes, but she has lost both her ability to practice law and the profits she made from the fraud."

"Quite simply, America's immigration system is not for sale," said Kenneth Smith, Special Agent in Charge of U.S. Immigration and Customs Enforcement's Office of Investigations in Atlanta. "The ICE Document and Benefit Fraud Task Force is working closely with its member agencies, to include the U.S. Department of Labor, Office of the Inspector General, the U.S. Department of State and U.S. Citizenship and Immigration Services, as well as other agencies to ensure that those who seek to enrich themselves by compromising the integrity of our nation's legal immigration system pay a price for their crimes."

LEE was sentenced to one year and one day in prison to be followed by two years of supervised release. LEE was also required to forfeit $100,000, which represents the attorney's fees that she generated through the fraud scheme. LEE pleaded guilty to the charge on November 18, 2009.

According to United States Attorney Yates, the charges and other information presented in court: Employers who can demonstrate a particular need for a foreign worker may apply to the United States Department of Labor for a labor certification for the foreign worker. Once the employer obtains a labor certification, the employer may apply for an immigrant visa and adjustment of status for the foreign worker. After the approval of the visa application and change of status, the foreign worker is afforded the benefit of lawful permanent residence in the United States and is expected to begin working for the employer who petitioned to bring the worker to the United States.

LEE, who was licensed to practice law in Georgia, charged one client who was an alien without lawful status in the United States $25,000 to substitute the client on an approved labor certificate that had been issued to an employer but for a different foreign worker. LEE then assisted her client in using the labor certificate to apply for Lawful Resident Status in the United States with knowledge that the client did not work for the employer and did not intend to work for the employer to which the labor certificate was issued, as is required by federal law. Based upon the fraudulent application, the client did obtain legal status as a Lawful Resident Alien. LEE's client never worked for the employer and the employer was not aware that LEE used the labor certificate to assist her client in obtaining legal status.

The investigation established that LEE assisted at least 16 other aliens in the same way. In some instances, aliens who hired LEE to help them obtain legal status did not know they were supposed to be working for a particular employer when they became legal resident aliens. In many instances, the employers did not know that LEE used labor certificates issued to them to assist her clients in obtaining lawful status through fraud.

This case was investigated by the Immigration and Customs Enforcement (ICE) Document Benefit Fraud Task Force made up of Special Agents with ICE, the United States Department of Labor-Office of the Inspector General, the FBI, and the United States Postal Inspection Service and Fraud Detection/National Security Officers of the United States Citizenship and Immigration Services.

Assistant United States Attorneys William L. McKinnon, Jr., Susan Coppedge and Mary Kruger prosecuted the case.
For further information please contact Sally Q. Yates, United States Attorney, or Charysse L. Alexander, Executive Assistant United States Attorney, through Patrick Crosby, Public Affairs Officer, U.S. Attorney's Office, at (404) 581-6016.

Figure 1-2 Sample Attorney Misconduct Case

Copyright © 2011 - GreenCard123.Com by UNorth® - All Rights Reserved

As you can see this was a famous attorney; just because one is advertising in the newspapers and on television does not necessarily mean he/she is a good attorney. If you're still unsure if an attorney can help you or not, see the table below:

What Can Immigration Lawyers do for you?
• Explain different options that you may have and recommend the best one for you
• Analyze your case, documents, and current status
• Complete and submit your application properly (sometimes they mess it up
• Catch obvious errors that maybe a big deal to the immigration officer but you may overlook easily
• Avoid certain delays for obvious mistakes (e.g. writing your brother's name in place of your wife's...)
• Discuss the status of the case and keep you updated
• Promptly act on your behalf at USCIS, embassy consulate, and/or represent you in court
• File necessary appeals and waivers
• Use the current laws, benefits, and regulations to your advantage

Again, unless you have some extraordinary immigration case that makes you otherwise ineligible to enter United States, the answer would be probably not. The Visa Lottery process is basically divided into two parts.

Part I involves submitting your application directly to USCIS or Consulate for the purpose of participating in the Visa Lottery program. This part does not require an attorney or agent, and can be done in a few easy steps that are provided in detail in this book.

Part II includes the steps after you're notified that your application is selected (i.e. you won the lottery). For this step, you may want to consult an attorney prior to visiting a US Consulate to make sure your documents are in order and if not find out the best thing to do. Most of the information an attorney can provide to you, along with examples of common scenarios are provided in this book, however.

H. UNITED STATES IMMIGRATION STRUCTURE

Although you might have heard that "US Immigration" or "Embassy" is in charge of immigration, behind the scenes, various government organizations are involved in the visa lifecycle to insure that the appropriate "checks and balances" are in place and at the same time everyone has a separate responsibility. As you read the book some common immigration related organizations in the United States are mentioned quite frequently. Although there is a glossary at the end of the book, some of the important ones are defined here in more detail:

USCIS: United States Citizenship and Immigration Service

- Previously known as INS (Immigration and Naturalization Service) U.S. Citizenship and Immigration Services (USCIS) is the government agency that oversees lawful immigration to the United States. USCIS owns and operates Service Centers around the United States and possesses certain responsibilities in the immigration process such as Green Cards, employment authorization, asylum and refugee status, citizenship, and Diversity Visa Lottery drawing. For example, in respect to the Diversity Visa Lottery, the Kentucky Service Center is in charge of receiving the DV applications, processing, selection and notification of the applicants.

TSA: Transportation Security Administration

- TSA is responsible for various tasks related to Transportation Security such as airport security, screening, etc.

CBP: Customs and Border Protection

Copyright © 2011 - GreenCard123.Com by UNorth® - All Rights Reserved

- CBP is a component of the Department of Homeland Security's largest and one of the most complex with a priority mission of keeping terrorists and their weapons out of the U.S. When you enter the United States, you'll need to go through the CBP officers who check to make sure your documents are legitimate, you're who you're claiming to be and other related tasks. CBP has the power to refuse your entry into the United States if they believe that you're otherwise inadmissible (even if you have been issued a visa and interview, etc.)

  CBP performs two crucial roles in facilitating trade to and from the US and around the globe: securing it from acts of terrorism and ensuring that goods arriving in the US are legitimate and that appropriate duties and fees are paid. Last year, CBP safely welcomed more than 300 million people into the US continuing America's tradition of being a welcoming country while also preventing dangerous individuals from entering.

ICE: Immigration and Customs Enforcement

- ICE's mission is to enforce the immigration and custom processes such as deportation, and removal proceedings; prosecuting removal court cases; handling Board of Immigration Appeal cases; providing litigation support to U.S. Attorney offices; assisting with removal order reinstatements, administrative removal orders, and expedited removals; reviewing legislative and regulatory proposals; providing legal training and ethics guidance to all ICE personnel; and representing ICE in court and administrative proceedings.

NVC: National Visa Center

- The NVC is a sub-division of the Department of State that processes all approved immigrant visa petitions after they are received from Citizenship and Immigration Services in the Department of Homeland Security (CIS) and retains them until the cases are ready for adjudication by a consular officer abroad.

  The NVC is responsible for the collection of visa application fees and visa application documentation. When an applicant's priority date meets the most recent qualifying date, the NVC will contact the applicant and petitioner with instructions for submitting the appropriate processing fees. After the appropriate processing fees are paid, the NVC will again contact the applicant and petitioner to request that the necessary immigrant visa documentation be submitted to the NVC.

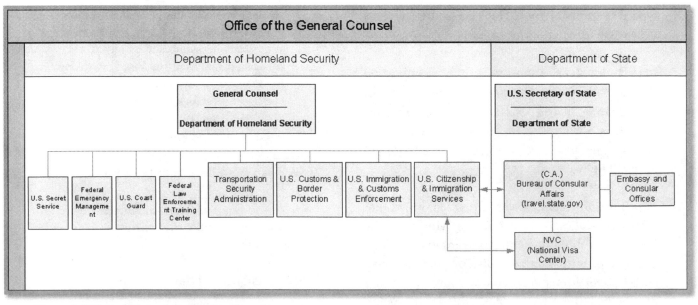

Figure 1-3 United States Immigration Structure

Copyright © 2011 - GreenCard123.Com by UNorth® - All Rights Reserved

Department of State (Travel):

- One of the responsibilities of the Department of State is to administer the US Consulates around the world. If you're applying from outside of United States, this is one place that you'll have your interview at. The Department of State is the only department that does the actual visa issuance (e.g. visa stamp on your passport).

- It also issues the travel documents that allow Americans to travel the globe and lawful immigrants and visitors to travel to America and provides essential cycle of life services to American citizens overseas.

I. GREEN CARD

A Legal Permanent Resident (or LPR, or Lawful Permanent Resident, a Green Card holder, Resident Alien) has certain benefits and privileges' that others who don't have the Green Card don't have. At the minimum you can visit the United States as often as you want.

A **United States Permanent Resident Card** (also known as Resident Alien Card), known informally as a **Green Card** (due to the color of earlier versions of the card), is an identification card attesting to the Permanent Resident of the United States status The Green Card serves as proof that its holder has been officially granted immigration benefits, which include permission to reside and take employment in the US. The holder must maintain permanent resident status, and can be removed from the United States if certain conditions of this status are not met.

Other benefits of a Permanent Resident include:

- Ability to enter and exit the United States as often as you wish. You're no longer considered a visa holder and don't need to get permission from the Embassy or Point of Entry (border) every time you enter the United States

- Permission to work in the United States
- Can sponsor spouse and family to United States
- Receive Social Security benefits (upon retirement)
- Paying resident fee rates for schools, colleges, and universities.
- Eligible for Educational Financial Aid
- And eligible to apply for United States Citizenship after five years
- Enjoy same rights as a citizen (with a few exceptions) You may legally own property and firearms
- Other tax benefits that only Green Card Holders and US Citizens can take advantage of

Who Issues Green Cards?

Green Cards were formerly issued by the Immigration and Naturalization Service (INS). During a re-organization process, that agency was merged with other departments and replaced by the Bureau of Citizenship and Immigration Services (BCIS), part of the Department of Homeland Security (DHS). Shortly after that re-organization, BCIS was renamed the U.S. Citizenship and Immigration Services (USCIS), which still retains the responsibility of issuing Green Cards.

An alien with a Green Card application can obtain two important permits while the case is pending after a certain stage is passed in Green Card processing (filing of I-485). The first is a temporary work permit known as the Employment Authorization Document (EAD), which allows the alien to take employment in the United States. The second is a temporary travel document, advance parole, which allows the alien to re-enter the United States. Both permits confer benefits that are independent of any existing status granted to the alien.

Copyright © 2011 - GreenCard123.Com by UNorth® - All Rights Reserved

- Figure 1-4 United States Permanent Resident Card

J. GREEN CARD EXPIRATION

Your Green Card normally expires in 10 years and you will need to renew your card. This does not mean that you have to go through the whole process of applying for it again. You just need to inform USCIS that you would like to renew your permanent resident status.

As a Green Card, holder you are assumed to be staying in the United States majority of your time. If you stay outside of the United States for a long time, you may lose your permanent residency privileges and you will need to go through the whole application process again.

Note: If your intention is to visit the United States on a short-term basis, don't bother going through the green card process. The purpose of becoming a Permanent Resident is to have your place of residence in the United States.

K. ABANDONMENT OR LOSS OF PERMANENT RESIDENT STATUS

Voluntarily Abandonment: A Green Card holder may abandon permanent residence by filing appropriate forms and filing at a US Embassy or Consulate.

Involuntarily Abandonment: Under certain conditions, permanent residence status can be lost involuntarily. This includes:

- Committing a criminal act that makes a person removable from the United States
- A person might also be found to have abandoned their status if he or she moves to another country to live there permanently, stays outside the USA for more than 365 days (without getting a re-entry permit before leaving) does not file an income tax return
- Status can also be lost if it is found that the application or grounds for obtaining permanent residence was fraudulent

A person who loses permanent residence status is immediately removable from the United States and must leave the country as soon as possible or face deportation and removal. In some cases the person may be banned from entering the country for three or seven years, or even permanently.

L. SEPTEMBER 11, 2011 AND RESULTANT CHANGES

After the unfortunate incident of September 11, there have been certain security-related changes by the Government of the United States. Obviously such changes act as a double-edge sword in sense that although they increase security and protection of the United States they also cause additional delays or frustration in the immigration process. In some way, these changes

Copyright © 2011 - GreenCard123.Com by UNorth® - All Rights Reserved

have limited or restricted certain processes and procedures and in others have delayed the normal process since additional screening became a requirement. Below are examples of the recent changes in the immigration system:

Special Registration Requirement: Recently, special rules have been implemented for nationals of designated countries. Effective September 11, 2002, certain non-immigrant foreigners traveling to or residing in the United States will be required to comply with extensive new registration requirements such as fingerprinting, interviews at INS offices, special rules regarding departure from the U.S. and special rules regarding filing the change of address card (AR-11). These special rules apply to all non-immigrant males aged 16 years or older who are currently in the United States, were last admitted to the United States before 9/10/02 and plan to remain past December 16, 2002.

The special registration rules currently apply to nationals or citizens of Iran, Iraq, Libya, Sudan or Syria*. These individuals must report to an immigration officer at one of several designated locations and they must do so before December 16, 2002. At this time, they will be required to provide documentation, answer questions from INS, be photographed and fingerprinted and then follow-up with other registration requirements.

*Attorney General of the United States may add or remove countries from the list. Check USCIS.gov website for latest list of special registration rules.

Security Clearance / Background Check Requirement: The Enhanced Border Security and Visa Entry Reform Act of 2002 bars the issuance of non-immigrant visas to nationals of seven countries, unless it is deemed that the person does not pose a security threat. This particular list includes: Cuba, Iran, Iraq, Libya, North Korea, Sudan and Syria. Nationals of these countries must interview with a consular office before a visa will be issued.

Department of Homeland Security: As explained previously, the old Immigration and Naturalization Service (INS) was absorbed into the Department of Homeland Security (DHS) which by itself has many different sections. The responsibilities and duties of the INS is replaced by the following organizations:

- USCIS (United States Citizenship and Naturalization Service)
- ICE (Immigration and Customs Enforcement)
- CBP (Customs and Border Protection)

Diversity Visa Records keeping: It is known that Kentucky Service Center has begun to keep records of all applicants from prior years. This would be a security measure to identify if list of people who pose a security threat to the United States match of those that apply lottery. It also lengthens the fraudulent application and duplicate record check of applicants.

Note: *Diversity Visa winners may also face additional delays during the background check process if applicant is from a sponsor-of-terrorism designated country.*

As of the time of writing this Book, President Barack Obama, Congress, and Senate are working closely on a Bill to make certain changes in the immigration procedure. The focus is on illegal immigrants, border and customs protection and increase in security of the United States.

M. TO BE ADMISSIBLE OR NOT TO BE

No matter the type of visa that you're applying, the United States maintains strict standard on who can enter and who cannot. The US

Copyright © 2011 - GreenCard123.Com by UNorth® - All Rights Reserved

Government may restrict entrance of individuals due to:

- **Health related grounds:** Lack of required vaccination or suffering any communicable diseases of public health significance such as tuberculosis, cancroids, leprosy, or any other communicable disease as determined by the US Secretary of Health and Human Services *
- **Criminal and related violations:** Members of criminal organizations, families and relatives of the criminal organizations, a Person who is involved in moral turpitude
- **Security related violations:** Persons who poses a security risk to the United States (e.g. terrorists and relatives). Members of Communist party or other totalitarian parties, Nazis, spies, etc.
- **Illegal immigrants:** Persons who enter United States without being admitted legally or those who overstay a valid visa. Persons who willfully and knowingly made misrepresentations or committed immigration fraud in order to obtain immigration benefit (e.g. visa).
- **Miscellaneous grounds:** Such as practicing Polygamy, international child abductors and their relatives, and other fraudulent activities against the US Government.

* For Latest and complete list of inadmissibility grounds, visit USCIS.gov

In your Visa form, you need to specifically check each item of inadmissibility and confirm that whether or not those would apply to you. Among the list of inadmissibility grounds, some of the inadmissibility grounds are appealable, ("Waiver of Inadmissibility"). If your situation falls under any of the inadmissibility grounds above, consult an attorney prior to filing your case.

N. IMMIGRATION AND CHANGES IN LAW

The immigration laws of the United States change quite frequently. Although the main framework of the law remains the same, the new addition or modifications of the law are unavoidable. Attorneys generally check USCIS website on a daily basis to be up to date on the latest changes, forms, and modifications.

Copyright © 2011 - GreenCard123.Com by UNorth® - All Rights Reserved

2. WHAT IS THE VISA LOTTERY?

Visa Lottery Alert!

Did you know over 2million Lottery applications were rejected last year due to incorrect data entry or duplicate submission?

Fiction: You can increase your chances in Lottery by submitting your application more than once
Fact: Duplicate submission of your application can only hurt your chance and in fact can eliminate you from the lottery program entirely. There are, however, other ways to legally increase your chances for the lottery. Read on!

A. VISA LOTTERY PROGRAM

The US Green Card Lottery program, is a Congress-mandated Lottery Program to provide 50,000 United States Permanent Resident Cards to the winners of the lottery each year. The primary purpose of this program is to promote diversity in the United States and thus certain countries are not eligible to participate in the lottery program. In addition, unlike most other US Visas, the lottery program visa requires sets minimum application requirements for education and country of origin.

To further promote the diversity and number of applicants, participation in the Visa Lottery is totally FREE. The winners of lottery, subject to certain conditions, will be issued a permanent resident card for the applicant, spouse, and unmarried children under age of 21 and upon issuance of the card are considered "Permanent Residents." Permanent residents get all the benefits of a United States Citizen, except voting*. A Permanent Resident may optionally apply for United States Citizenship after five years. The Diversity Program is known to be the easiest way to become a United States Permanent Resident.

Since the 2005 Lottery program, the entire application process is performed online only and upon submission a computer generated, random lottery drawing chooses selectees for the Diversity Visa Lottery. Interestingly, the number of winning applicants that are randomly selected is approximately 100,000 (double the number of actual visas available); the assumption is that by the time the Visa is actually issued many of the winners may change their mind or will not have the necessary documentations or their documentation would not be ready by the visa issuance deadline.

US Citizen or Permanent Resident?

In addition to voting rights, there are certain other limitations for Permanent Residents such as working for the government, becoming a president, and higher visa quota for relatives. A Permanent Resident privileges may also be revoked if the holder commits a felony and is ordered to depart United States by the Immigration court or if the holder is no longer interested to be a "resident" in of the United States.

B. LEGAL BACKGROUND

The lottery program is administered on an annual basis by the U.S. Department of State and conducted under the terms of Section 203(c) of the Immigration and Nationality Act (INA), Section 131 of the Immigration Act of 1990 (Pub. L. 101-649) amended INA 203 to provide for a new class of immigrants known as "diversity immigrants" (DV immigrants). The Act makes available 50,000 permanent resident visas annually to persons from countries with low rates of immigration to the United States. [*See Appendix – Getting Technical*]

Those born in any territory that sent more than 50,000 immigrants to the United States in the

Copyright © 2011 - GreenCard123.Com by UNorth® - All Rights Reserved

previous five years are not eligible to receive a diversity visa.

The term 50,000 "immigrants" is partial and refers only to people who immigrated via the family-sponsored, employment, or immediate relatives of U.S. citizen categories, and does not include other categories such as refugees, asylum seekers, , or previous diversity immigrants. It is for this reason that Cuba, Ukraine, Iran, Ethiopia, Bangladesh, Nigeria, Russia and Venezuela are not on the ineligible list despite sending over 50,000 immigrants in the previous five years.

C. ELIGIBILITY

As mentioned above, there are only a few requirements that an applicant must have in order to apply for the Visa Lottery. First, you need to have been born in an eligible country, and second, you must possess a minimum high school diploma or two years work experience in a specialized field.

As of the date of writing this book, natives of the following countries are not eligible to apply because the countries sent a total of more than 50,000 immigrants to the United States in the previous five years:

BRAZIL, CANADA, CHINA (mainland-born), COLOMBIA, DOMINICAN REPUBLIC, ECUADOR, EL SALVADOR, GUATEMALA, HAITI, INDIA, JAMAICA, MEXICO, PAKISTAN, PERU, PHILIPPINES, POLAND, SOUTH KOREA, UNITED KINGDOM (except Northern Ireland) and its dependent territories, and VIETNAM. *

*(Persons born in Hong Kong SAR, Macau SAR, and Taiwan are eligible.)

USCIS may change this list every year.

Exception: If you're born in one of the countries above but one of your parents or your spouse is born in an eligible country, you may still apply for the Diversity Visa Lottery.

D. PROS AND CONS OF THE VISA LOTTERY

There are, of course, both advantages and disadvantages of using the Diversity Visa Lottery. Table below summarizes the important Pros and Cons of this type of visa:

Advantage	Disadvantage
• Free to apply	• Does not guarantee you will get the card
• No attorney or agent or third-party company is needed	• It takes months to know the status of your application
• It is issued for the whole family (applicant, spouse, and children under 21 years of old at the time of applying)	• Short Deadline: Even if you win the lottery, if you don't respond quickly, you may miss the deadline and miss your chance
• Has the minimum requirement to apply (Education of high school diploma for the applicant or 2 years experience)	• Low chance of getting it (although this maybe an advantage if you don't have any other choice)
• No minimum age to apply (but you need high school diploma or 2 years experience as described above)	• Even if you win the lottery, and you don't apply soon, there is a chance that visas would run out before yours is given out
•	

Table 2-1 Pros Cons of Visa Lottery

E. REGISTRATION

There is a strict time frame to apply for Diversity Visa. It starts in October every year and stays open until November. Since the visa application

Copyright © 2011 - GreenCard123.Com by UNorth® - All Rights Reserved

is entirely online, once the deadline is reached, the application will not be available.

The Department utilizes special technology and other means to identify those who commit fraud for the purposes of illegal immigration or those who submit multiple entries.

F. WINNING

A computer-generated, random lottery drawing chooses selectees for the Diversity Visa. The visas are distributed over six geographic regions, with a greater number of visas going to regions with lowest rates of immigration. Within each region, no single country may receive more than seven percent of the available Diversity Visas in any one year.

G. REQUIREMENTS

Besides the qualification needed for country of origin, you must also possess a high school diploma or two years work experience in a qualified job.

H. APPROXIMATE CHANCES OF WINNING

There are 55,000 visas available out of these 55,000 visas, 5000 visas are specifically for Nicaragua and parts of South America. That leaves 50,000 visas for the rest of the world. Through some sort of internal systems, USCIS will determine which region will get how many of the visas and how many are available for which country. These allocations change every year due to immigration visa availability and number of applicants and winners.. At any point, none of the countries can receive more than 7% of the total.

Option	Probability
• Average Chance of Winning a Single Person Worldwide	1% (1 in 100)
• If You and Spouse apply	2% (1 in 50)
• A Child under 21 years old applies separately, and the parents also apply for her on their own application	3% (1 in 33)

Table 2-2 Winning Probability

That being the case, considering you apply every year, this would be the probability of you winning the Lottery:

Apply Consecutively	Winning Probability
• You Apply Alone - 1st Year	1%
• You Apply Alone – 2nd Year	2%
• You Apply Alone – 3rd Year	3%
• You Apply Alone – 4th Year	4%
• You Apply Alone – 5th Year	5%
• You and Your Spouse Apply (Separate Application) – 1st Year	2%
• You and Your Spouse Apply (Separate Application) – 2nd Year	4%
• You and Your Spouse Apply (Separate Application) – 3rd Year	6%
• You and Your Spouse Apply (Separate Application) – 4th Year	8%
• You and Your Spouse Apply (Separate Application) – 5th Year	10%
• If your application is submitted twice (e.g. you wanted to increase your chance of winning)	0%

Table 2-3 Winning Probability

Copyright © 2011 - GreenCard123.Com by UNorth® - All Rights Reserved

Based on the graph above, we can conclude two things:

- The probability of winning almost doubles if you and your spouse (if available) file separate applications
- The more you apply the better chance of winning the lottery. As you can see in the chart, if you apply for 5 years consecutively, you can increase your chances by almost 1 out of 20.
- If you supply incorrect data or multiple applications, you automatically get disqualified

The Average number of Visas issued since 1999 are provided below:

Year	Number of Visas Issued
1999	47,535
2000	50,920
2001	41,989
2002	42,820
2003	46,335
2004	50,084
2005	46,234
2006	44,471
2007	42,127
2008	41,761

Table 2-4 Average Number Visa Issued

Approximately 10 million people apply every year to Diversity Visa Lottery. Out of these applicants, about 3-5 million are disqualified every year and that counts about 30-50% of the applicants.

On average, about 84,000 applicants were selected in the random drawing since 1999 and about half of that them were issued a visa. If you're wondering why one would waste his/her chance of getting the visa once he/she is selected from more than 10 million applicants, here are some reasons that an applicant may be taken out of the final Visa list:

- Incorrect information was submitted in the lottery application (e.g. your application is selected but name or address is incorrect and you never get to know since you cannot won't check your status on the internet)
-
- Duplicate Submission (Application form was submitted more than once per DV year and application is denied)
- Change of Mind (no longer interested to migrate to the United states) or Death of the primary applicant
- Not Qualified (e.g. does not possess high school degree or two years work experience, or is not from eligible country but applied anyways)
- Applicant is Inadmissible: There are certain rules that grounds for inadmissibility to the United States (such as criminal background, illegal/excessive overstaying in the US, previous deportation, etc.). Even if the individual is selected as a winner in the lottery, as long as he/she is inadmissible, they cannot enter United States.

I. DATES AND DEADLINES

Over 13.6 million applications for the 2008 Diversity Visa Lottery (DV-2010) were submitted — an increase of 4.5 million, or 50%, from the 9.1 million applications submitted in the 2007 Diversity Visa Lottery (DV-2009).[6]

Starting with the DV-2008, several questions and options for answers have been added. Applicants are now required to provide information, such as the country where they currently live and their highest level of education achieved, in the Electronic Diversity Visa Entry Form (E-DV Entry Form).

Copyright © 2011 - GreenCard123.Com by UNorth® - All Rights Reserved

Region	Applicants (%)	Applicants (approximate)	Winners	Winning chance (estimate)
• Africa	41%	2,624,000	52,824	2.01%
• Asia	38%	2,432,000	14,142	0.58%
• Europe	19%	1,216,000	26,149	2.15%
• North America			17	
• Oceania			1,713	
• South and Central America and the Caribbean	2%	128,000	1,845	1.44%
Total	**100%**	**6,400,000**	**96,690**	**1.51%**

Table 2-5 Diversity Visa Application Statistics 2007

J. FRAUD: BEWARE

As discussed in Appendix VII there is no charge for the Diversity Visa Lottery application. In other words, if anyone is soliciting a fee to perform the registration for the Diversity Visa Lottery, the fee is not collected by the USCIS at all. More information is provided in Chapter 3 - Registering for Visa Lottery.

With this in mind, and considering the large number of applicants, close to 13million every year, registration service for the visa lottery presents a great business for many individuals or businesses. The service charges a fee to register for the visa lottery that is otherwise free. Although there are many legitimate businesses that perform this service, unfortunately there have been large numbers of misconduct by various businesses and this makes the selection very difficult. If an individual elects to use an agent instead of self-registration, he/she must perform a very careful research on the agency. Also keep in mind that even though you are hiring an agent to file your application, in the eyes of USCIS, you are applying for your application and you're ultimately responsible for any falsifying information.

Example: John would like to register for Diversity Visa application and he finds and offer to have an agent perform the registration for $50 with promise of increasing his chance of winning. Without any research on the business, John decides to have the business file the registration for him. The business submits John's application multiple times with slight changes in address to increase his chance of winning. Once USCIS receives the application, it automatically flags John's application as fraudulent and he is disqualified, but he thinking that he is indeed in the random selection. USCIS may even disqualify him from participating in the future.

The most important note about having an agent to perform the registration for you is to keep in mind that

A) It is absolutely impossible to increase someone's chance and

B) There is no Lottery registration agent or company that is related to US Government.

USCIS has tried to provide an easy self-service tool so anyone can use the application process.

Make sure to visit **Appendix IX – Fraud and Warnings** for more information on visa Fraud related to Diversity Visa Lottery.

Copyright © 2011 - GreenCard123.Com by UNorth® - All Rights Reserved

K. QUESTIONS AND ANSWERS

What is the Visa Lottery program?

- The Diversity Visa program, started in 1990, provides up to 50,000 visas to eligible countries via lottery (random selection). There is no specific requirement to participate in the lottery other than minimum high school education and country of birth, and participation is free. Once selected, Candidates are allowed to apply for Green Card and become permanent residents of the United States. If a candidate is selected, his/her spouse, and unmarried children under 21 years of age are also considered eligible to apply for Green Card.

Why is Visa Lottery is identified "DV-20XX" Visa?

- DV in the name stands for "Diversity Visa" since the Visa is to promote diversity in the American population. The four digits following the DV letters are the identification of the year that the visa is to be issued. For example, DV-2011 means that by end of the fiscal year 2011 (September 2011) the visas are awarded.

What are the Visa Lottery Time Lines?

- The Timeline of Visa Lottery may change from year to year. For DV-2012 Timeline is as follows. Most likely, the following years would follow the similar timeline:

- **October 05, 2010** - Registration Started
- **November 03, 2010** - Registration Deadline
- **May 2011** - Winners Notified
- **May 2011-Sep 2012** - Interviews and Issuance of Visas

Once the visa is issued, how long do I have to visit United States?

- Visas are generally issued for a six-month basis. In other words, if you're issued a Visa on September 01, 2011 you have time until March 01, 2011 to enter the United States. After this date your visa is expired and unless under very specific circumstances you can kiss your visa goodbye.

What are the Eligible or ineligible Countries?

- Eligible or ineligible refers to the born city of the applicant. In other words, if you or your spouse were born in one of the countries listed under Eligible, you are allowed to participate in the visa lottery.

List of Ineligible Countries as of DV-2012:

BRAZIL, CANADA, CHINA (mainland-born), COLOMBIA, DOMINICAN REPUBLIC, ECUADOR, EL SALVADOR, GUATEMALA, HAITI, INDIA, JAMAICA, MEXICO, PAKISTAN, PERU, PHILIPPINES, POLAND, SOUTH KOREA, UNITED KINGDOM (except Northern Ireland) and its dependent territories, and VIETNAM

What is the difference between Diversity Visa Lottery program and other Visas?

- The Diversity Visa program) is not a "Visa" by itself. Once you go through the process of registration and you are selected in a random drawing, you will have the option to request a Visa to the United States of America.

How USCIS calculates the number of visas available for each country

- Every year USCIS analyzes the number of Green Cards (Permanent Resident Status) granted by all countries*. Based on the visas that were issued in the past 5 years, a list of ineligible countries is generated.

The groups of countries are then divided by "regions."

Once USCIS figures out what percentage of the total Permanent Residents were from which countries/regions, (for example 40% from china, 40% from Mexico, and 20% all other countries) they'll allocate 80% of the diversity visas available (80% x 50,000 = 40,000 visas) to all other countries.

Bottom line, about 85% of the visas are actually awarded because of the lack of documentation submitted, incorrect data submission, not sending paperwork, etc.

Copyright © 2011 - GreenCard123.Com by UNorth® - All Rights Reserved

THIS PAGE WAS INTENTIONALLY LEFT BLANK

Copyright © 2011 - GreenCard123.Com by UNorth® - All Rights Reserved

3. REGISTERING FOR THE VISA LOTTERY

ROADMAP TO PREMANENT RESIDENCY VIA VISA LOTTERY:

   I.   Visa Lottery Information ✔
  II.   Register for Visa Lottery
      a. Get the information needed for registration
      b. Register for Visa Lottery Application via State Lottery Website
 III. Checking Status and Winning
 IV. Getting your green card
  V. Entering the United States
 VI. Now that you have your green card

BEWARE!

There is only one way to enter the Diversity Visa Program and that is by submitting your DV application online, at the state website http://dvlottery.state.gov. Any agency that promises to increase your chance or have affiliation with the US Government is fraudulent.

ow that you've decided to participate in the Visa Lottery, it's time to go over the high-level steps needed from beginning to the end of this process. The Diversity Visa lottery process is broken down to:

1) Get the information needed for registration
2) Register for Visa Lottery via State Lottery website (travel.state.gov)
3) Wait approximately 6-8 months
4) Check status of your application (or wait for winning letter)

Assuming you'll win:
1) Prepare the Green Card forms
2) Interview at the Embassy/Consulate (or USCIS Service Center in case you are in the United States)
3) Receive your visa
4) Enter United States before the visa expiration
5) Wait for your actual Green Card to arrive in the mail

And other optional processes:

1) Apply for Social Security Number
2) Become a US Citizen after 5 years.

Figure 3-1 provides an easy to follow flowchart for the Visa Lottery Registration process

Note: Immigration Laws in the United States change over time and Visa Lottery is not an exception either. For latest information, check Department of State website available at http://travel.state.gov and search for "Diversity Visa" (without the quotes).

We go through the above steps in detail in this and upcoming chapters.

In this chapter we focus on the first three steps:
- Getting the information needed
- Going to the State Lottery website http://dvlottery.state.gov
- Registering for visa lottery on website for FREE

Note: No fees are charged for the electronic lottery entry in DV program. U.S. government employs no outside consultants or private services to operate the DV program. Any intermediaries or others who offer assistance to prepare DV entries do so without the authority or consent of the US government. Use of any outside intermediary or assistance to prepare a DV entry is entirely at the entrant's discretion.

A. GATHERING THE INFORMATION NEEDED

Assuming that you do not want your application to be tossed out due to incorrect or duplicate submission, the best way would be to prepare the information needed in advance and apply for the visa lottery once everything is in place.

Although immigration forms generally look scary, if you have gathered the information prior to filling the form, they won't look scary at all. Particularly in regards to the Diversity Visa Lottery, you only need basic personal information about yourself and your family to complete the forms.

Copyright © 2011 - GreenCard123.Com by UNorth® - All Rights Reserved

---

TYPOGRAPHICAL ERRORS

To make sure there is no typographical error in the application, we recommend that you use the information in your passport or other government official documentation. Any non-consistent information may cause additional delay or denial of your application if your application is chosen as winner.

Free Tips!
Filling Immigration Forms

Just a couple of easy to use tips can save your application from getting disqualified:

- Use all CAPITAL words
- Match the information with your passport
- Verify your entries for typos

The list below is all the information you need to know about yourself and your family before going to DV website to submit your application. The form is designed to cover the questions that are asked in the application page.

Personal Information
- Full Name (Last Name, Middle Name, First Name)
- Gender
- Date of Birth (US Calendar)
- City of Birth
- Country of Birth
- Photos
- Country of Chargeability (Country that makes you eligible to apply - typically your birth country)
- Country that you are currently living in
- Marriage Status (Single, Married, Divorced, Windowed, etc)
- Spousal Information (if applicable):
  - Full Name (Last Name, Middle Name, First Name)
  - Gender

- Date of Birth (US Calendar)
- City of Birth
- Country of Birth
- Photos
- Number of Children (if applicable)
  Children Information:
  - Full Name (Last Name, Middle Name, First Name)
  - Gender
  - Date of Birth (US Calendar)
  - City of Birth
  - Country of Birth
  - Relationship to Parent
  - Photos

Education / Work
- (Latest Degree Completed): Your options are limited to Primary School Only, High School - No Degree, High School - Degree, Vocational School, Some University Courses, University Degree, Some Graduate Courses, Master Degree, Some Doctorate Courses, Doctorate Degree

Contact Information / Mailing Address
- Recipient Name:
- Address:
- City:
- State or Province (if applicable):
- Country:
- Zip Code:
- Telephone (+ International Code):
- Email Address

B. THE IMPORTANCE OF BEING TRUTHFUL

As noted earlier, USCIS utilizes extremely sophisticated computerized systems to identify fraudulent applications, including duplicate submissions, etc. As a result, pay close attention to the spelling of your name and enter it the same way as spelled in your passport. One common method by applicant is to apply with same name but modify it a little so that they can get a better chance of winning, but not knowing that USCIS automatically disqualifies their application.

Copyright © 2011 - GreenCard123.Com by UNorth® - All Rights Reserved

Because the rate of duplicate applications can be quite high (of course for those who don't know their application may get tossed out!), USCIS Kentucky Center (also known as Kentucky Consular Center) is dedicated to all the matters related to Diversity lottery visa. This includes entering, accepting, rejecting, and monitoring for fraud or duplicate submissions. KCC even employs face recognition methods to identify your face.

Example: Mary applies for 2010 diversity visa with her name, Mary Robinson. However, later she learns that the chances of winning lottery is 1 in 100 and so she thinks if she submit another application with slightly different name, she will double her chance, so she submits another application with name Mary Robinson (notice "I" and "n" are misplaced). She thinks that if later she is chosen, she can claim that this was a typo and everything will be fine. However, USCIS systems automatically toss out both of her applications and she loses her chance completely to win. She has to apply next year.

Example: Maria and Robert are living in Kuwait and would like to apply for Green Card Visa Lottery. They have been applying for the past five years. Later they learn that their uncle that is Citizen of the United States have been, without telling them, applying for them for the past four years! USCIS had every year been disqualifying them from the lottery and they have been losing their chance to be one of the winners.

C. REGISTER ON USCIS WEBSITE FOR FREE

As of 2010, Diversity Visa Lottery Application is split in two parts:

- Part I for entrant information, and

- Part II for dependents (if any)

MYTH: HIRING AN AGENT CAN IMPROVE YOUR CHANCES

A qualified electronic entry submitted directly by an applicant has an equal chance of being randomly selected by the computer at the KCC as does a qualified electronic entry received from an outside intermediary on behalf of the applicant. However, receipt of more than one entry per person will disqualify the person from registration, regardless of the source of the entry

Once you enter the State Website at http://dvlottery.state.gov/ and enter the Lottery application page, you'll see a screenshot similar to the Figure 3-1

Form 3-1 and 3-2 Provides scratch note to prepare the information you need for the registration of the Visa Lottery. Once you fill-in the information in the form ahead of time, you may simply copy those to the registration form. Form is broken down to:

Part I – Personal Information
- Information about the applicant

Part II – Dependent Information – Spouse
- If married, information about your spouse

Part II – Dependent Information - Child #1
- If you have a child, information about your child

Part II – Dependent Information - Child #2
- If you have another child, information about your second child,
- And additional children as applicable.

For easier understanding, sample information is filled for Mr. John Smith's family (Form 3-3) and will be used for Lottery Registration.

Copyright © 2011 - GreenCard123.Com by UNorth® - All Rights Reserved

- Figure 3-1 Travel.state.gov Lottery Registration Website

Copyright © 2011 - GreenCard123.Com by UNorth® - All Rights Reserved

Form 3-1 Sample Form to Fill prior to Registration
Copyright © 2011 – green card 123.Com – UNorth LLC – All rights Reserved

PART I – Personal Information

Personal Information	
▪ Full Name (Last Name, Middle Name, First Name)	
▪ Birth Date (US Calendar)	
▪ Gender	
▪ City Where You Were Born	
▪ Country Where you Were Born	
▪ Country that makes you eligible to apply	
▪ Photograph	
▪ Mailing Address	
• In Care Of	
• Address Line	
• City/Town	
• District/County/Province/State	
• Postal Code/Zip code	
• Country	
▪ Country that you are currently living in	
▪ Phone Number	
▪ Email Address	
▪ (Latest Degree Completed):	
▪ Marriage Status	
▪ Number of Children	

Part II – Dependent Information - Spouse

Spouse	
▪ Spouse Name (Last Name, Middle Name, First Name)	
▪ Birth Date (US Calendar)	
▪ Gender	
▪ City Where Your Spouse Was Born	
▪ Country Where Your Spouse Was Born	
▪ Spouse's Photograph	

Part II – Dependent Information – Child #1

Child	
▪ Child Name (Last Name, Middle Name, First Name)	
▪ Birth Date (US Calendar)	
▪ Gender	
▪ City Where Your Child #1 Was Born	
▪ Country Where Your Child #1 Was Born	
▪ Child #1's Photograph	

Part II – Dependent Information – Child #2

Child #2	
▪ Spouse Name (Last Name, Middle Name, First Name)	
▪ Birth Date (US Calendar)	
▪ Gender	
▪ City Where Your Spouse Was Born	
▪ Country Where Your Spouse Was Born	
▪ Spouse's Photograph	

Copyright © 2011 - GreenCard123.Com by UNorth® - All Rights Reserved

Form 3-2 Sample Form to Fill Prior Registration
Copyright © 2011 – green card 123.Com – UNorth LLC – All rights Reserved

PART I – Personal Information

Personal Information		
▪ Full Name (Last Name, Middle Name, First Name)	
▪ Birth Date (US Calendar)	
▪ Gender	
▪ City Where You Were Born	
▪ Country Where you Were Born	
▪ Country that makes you eligible to apply	
▪ Photograph	
▪ Mailing Address	
● In Care Of	
● Address Line	
● City/Town	
● District/County/Province/State	
● Postal Code/Zip code	
● Country	
▪ Country that you are currently living in	
▪ Phone Number	
▪ Email Address	
▪ (Latest Degree Completed):	
▪ Marriage Status	
▪ Number of Children	

Part II – Dependent Information - Spouse

Spouse		
▪ Spouse Name (Last Name, Middle Name, First Name)	
▪ Birth Date (US Calendar)	
▪ Gender	
▪ City Where Your Spouse Was Born	
▪ Country Where Your Spouse Was Born	
▪ Spouse's Photograph	

Part II – Dependent Information – Child #1

Child #1		
▪ Spouse Name (Last Name, Middle Name, First Name)	
▪ Birth Date (US Calendar)	
▪ Gender	
▪ City Where Your Spouse Was Born	
▪ Country Where Your Spouse Was Born	
▪ Spouse's Photograph	

Part II – Dependent Information – Child #2

Child #2		
▪ Spouse Name (Last Name, Middle Name, First Name)	
▪ Birth Date (US Calendar)	
▪ Gender	
▪ City Where Your Spouse Was Born	
▪ Country Where Your Spouse Was Born	
▪ Spouse's Photograph	

Copyright © 2011 – GreenCard123.Com by UNorth® – All Rights Reserved

Form 3-3 Sample Pre-Form Filled for Mr. John Smith's Family
Copyright © 2011 – green card 123.Com – UNorth LLC – All rights Reserved

PART I – Personal Information

Personal Information		
	Full Name (Last Name, Middle Name, First Name)	SMITH, M, JOHN
	Birth Date (US Calendar)	OCTOBER 20, 1970
	Gender	MALE
	City Where You Were Born	PARIS
	Country Where you Were Born	FRANCE
	Country that makes you eligible to apply	FRANCE
	Photograph	---READY---
	Mailing Address	
	• In Care Of	JOHN AND JANE SMITH
	• Address Line	2, AVENUE GABRIEL
	• City/Town	PARIS
	• District/County/Province/State	PARIS
	• Postal Code/Zip code	75016
	• Country	FRANCE
	Country that you are currently living in	FRANCE
	Phone Number	(33) 1 22 3344 55
	Email Address	johnsmith@example.com
	(Latest Degree Completed):	UNIVERSITY DEGREE
	Marriage Status	MARRIED
	Number of Children	2

Part II – Dependent Information - Spouse

Spouse		
	Spouse Name (Last Name, Middle Name, First Name)	SMITH, JANE
	Birth Date (US Calendar)	DECEMBER 10, 1973
	Gender	FEMALE
	City Where Your Spouse Was Born	SHANGHAI
	Country Where Your Spouse Was Born	CHINA
	Spouse's Photograph	---READY---

Part II – Dependent Information – Child #1

Child #1		
	Spouse Name (Last Name, Middle Name, First Name)	SMITH, ROBERT JR
	Birth Date (US Calendar)	JANUARY 10, 1994
	Gender	MALE
	City Where Your Spouse Was Born	PARIS
	Country Where Your Spouse Was Born	FRANCE
	Spouse's Photograph	---READY---

Part II – Dependent Information – Child #2

Child #2		
	Spouse Name (Last Name, Middle Name, First Name)	SMITH, SARAH
	Birth Date (US Calendar)	MARCH 18, 1996
	Gender	FEMALE
	City Where Your Spouse Was Born	PARIS
	Country Where Your Spouse Was Born	FRANCE
	Spouse's Photograph	---READY---

Copyright © 2011 - GreenCard123.Com by UNorth® - All Rights Reserved

PART 1

1. Name

Explanation: Enter Your Full name here. Family name first, then first name, and lastly your middle name.

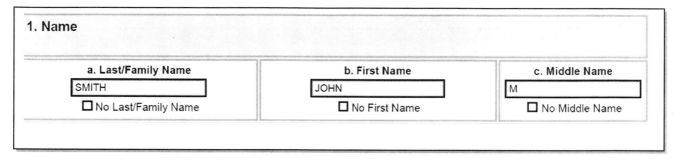

If your name does not include any of the pieces, mark the checkbox below the name.

Example: John Robertson does not have a middle name. He enters ROBERTSON for his last name, JOHN for his first name, and marks the "No Middle Name" choice.

In some countries, the name may be longer that the maximum characters available in the text-fields. In such cases, enter as many characters as it fits in the field and omit the remaining portion.

Name Definition

If you are not familiar with western culture, the name conversion can be difficult. For example, different part of the world may refer to "Family Name" as "Surname" or "Last Name". If you need more information, refer to the table below

- **Family Name:** (in Western contexts often referred to as a last name) is a type of surname and part of a person's name indicating name indicating the family to which the person belongs. The use of family names is widespread in cultures around the world. Each culture has its own rules as to how these names are applied and used. Don't mistake Families that have more than one word with middle name.
- **First Name:** is a given name or personal name that name that specifies and differentiates between members of a group of individuals, especially in a family, all of whose members usually share the same family name (surname). A given name is a name given to a person, as opposed to an inherited one such as a family name.
- **Middle Name:** In some countries, people's names include one or more middle names, placed between the First Name and Last Name. In most countries, except Northern America, this notion of middle name does not exist, and those names are considered as a second, third, etc. given name. In the USA and Canada there is usually only one middle name, often abbreviated by its possessor to the middle initial (e.g. James Ronald Smith becomes James R. Smith). In other English speaking countries people will have more than one given name, although they are usually known by one only. In some other countries, the term middle name is only used for names that are originally last names, but not part of the last name of the bearer (for instance one can have one's mother's maiden name as a middle name).

2. Birth Date

Explanation: Enter Your Full name here. Family name first, then first name, and lastly your middle name.

Copyright © 2011 - GreenCard123.Com by UNorth® - All Rights Reserved

2. Birth Date		
19	October	1970

Date Conversion: To convert your birthday, perform a search on internet for "Calendar Converter" or go to the website http://www.fourmilab.ch/documents/calendar/ The US Calendar is also known as the "Gregorian Calendar". Other calendars in use include Julian, Hebrew, Islamic, Persian, Mayan, Baha'i, Indian Civil, and ISO8601.

3. Gender

Explanation: Select your gender from the list.

3. Gender		
⊙ Male	O Female	

4. City Where You Where Born

Explanation: type the city in which you were born in the appropriate text box. If the birth city/town is not known, mark the appropriate checkbox.

4. City Where You Were Born
Paris
☐ Birth City/Town Unknown

5. Country Where You Where Born

Explanation: type the Country in which you were born in the appropriate text box.

Copyright © 2011 - GreenCard123.Com by UNorth® - All Rights Reserved

---

5. Country Where You Were Born

France

---

6. Country of Eligibility for the DV Program

Explanation: In most cases, your country of birth is same as the country of your chargeability. However, if your country of birth does not qualify you to enter the Diversity Visa program (e.g. in the list of countries that cannot apply) there are two situations that you may be able to select another country for your chargeability:

- First, if you were born in a country whose natives are ineligible but your spouse was born in a country whose natives are eligible, you can claim your spouse's country of birth - provided that both you and your spouse are on the selected entry, are issued visas, and enter the United States simultaneously. If your country of eligibility is not same as the country you were born, select "NO" and" and then choose the country that makes you otherwise eligible from the drop down menu.
- Second, if you were born in a country whose natives are ineligible, but neither of your parents was born there or resided there at the time of your birth, you may claim nativity in one of your parent's countries of birth if it is a country whose natives qualify for the Diversity Visa Program.

---

6. Country of Eligibility for the DV Program

Your country of eligibility will normally be the same as your country of birth. Your country of eligibility is **not** related to where you live. If you were born in a country that is not eligible for the DV program, please go to Explanation of Country of Eligibility (this link will open in a new window) to see if there is another option available in your case.

Are you claiming eligibility based on the country where you were born?

◉ Yes ○ No

If not, you must enter the country from which you are claiming eligibility.

France

---

7. Entrant Photograph

Explanation: Refer to the **Appendix I** for photographs requirement and instruction. For the purpose of Diversity Visa application, there are two primary ways to import your Photograph into the USCIS system:

Copyright © 2011 - GreenCard123.Com by UNorth® - All Rights Reserved

- If you have a digital camera, you may take a new photo; import your picture directly from the digital camera into your computer, and to the DV website.
- If you have a digital scanner, you may scan your photo; import your picture directly from the digital scanner into your computer, and to the DV website.

---

7. Entrant Photograph

Photographs must be submitted at the time of E-DV entry. Photographs that do not comply with all specifications, including but not limited to recency of the photos, composition of the photos, and unacceptable backgrounds are grounds for disqualification of the entire entry. Any manipulation of photographs that alters the facial characteristics is grounds for disqualification of the entire entry. See examples on the Photo Validation {this link will open in a new window} page.

Please refer to the Instructions for the 2009 Diversity Immigrant Visa Program (DV-2009) for technical specifications and compositional specifications for the digital image.

You will use one of the following methods to enter the image into eDV:

- Take a new digital image.
- Use a digital scanner to scan a submitted photograph.

Link to photo instructions/photo validation page {this link will open in a new window}

Photograph File Name `C:\Users\jsmith\Documents\jsmith.jpg` [Browse...]

If you know the location in the computer and the name of the file which is storing the photograph, enter in the box to the left of the 'Browse' button. If you are not sure of the location in the computer or the name of the file, clicking the 'Browse' button will allow you to look for and choose the file which is storing the photograph, and after you choose the file its name will appear in the box above.

---

8. Mailing Address

Explanation: Mailing address is another piece of information that varies from country to country. Pay extra attention to this section as any incorrect address information may jeopardize the notice delivery should you win the Visa Lottery and by now I'm sure it's not what everyone's after!

If you are already in the United States, use your United States address. If you are outside of the United States, the fastest way to receive any notice from USCIS is to have an address of a relative or friend in the United States. You may also use the mailing address in any country or your own.

Note: *In the United States, Postal Service will not deliver the mail to the destination unless the name of the recipient matches the resident on record, thus make sure to enter the in-care-of name correctly.*

Copyright © 2011 - GreenCard123.Com by UNorth® - All Rights Reserved

- **In care of:** It's the name of the recipient of the mail; if the recipient is same as applicant, enter the applicant's name; otherwise (e.g. if an address from another person is being used), enter the recipients full name in this field.

Example: *Ron is an applicant from Paris France. Although he can use his own address in Paris, he is travelling most of the time, thus he decides to use his cousin's address, Albert Robinson, in New York, United States. Ron enters the "Mailing Address as follows:*

In Care of: ALBERT ROBINSON
Address 1: 123 FIRST ST
Address 2: APT # 1003
City: NEW YORK
State: NY
Postal Code*: 10001
Country: UNITED STATES

In some countries that do not have political relations with United States, (such as Iran, Iraq, Libya, Sudan and Syria) mails from United States government may encounter difficulties in reaching the residents due to government control of the postal system. If you are a resident of such a country, it is recommended that you use an address from a friend or relative in the United States or another country that does not have such difficulty.

- ***Postal Code:** A postal code (known in various countries as a post code, postcode, or ZIP code) is a series of letters and/or digits appended to a postal address for the purpose of sorting mail. If your country's postal system does not support Postal Code, you may omit this portion and check the box "No Postal Code/Zip Code" in the application

8. Mailing Address

8a. In Care Of	JOHN AND JANE SMITH
8b. Address Line 1	2, AVENUE GABRIEL
8c. Address Line 2	
8d. City/Town	PARIS
8e. District/County/Province/State	PARIS
8f. Postal Code/Zip Code	75016 ☐ No Postal Code/Zip Code
8g. Country	France

(NOTE: This is the address that will be used to notify you if you are selected.)

Copyright © 2011 - GreenCard123.Com by UNorth® - All Rights Reserved

9. Country Where You Live Today

Explanation: Select the country that is your primary place of residence. Although not USCIS definition but country of residence is defined as the country where a person has lived for most of the past 12 months. Tourists and vacation places are defined as non-residents/residents according to the country of residence.

---

9. Country Where You Live Today

> France

---

10. Phone Number

Explanation: Although it happens extremely rare that USCIS would want to talk to you over the phone, it does provide alternate method of communication and security validation. This entry is optional and if filled make sure that you enter the full country code, state/city code, and phone number.

---

10. Phone Number

> (33) 1 22 3344 55   *Optional*

It is recommended that you separate the codes from the phone number, or follow a format similar to this

(+Country Code) (State Code, City Code) (Phone Number)

Example: If you live in the United States, California, San Francisco, your phone number will be as follows:

Country Code: +1
State Code/City Code: (408)
Phone Number: 392-2223

Your entry would look like this:
(+1) (408) 392-2223Country: UNITED STATES

Copyright © 2011 - GreenCard123.Com by UNorth® - All Rights Reserved

11. Email Address

Explanation: Due to the fraud, email communication is currently not being used to inform you about winning the lottery but USCIS/KCC has future plans to use email for communications post winning. If you have an email you may enter it at this text box.

---

11. E-mail Address

Electronic delivery of DV correspondence may be offered in the near future. Please enter an email address in the box below if you would prefer to receive correspondence electronically.

johnsmith@example.com   *Optional*

If you do not have an email address, you may create one at one of the popular email services for free. Common email systems include Yahoo!®, Gmail®, and Hotmail®.

BEWARE!! Read our fraud appendix regarding the fake emails and how to identify them. At the time of writing this book KCC and USCIS do not communicate to you via email so if you receive an email informing you that you are a winner of lottery is fake. Visit http://travel.state.gov for updated information.

---

12. Highest Level of Education Completed

Explanation: Select the highest level of education achieved <u>as of the date completing the application.</u> As shown in the figure, your selection is limited to the followings:

- Primary school only
- High school, no degree
- High school degree
- Vocational school
- Some university courses
- University degree
- Some graduate level courses
- Masters degree
- Some doctorate level courses
- Doctorate degree

As explained earlier, a definite requirement for Visa Lottery is possessing a high school diploma reflecting the completion of a full course of study (vocational schools the like are not acceptable by USCIS). An alternative to possessing minimum high-school diploma is to be qualified as a "skilled worker" in an

Copyright © 2011 - GreenCard123.Com by UNorth® - All Rights Reserved

occupation that requires two years of training or experience. Additional information is provided in Appendix - One job List

---

12. What is the highest level of education you have achieved, as of today?

- O Primary School Only
- O High School, no Degree
- O High School Degree
- O Vocational School
- O Some University Courses

- ⦿ University Degree
- O Some Graduate Level Courses
- O Master Degree
- O Some Doctorate Level Courses
- O Doctorate Degree

You must have a minimum of a high school diploma reflecting the completion of a full course of study (vocation schools or equivalency degrees are not acceptable) or be a skilled worker in an occupation that requires at least two years of training or experience to qualify (visit http://online.onetcenter.org/ {this link will open in a new window} to see if your occupation qualifies) for a Diversity Visa.

---

13. Marital Status

Explanation: A person's marital status indicates whether the person is married. In the simplest sense, the only possible answers are "single" or "married". However, other options are often included, such as "divorced", "widowed", and "legally separated".

---

13. What is your current marital status?

- O Unmarried *(no spouse info required)*
- ⦿ Married *(spouse info required)*
- O Divorced *(no spouse info required)*
- O Widowed *(no spouse info required)*
- O Legally Separated *(no spouse info required)*

Legal separation means that a court has formally declared that you and your spouse are legally separated. Legal separation means that your spouse would not be eligible to immigrate as your derivative.

Select your marriage status from the list of options:
- Unmarried
- Married
- Divorced
- Windowed
- Legally Separated

Copyright © 2011 - GreenCard123.Com by UNorth® - All Rights Reserved

Because USCIS takes fraud very seriously, it wants to make sure you provided all the info about yourself and your family (e.g. your spouse, and children unmarried under 21 years of age) accurately. This information basically ensures the correct person is winning the game and two people with the same name are not mistaken. It is also a test of your honesty and truthfulness!

Note: Listing of the children and/or your spouse on your application does not necessarily mean that they must travel with you. It's optional and they can decide later if you find out you won the Lottery. However the reverse is not true; if you do not include them on your application and later you win the Lottery and they now have changed their mind to come to United States that will not be possible. In fact, if you provide incorrect information you may disqualify yourself from receiving permanent resident card entirely.

Unmarried (no spouse info required)

- In legal definitions for interpersonal status, a single person is someone who has never been married. A person who was previously married and was divorced or widowed is usually considered an "unmarried" person.

- Since in case of unmarried person, no spouse exists, you'll not be required to answer the spouse related questions in the Part II

Married (spouse info required)

- To be "married," a spouse is a legally wedded husband or wife, merely living together does not qualify a marriage for immigration. Common-law spouses may qualify as spouses for immigration purposes depending on the laws of the country where the common-law marriage occurs.

Marriages that are not recognized by USCIS

In the immigration law, some marriages are not recognized by the USCIS and thus spouse is not qualified to enjoy immigration benefits with the individual:

- **Same Sex Marriage:** As of the time writing the book, USCIS does not recognize same-sex marriages for the purpose of immigration to the United States; this is true, even if one of the US States has issued the marriage license.
- **Common Law Marriage:** Common-law marriages are normally not recognized by USCIS; however, common-law spouses may qualify as spouses for immigration purposes depending on the laws of the country where the common-law marriage occurs. For example, if the country that common-law marriage occurred accepts this type of marriage as official and legal, USCIS may also accept it for immigration purposes. Same rule applies to Customary marriages
- **Polygamy Marriage:** In some countries, the law allows the husband or wife to have more than spouse simultaneously. The Polygamy is a form of marriage in which a person has more than one spouse at the same time. USCIS does not recognize polygamy marriages. In cases of polygamy, only the first spouse may qualify as a spouse for immigration.
- **Immediate Family Member Marriage:** Marriage between immediate family members (e.g. brother and sister, etc), also known as Incest marriage is generally not recognized by the USCIS. The only exception is if the destination state accepts such marriage.
- **Proxy Marriage:** Proxy marriage is a marriage that occurred without the parties being physically present. This type of marriage is generally not recognized by the USCIS. If your marriage was conducted through proxy, consult a lawyer to see if any exception applies to your case.

Widowed (no spouse info required)

- Widowed is a husband or wife whose spouse has died. A widow is a woman whose spouse has died. A man whose spouse has died is a widower.

Copyright © 2011 - GreenCard123.Com by UNorth® - All Rights Reserved

Divorced (no spouse info required)

- Divorce (or the dissolution of marriage) is the final termination of a marital union, cancelling the legal duties and responsibilities of marriage and dissolving the bonds of matrimony between the parties. In most countries divorce requires the sanction of a court or other authority in a legal process.

Legally separated (no spouse info required)

- In some countries, including United States, there is a marital status called "Separation." Separation is a legal process by which a married couple may formalize a de facto separation while remaining legally married. A legal separation is granted in the form of a court order, which can be in the form of a legally-binding consent decree. The most common reason for filing with the courts for a legal separation is to make interim financial arrangements for the two of them, such as deciding which one will pay which bills, possess which property, and whether one of them shall pay the other temporary financial support. Decision by a married couple alone does not constitute as a "separation," but it rather requires a Court Order.

  If you are <u>legally</u> separated, you would select this option and your spouse information would not be required. Legal separation means that your spouse would **not** be eligible to immigrate with you as your derivative.

Scenario	Who's Filing?	Marital Status	Spousal Information	Explanation
Peter and Kellie are engaged and planning to marry next month. Peter has never married previously but Kellie was married and divorced last year.	Peter	Unmarried	Not Required	At the time of filing the DV Lottery, they are not married so the correct status should be selected. *However, should they get married and Peter wins the diversity visa Lottery, their status is now "married." he can apply for his new wife as well due to change of status.*
Peter and Kellie are engaged and planning to marry next month. Peter has never married previously but Kellie was married and divorced last year.	Kellie	Divorced	Not Required	At the time of filing the DV Lottery, they are not married so the correct status should be selected. *However, should they get married and Kellie wins the diversity visa Lottery, their status is now "married." she can apply for his new wife as well due to change of status.*
John and Mary were married last year but their marriage is not working. They are planning to file divorce very soon	Either one	Married	Required	At the time of filing the DV Lottery, they are still married so the correct status along with the Spousal information must be entered. *However, should they decide to divorce and either one win the Lottery, their status is now "divorce" and the primary applicant can immigrate, but the other spouse cannot immigrate as part of Diversity Visa*

Copyright © 2011 - GreenCard123.Com by UNorth® - All Rights Reserved

• Robert and Stephanie have not filed divorced yet but the court has issued a "legally separated" status to them	Either one	Legally Separated	Not Required	At the time of filing the DV Lottery, they are considered legally separated so the correct status must be selected. *Legal separation means that the spouse would **not** be eligible to immigrate as the derivative.*
• Gary's wife passed away ten years ago and he has not married since	Gary	Widowed	Not Required	At the time of filing the DV Lottery, Gary is considered Widowed so the correct status must be selected
• Jerry and Monica had been married for 15 years but they filed for divorce and court just issued their final divorce ruling papers.	Either one	Divorced	Not Required	At the time of filing the DV Lottery, Jerry and Monica are considered "divorced" so the correct status must be selected. They can no longer claim each other as spouse and so the spousal information is not required.

Table 3-1 Marriage Scenario and Selection in DV Lottery Registration

14. Number of Children

Explanation: In USCIS terms, a child is defined as being unmarried and under 21, whereas a "son" or "daughter" is defined as being married and/or 21 or over. For immigration purposes, a child can be any of the following:

- A biological child born in wedlock
- A biological child born out of wedlock
- A step-child, as long as the marriage creating the step-relationship occurred before the child turned 18
- An adopted child if the child was adopted prior to age 16 (one exception is if siblings are adopted, as long as one was under 16, the other could be older than 16 but younger than 18), AND the adopted child has resided in the legal and physical custody of the adoptive parent for 2 years prior to filing (the legal and physical custody do not have to be the same time period, but each must be met for 2 years)
  Most adoption-based immigration occurs through the orphan inter-country or Hague processes.

Note: If you or your child, son or daughter currently serves in the U.S. military, special resources and conditions may apply. See the "Military Personnel and Their Families" link to the right.

When counting children, you MUST include all natural children, as well as all legally adopted children and stepchildren who are unmarried and under the age of 21 on the date of your electronic entry (do not include children who are already U.S. citizens or Lawful Permanent Residents), even if you are no longer legally married to the child's parent, and even if the spouse or child does not currently reside with you and/or will not immigrate with you.

Copyright © 2011 - GreenCard123.Com by UNorth® - All Rights Reserved

---

14. Number of Children

2

Children include all biological children, legally adopted children, and stepchildren who are unmarried and under the age of 21 on the date that you submit your entry. Failure to include all children or inclusion of children who are not your biological children, legally adopted children, and stepchildren (regardless of whether they live with you and/or intend to apply for a visa as your derivative) is grounds for disqualification of the entire entry.

Legal Permanent Residents (LPR) and American Citizens should not be included.

Note: *Failure to list all children who are eligible will result in disqualification of the principal applicant and refusal of all visas under the case at the time of the visa interview.*

Child turning 21: *Note that married children and children 21 years or older are not eligible for the DV; however, U.S. law protects children from —aging out‖ in certain circumstances. If your electronic DV entry is made before your unmarried child turns 21, and the child turns 21 before visa issuance, he/she may be protected from aging out by the Child Status Protection Act and be treated as though he/she was below 21 years of age for visa-processing purposes. Refer to previous chapter for additional information*

Example: Ron Smith and Julie Smith are parents of the following children:

Child Name	Relative	Age	Marital Status	Residency	Should be listed in your DV Application?
John Jr. Smith	Ron and Julie's child	17	Single	Currently living with parents	Yes, John is under 21 and single so considered a child and should be listed, even if he doesn't plan to migrate to US
Jerry Schneider	Julie's child from previous husband (Ron's step son)	23	Single	currently living with parents	No, Jerry is over 21 years old
Mary Smith	Ron and Julie's child	19	Single	US Resident, living in US	No, Mary is already a US Resident and should not be included in DV Application
George Smith	Ron and Julie's child	20	Married	Currently living with parents	No, George is married and is no longer considered a "child" thus should not be included in the DV application

Table 3-2 Children Scenario

Copyright © 2011 - GreenCard123.Com by UNorth® - All Rights Reserved

Official Explanation by Travel.State.Gov:

On your entry you must list your spouse (husband or wife) and all unmarried children under 21 years of age, with the exception of children who are already U.S. citizens or Lawful Permanent Residents. You must list your spouse even if you are currently separated from him/her, unless you are legally separated (i.e., there is a written agreement recognized by a court or a court order). If you are legally separated or divorced, you do not need to list your former spouse. You must list ALL your children who are unmarried and under 21 years of age at the time of your initial E-DV entry, whether they are your natural children, your spouse's children, or children you have formally adopted in accordance with the laws of your country, unless such child is already a U.S. citizen or Lawful Permanent Resident. List all children under 21 years of age at the time of your electronic entry, even if they no longer reside with you or you do not intend for them to immigrate under the DV program. The fact that you have listed family members on your entry does not mean that they must travel with you. They may choose to remain behind. However, if you include an eligible dependent on your visa application forms that you failed to include on your original entry, your case will be disqualified. This only applies to those who were family members at the time the original application was submitted, not those acquired at a later date. Your spouse may still submit a separate entry, even though he or she is listed on your entry, as long as both entries include details on all dependents in your family. (source: travel.state.gov)

PART 2

13. Spouse Information

Explanation: This section is only available to you if your marital status is married and/or you have a child listed in your application. We have omitted duplicate instruction. Follow the same instruction provided above

13a-13c Spouse Name
Explanation: Enter full name of your spouse here. Family Name First, then First Name, and lastly your Middle Name

13d Birth Date
Explanation: Enter your spouse's birthday based on the information from the passport

13e Spouse Gender
Explanation: Select Spouse's Gender
13f City Where Spouse was born
Explanation: Enter City name that your spouse was born. If the city is not known mark the appropriate checkbox

13g Country Where Spouse Was Born
Explanation: Select the country that your spouse is born from list of available countries.

13th Spouse Photographs

Copyright © 2011 - GreenCard123.Com by UNorth® - All Rights Reserved

Explanation: Upload photographs using the same procedure and requirements described in the previous section.

---

13. Spouse Name

a. Last/Family Name	b. First Name	c. Middle Name
SMITH	JANE	
☐ No Last/Family Name	☐ No First Name	☑ No Middle Name

13d. Birth Date

10	December	1973

13e. Gender

○ Male	⊙ Female	

13f. City Where Spouse Was Born

SHANGHAI
☐ Birth City/Town Unknown

13g. Country Where Spouse Was Born

China, People's Republic Of

PART 2

14. Child Information

Explanation: This section will only be available to you if you have entered a child number in the related question. Depending on the number of children that you have entered, you need to fill-in the information. The forms distinguish between the children by placing a #placing#1, #2 after the child.

14a-14c Child #1 Name
Explanation: Enter full name of your child here. Family Name first, then First Name, and lastly your Middle Name.

14d Birth Date
Explanation: Enter your first Child birthday based on the information from the passport

14e Child Gender

Copyright © 2011 - GreenCard123.Com by UNorth® - All Rights Reserved

Explanation: Select Child #1's Gender

14f City Where Child #1 was Born
Explanation: Enter City name that your Child #1 was born. If the city is not known mark the appropriate checkbox

14g Country Where Child #1 Was Born
Explanation: Select the country that your Child #1 is born from list of available countries.

14th Child #1 Photographs
Explanation: Upload photographs using the same procedure and requirements described in the previous section.

---

14. Child #1 Name

a. Last/Family Name	b. First Name	c. Middle Name
SMITH	ROBERT	JR
☐ No Last/Family Name	☐ No First Name	☐ No Middle Name

14d. Birth Date

10	January	1994

14e. Gender

◉ Male	○ Female	

14f. City Where Child Was Born

PARIS
☐ Birth City/Town Unknown

14g. Country Where Child Was Born

France

After completing the information, click on Continue to proceed to the Review page. At this point, you may review your application for accuracy and compare the dates and other information to the information in the scratch table you prepared above.

And Walla! You are done! You'll see a screenshot similar to the one shown.

Copyright © 2011 - GreenCard123.Com by UNorth® - All Rights Reserved

Note: *Either print the application or take a note of the case number, date/time, etc. make sure to get to a page similar to this otherwise your application may not have been submitted.*

Submission Confirmation Page

Besides applying for the Lottery Application, the next most important thing is to write down or print your confirmation number. This is the only way to check your application status, should you not receive the formal mail from KCC

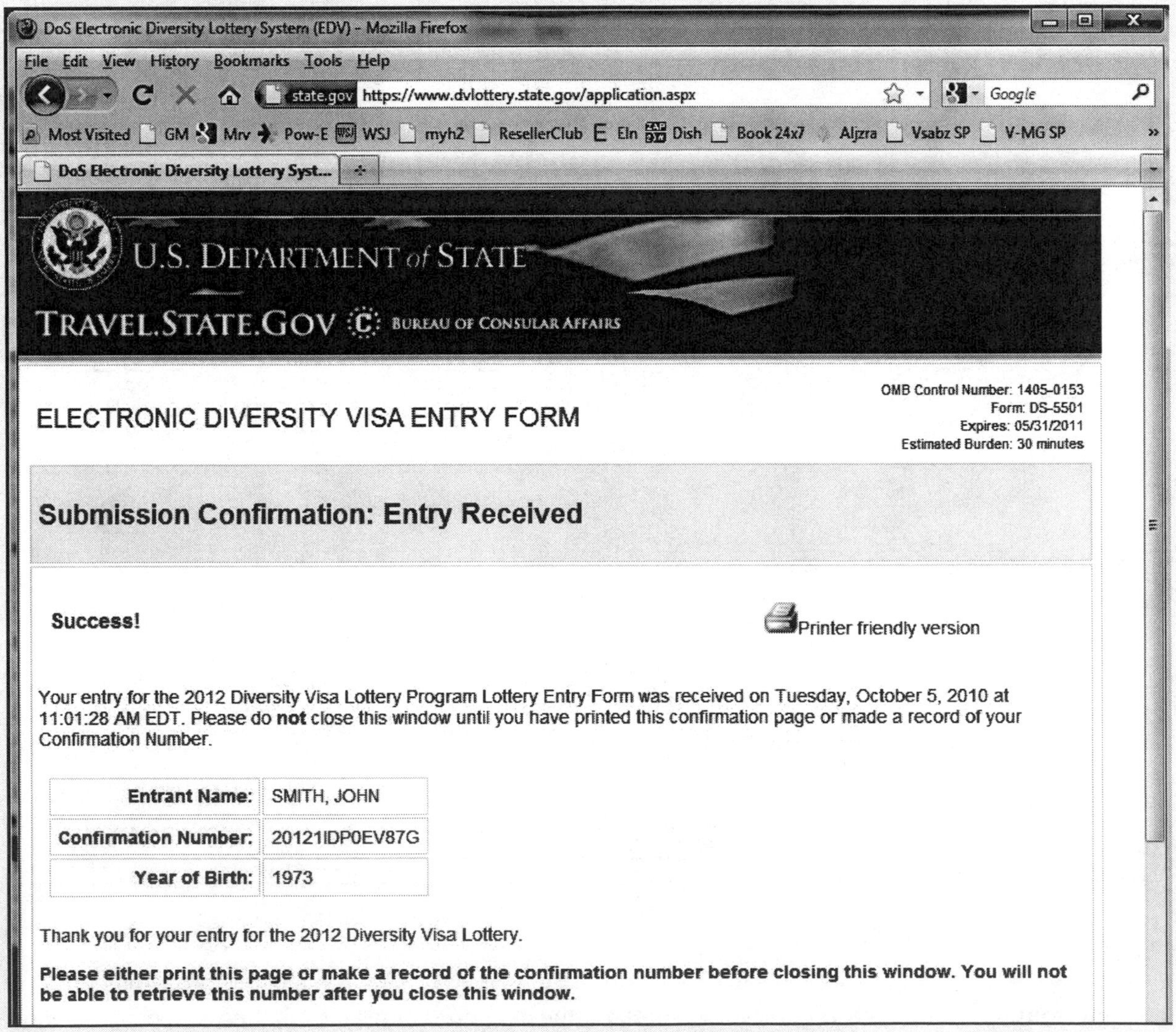

Figure 3-3 Submission Confirmation Page

Copyright © 2011 – GreenCard123.Com by UNorth® – All Rights Reserved

D. HOW MANY APPLICATIONS CAN BE SUBMITTED?

As rule of thumb, you can make one application per person only. You cannot apply twice, thrice, etc.

Using the rule above, if you have a spouse your spouse may also file an application and list you as spouse. You just increased your chance of winning, for free!

Example 1: Mary and Rob just married and they are thinking of applying for the Green Card Lottery. After all, nothing to lose! Mary has Bachelor of Science in Psychology but Rob had left his high-school unfinished and doesn't have any experience. Rob and Mary can only file one Green Card Lottery application because only Mary is a qualified applicant for Green Card Lottery. Mary has to be the primary applicant and add Rob as spouse in her application

Example 2: Rey and Anna have a 9 years old son. They don't have high-school diploma but have been working in their field for the past 5 years. Rey can apply for Green Card lottery application and put Anna as his spouse. Anna can also file a separate Green Card Lottery application and put Rey as her spouse. This way they are doubling their chances to win the Lottery!

Example 3: Ahmad and Lily have been married for over 30 years. They have one son (19 years old) and one daughter (22 years old). They both finished their high school and have long work experience. Ahmad can file one Green Card Lottery application, and put Lily at his spouse and their son on the application. Lily can also file another Green Card Lottery application and put her spouse (Ahmad) and their son on the application. Their daughter must file a separate Green Card Lottery application because she is over 21 years old. Should Ahmad and Lily win the Lottery, Ahmad, Lily and their son can apply to get Green Card visa to United States. The 22 Years old daughter is considered adult and will not be issued a visa with them (She has to win separately).

Similarly, if their daughter wins the Lottery, she will be allowed to apply for Green Card visa but her parents and her brother cannot (assuming they didn't win).

Example 4: Michael and Peggy have been married for over 20 years. They have a son, Omid, who is 19 years of age but he is married as well. Michael and Peggy would like to apply for Green Card Lottery. They are both qualified for the minimum education requirement so they submit two applications, one for Michael and listing Peggy as spouse, and one for Peggy, listing Michael as spouse. Omid cannot be on their Green Card Lottery application because he is married. He must be filing a separate application with his spouse should he be interested to come to US via Green Card.

Copyright © 2011 - GreenCard123.Com by UNorth® - All Rights Reserved

THIS PAGE WAS INTENTIONALY LEFT BLANK

Copyright © 2011 – GreenCard123.Com by UNorth® – All Rights Reserved

4. CHECKING STATUS AND WAITING

ROADMAP TO PREMANENT RESIDENCY VIA VISA LOTTERY:

   I.   Visa Lottery Information ✔
  II.   Register for Visa Lottery ✔
 III.   Checking Status and Winning
      a.   Wait approximately 6-8 months
      b.   Check status of your application (or wait for winning letter). Assuming you've won:
      c.   Winning!
 IV.   Getting your green card
  V.   Entering the United States
 VI.   Now that you have your green card

BEWARE

There is only one way to enter the Diversity Visa Program and that is by submitting your DV application online, at the state website http://dvlottery.state.gov. Any agency that promises to increase your chance or have affiliation with the US Government is fraudulent

A. AFTER SUBMISSION OF YOUR APPLICATION

Once you submit your application and verified by KCC, it would go through various screenings to check for various fraud checks (e.g. name checks, incorrect spelling check of your name, previous candidate fraud history, picture test, etc) and once verified that your application is not submitted fraudulently, it will go through a closely-monitored random drawing by Kentucky Service Center.

B. WAITING, WAITING, AND MORE WAITING

Once you successfully apply for Diversity Visa Lottery as instructed in previous chapters, there is not much you can do other than waiting and keeping your fingers crossed and hope to win the Lottery! The process of random selection takes approximately 6-8 months after the date of submission.

C. SELECTION OF APPLICANTS

The computer will randomly select individuals from among all qualified entries. Normally, the selected individuals will be notified by mail between May and July of the following year

Example: Applications submitted on December 2010, random selection takes place shortly after, and winners will be notified May through July of the following year, 2011.

The notification letters will provide further instructions, including information on fees connected with immigration to the United States.

D. YOUR CHANCES

The purpose of this book is not to give you a false hope, but rather a realistic one; considering that about 3 million applications are tossed out due to error or duplicate submission, your chance of Lottery increases as more people make mistake on their application.

E. YOUR WINNING ODDS

While most people think the chances of winning a Lottery are quite slim, compared to others, you have a better chance of winning here. To give you a better idea, see the table below

As explained in Chapter 2, you can also increase your chance of winning up to 5% (if single), 10% (if married and both of you apply), and 33% (if a child and applying on his/her own application in addition to parents applying separately) in period of 3-5 years.

Copyright © 2011 – GreenCard123.Com by UNorth® – All Rights Reserved

Activity	Winning Probability Percentage	Odds of Winning
Winning Mega Million US Lottery (~ $80,000,000)	0.0000006%	1 in 175,000,000
Winning California Super Lottery (~$7,000,000)	0.000001%	1 in 11,000,000
Odds of being killed by falling out of bed	0.00001%	1 in 2,000,000
Being struck by Lightening	0.00005%	1 in 500,000
Odds of dating a supermodel in average lifetime	0.00020%	1 in 90,000
Odds of winning an Olympic Medal	0.00111%	1 in 600,000
Hitting Jackpot on Average Slot Machine in Las Vegas	0.00017%	1 in 32,768
Odds of getting the golf ball in the hole in one hit	0.00305%	1 in 5,000
Odds of injury from Shaving	0.02000%	1 in 7,000
Having your car Stolen	0.01429%	1 in 150
Be Selected as Winner of Diversity Visa Lottery, and be eligible to apply for Diversity Visa	1%	1 in 100

Table 4-1 Diversity Visa Lottery Approximate Odds

Now feel better! Your chance of winning is actually much better than many other probabilities that you encounter on daily basis. At the same time, if you took the time and made sure your application was submitted correctly, there is nothing else you can do other than to wait. Unfortunately, to keep the process fair, secure, and aligned with the guidelines, there is no way to expedite processing of your drawing result or check status prior to result being fully available.

F. IMPORTANT THINGS TO REMEMBER

- Those selected in the random drawing are NOT notified by e-mail.
- Those individuals NOT selected will NOT receive any notification.
- It's absolutely impossible to get the results earlier than officially available by KCC (in which time it becomes publicly available and mails are sent out). If you receive any offer that it's claimed they can let you know about status of your app earlier than others, it is fraud.
- U.S. embassies and consulates will not provide a list of successful entrants.

G. CHECK STATUS OF YOUR APPLICATION ONLINE OR RECEIVE A LETTER

Kentucky Service center will send a physical mail to all winners whose name was drawn during the random Lottery drawing, approximately 100,000 of them. If you kept a copy of your submission confirmation, you can also check the result of your application online at the State website.

Although extreme caution is exercised by the KCC service center, occasionally errors may occur. That includes incorrect application/confirmation query or website problem on the website, or accidental mail drop in another address by your mailman. Taking all these into consideration, the best way is to check

Copyright © 2011 - GreenCard123.Com by UNorth® - All Rights Reserved

the status of your application via internet. In addition, this is the fastest possible way to know whether or not you have won.

If your application is not selected for this year's lottery, you'll see a message similar to this:

Based on the information provided, the Entry HAS NOT BEEN SELECTED for further processing for the 200x Electronic Diversity Visa program.

Please verify that you have entered all information correctly. You may re-check the Entry status by clicking on the Return to Entrant Status Check Main Page link below.

And finally, if your application is among the winners, you'll receive a message similar to the text below:

Based on the information and confirmation number provided, you should have received a letter by mail from the United States Department of State's Kentucky Consular Center (KCC) notifying you that your Diversity Visa entry was selected in the DV-2012 lottery.

If you have not received a letter instructing you on how to proceed by August 1, 2012, please contact KCC by email at kccdv@state.gov This e-mail

---

address is being protected from spambots. You need JavaScript enabled to view it.

Please remember that you do not have to pay until you apply for a visa at a U.S. consulate or embassy The U.S. government will not ask you to send money by mail or by courier service.

As mentioned earlier in the book, you'll only be notified if your application is selected as a winner in the drawing. You'll not receive any notification from KCC indicating that you did not win or your application was duplicate, etc.

For those who do not have access to the internet or would like to rather receive the mail, KCC will send you a letter similar to what is shown in the Form 4-1.

Checking your application status on Secretary of State Website

While the Secretary of State website does provide fastest status check regarding your application, it only indicates whether or not you are the winner of the Lottery; it does not provide the documentations, rank number, and forms that you need to file. See next chapter for more information.

Copyright © 2011 - GreenCard123.Com by UNorth® - All Rights Reserved

May 09, 2011

JOHN AND JANE SMITH
2, AVENUE GABRIEL
PARIS, FRANCE 75016

Dear John Smith:

You are among those randomly selected and registered for further consideration in the DV-2012 diversity immigrant program for fiscal year 2011 **(October. I, 2011 to September 30. 2012).** Selection does not guarantee that you will receive a visa because the number of applicants selected is greater than the number of visas available. Please retain this letter and take it with you to your visa interview.

Approximately 100,000 individuals were registered for further processing. However there are only between **50,000 & 55,000** diversity visas available under the **FISCAL YEAR 2012 DIVERSITY VISA PROGRAM.** Therefore, it is most important that you carefully follow these instructions to increase your chances of possible visa issuance.

Please read and follow all the enclosed instructions very carefully. **ALL FORMS AND CORRESPONDENCE** must be sent to the Kentucky Consular Center al the above address. Please notify the Kentucky Consular Center of any change in address, addition or deletion of any family members, and any other information which you believe may
effect your application.

PL.EASE COMPL.ETE AND RETURN FORM S 230 PART I. 230 PART II. AND OSP-122 FOR YOURSELF AND FORMS 230 PART I AND 230 PART II FOR ALL. ACCOMPANY ING FAMILY MEMBERS TO THE KENTUCKY CONSUL.AR CENTER. WRITE THE CASE NUMBER IN THE UPPER RI GHT HAND CORNER OF EACH FORM. PL.EASE MAKE SURE A.L.L. BLOCKS ARE COMPL.ETED.

Please be advised that even though you send all of the above listed documents to the KCC, your case may not be scheduled for an interview appointment until a visa number is available. You will only be contacted by the KCC when a visa appointment is scheduled. Please do not call us to check when your case will be scheduled.

If it should be necessary to contact the Kentucky Consular Center by telephone **YOU MUST ALWAYS REFER TO YOUR NAME AND CASE NUMBER EXACTLY AS THEY APPEAR BELOW.** Your case number should be clearly written in the upper right hand comer of ALL documents and correspondence sent to the Kentucky Consular Center.

Case Number:	2012EU00099999
PA Name:	JOHN SMITH
Preference Category:	DV DIVERSITY
Foreign Slate Chargeability:	FRANCE
Post:	PARIS

The Kentucky Consular Center telephone number is 606-526-7500
or send E-mail inquiry to KCCDV@State.gov

Figure 4-1 Sample Winning Letter

Copyright © 2011 – GreenCard123.Com by UNorth® – All Rights Reserved

THIS PAGE WAS INTENTIONALLY LEFT BLANK

Copyright © 2011 - GreenCard123.Com by UNorth® - All Rights Reserved

5. WINNING! NOTIFICATION AND FILING

ROADMAP TO PREMANENT RESIDENCY VIA VISA LOTTERY:

VII. Visa Lottery Information ✔

VIII. Register for Visa Lottery ✔

IX. Checking Status and Winning
- a. Wait approximately 6-8 months✔
- b. Check status of your application (or wait for winning letter). ✔
- c. **Winning!**

X. Getting your green card

XI. Entering the United States

XII. Now that you have your green card

I WON!

If you're are reading this chapter, it is assumed that you have received the letter from USCIS Kentucky informing you that your name has been selected in the lottery or saw your application status in the lottery website. Congratulations! You're are now one step closer to entering United States of America!

A. YOUR WINNING LETTER

A sample notification letter from USCIS is shown on the Figure 5-1. Note that the format and layout of the letter may change from year to year but the main content remains the same.

Your winning letter notification shows your case number (aka Rank number), your name, and address. Your case (Rank) number indicates your position on the list of winners. Recall that every year, 50,000 visas are available but approximately 100,000 winners are notified. In addition, the visa allocation number includes family of the winner, if any. In other words, family of 3 will take 3 out of allocated visa numbers.

Example: John and Mary are married. They have a son (5 years old) and a daughter (17 years old). John applied for Diversity Visa Lottery in 2009 and in 2010 he was notified that he is a potential winner with rank number 88,123 (88,123rd). Since John had included Mary and their son and daughter in the application when they registered for visa Lottery, they'll apply as a family to the consulate. If they're issued a visa, they'll take four out of 50,000 allocated visa numbers and thus available visas would be reduced to 49,996.

Note:

(!) Don't presume that your Winning Letter is a guarantee that you will be issued a visa. Besides the number, many other factors influence your availability of visa. For example, even though your rank number may be at the bottom portion (e.g. > 75,000), you'll still go through the process and most likely will be issued, assuming that your documentation and other visa issuance requirements are met. This is because even though there is 50,000 maximum visa available worldwide, there is a per-country quota of 3,500. That means that maximum visa available for each country cannot exceed 3,500 any year. In addition, many people will be disqualified or would change their mind during the process so while the actual number of visa recipients stays around 50,000 almost all the winners will eventually be eligible to apply. That being said, you must apply as early as possible to increase your chances of completing your application for visa on time.

As indicated on the letter (sample below), you have been selected as a possible immigrant to the United States. You must still complete the following to be issued a visa:

- Register for lottery application
- Wait and check status
- Receive notification and winning
- Apply for Green Card
- Complete post application tasks such as medical test, visa fee, documents and evidences
- Attending interview
- Receive visa before available visas run out
- Enter United States

Copyright © 2011 - GreenCard123.Com by UNorth® - All Rights Reserved

May 09, 2011

JOHN AND JANE SMITH
2, AVENUE GABRIEL
PARIS, FRANCE 75016

Dear John Smith:

You are among those randomly selected and registered for further consideration in the DV-2012 diversity immigrant program for fiscal year 2011 **(October. I, 2011 to September 30. 2012)**. Selection does not guarantee that you will receive a visa because the number of applicants selected is greater than the number of visas available. Please retain this letter and take it with you to your visa interview.

Approximately 100,000 individuals were registered for further processing. However there are only between **50,000 & 55,000** diversity visas available under the **FISCAL YEAR 2012 DIVERSITY VISA PROGRAM**. Therefore, it is most important that you carefully follow these instructions to increase your chances of possible visa issuance.

Please read and follow all the enclosed instructions very carefully. **ALL FORMS AND CORRESPONDENCE** must be sent to the Kentucky Consular Center al the above address. Please notify the Kentucky Consular Center of any change in address, addition or deletion of any family members, and any other information which you believe may
effect your application.

PL.EASE COMPL.ETE AND RETURN FORM S 230 PART I. 230 PART II. AND OSP-122 FOR YOURSELF AND FORMS 230 PART I AND 230 PART II FOR ALL. ACCOMPANY ING FAMILY MEMBERS TO THE KENTUCKY CONSUL.AR CENTER. WRITE THE CASE NUMBER IN THE UPPER RI GHT HAND CORNER OF EACH FORM. PL.EASE MAKE SURE A.L.L. BLOCKS ARE COMPL.ETED.

Please be advised that even though you send all of the above listed documents to the KCC, your case may not be scheduled for an interview appointment until a visa number is available. You will only be contacted by the KCC when a visa appointment is scheduled. Please do not call us to check when your case will be scheduled.

If it should be necessary to contact the Kentucky Consular Center by telephone **YOU MUST ALWAYS REFER TO YOUR NAME AND CASE NUMBER EXACTLY AS THEY APPEAR BELOW.** Your case number should be clearly written in the upper right hand comer of ALL documents and correspondence sent to the Kentucky Consular Center.

Case Number:	2012EU00099999
PA Name:	JOHN SMITH
Preference Category:	DV DIVERSITY
Foreign Slate Chargeability:	FRANCE
Post:	PARIS

The Kentucky Consular Center telephone number is 606-526-7500
or send E-mail inquiry to KCCDV@State.gov

Figure 5-1 Sample Winning Letter

Copyright © 2011 – GreenCard123.Com by UNorth® – All Rights Reserved

B. TIME SENSITIVENESS

Diversity Visa Program is extremely time-sensitive. If you are notified that your name has been drawn in the lottery, try to get the information to Consulate/USCIS as soon as possible.

- As of 2010, once you are notified as a winner of the DV Lottery, Visa issuance will be started from October of that year until September 30th of the following year. For example DV-2011 winners are notified around May 2010, and visas will be issued between October 1, 2010, and September 30, 2011.

- Processing of entries and issuance of DVs to successful individuals and their eligible family members MUST occur by midnight on September 30, 2011.

Note that the last two are the trickiest ones. Even though your name is drawn in the Random drawing, your visa issuance depends on 1) You applying for visa as soon as possible and 2) There are enough visas available to be issued to you. You must receive your visa before the end of the Fiscal year (September 31st) of the year following your notification.

United States Citizenship and Immigration Services Website provides the following note regarding the deadline to receive Visa Lottery:

"...Under no circumstances can DVs be issued or adjustments approved after this date, nor can family members obtain DVs to follow-to-join the principal applicant in the United States after this date. In order to receive a DV to immigrate to the United States, those chosen in the random drawing must meet ALL eligibility requirements under U.S. law. These requirements may significantly increase the

level of scrutiny required and time necessary for processing for natives of some countries listed in this notice including, but not limited to, countries identified as state sponsors of terrorism..." (source: travel.state.gov)

C. SELECTION PROCESS

As explained in earlier chapters, although USCIS initially selects 100,000 winners for the Lottery application, the number of actual visas available is 50,000. In this calculation USCIS assumes that some winners:

- Will change their mind in migrating to United States
- May no longer be available (address return, death, etc.)
- May no longer be eligible (e.g. committed a crime, deported, etc.)
- Have submitted (or will submit) incorrect information and will be disqualified later on
- Will be disqualified during the interview process (e.g. medical test failure, etc.)
- Will apply late, past the deadline and so will be disqualified
- From the time their priority date becomes current to getting their interviews scheduled there will not be enough time to get their visa processed
- Some applicants may encounter envelope returns or for whatever reason may not receive the USCIS's notification (e.g. changing address). This would be resolved if you check your application status online.
- Death of the principal applicant (which cancels the application)
- Found inadmissible (e.g. committed fraud, money laundering, etc.)

Copyright © 2011 - GreenCard123.Com by UNorth® - All Rights Reserved

Inadmissibility Rules

Receiving the visa are the same reasons that would disqualify someone from applying at the first place (See inadmissibility rules in Chapter 1)

Basic List of Inadmissibility determination criteria is as follows:

- One who, inside or outside of the United States:
- Has a communicable disease that is of significant importance to public health, including those that fail to provide proof of vaccination and those who have physical or mental disorder posing safety to self or others.
- Is drug abusers and Drug Addicts
- Knowingly committed crime of moral turpitude or drug-related offense for which they have not been arrested
- Is a trafficker, or spouse or close relative of a trafficker and/or benefitted from the trafficking activities
- Is likely to become a public charge -- public charge refers to likeliness of someone receiving government benefits and public assistance due to lack of support.
- Is affiliated with Communist party or Totalitarian party, or engaged in Genocide or killing of any person for discriminative purposes.
- Has violated various immigration laws including failure to appear in Deportation hearing, been orders in Removal Proceeding, Removal order, making Frivolous applications.
- Is coming to United States to engage in various illegal activities, including polygamy (form of marriage in which a person has more than one spouse at the same time), prostitution, criminal offense, illegal gambling, kidnapping, trafficking, espionage, sabotage violating export control laws, terrorism, overthrowing the government of united states,...

(!) If you fall into any of the categories above, you may be able to file a waiver. It is recommended to consult an attorney to determine your options

D. CHANGE OF MIND

You may be wondering why a winner of the Lottery would want to change his/her mind. In real life, however, this happens quite often since life undergoes many changes...

Example: *John and Mary are married and have a 19 years old daughter named Erica. Erica had always dreamed of living in the United States but her parents were not interested. She finally convinces them to participate in the Visa Lottery. John and Mary apply and list Erica as their daughter in the Visa Lottery application.*
Erica later meets someone and marries her. They are later notified that their application is selected as winner; however, Erica is in a new life and no longer interested in migrating to the United States, and so are John and Mary. They'll not respond to the USCIS letter and they will not be issued a Visa.

E. NO TOLERANCE ON FALSIFYING INFORMATION

In addition to all the disqualifiers above, if you have submitted incorrect information and now you are applying for the visa, any inconsistent information with your original application can be a major problem. For example, if you mistyped your name or date of birth and now in your application you are correcting the information, USCIS will most likely flag your application as fraudulent and disqualify you. Although this may seem unfair at first, USCIS is mandated to adapt a fair and randomized process to select the winners of the Lottery. Every year over 2 million applicants get disqualified due to duplicate submission, incorrect data submission, and misuse the Lottery process. For example, in the past some applicants would submit two different Visa Lottery applications, one with the name "John Roberts" and the other with name "John

Copyright © 2011 - GreenCard123.Com by UNorth® - All Rights Reserved

Robert." thinking that by submitting two applications, their chances of winning in the Lottery doubles! (Notice that in the later name, characters "n" and "h" are reversed.) That's why USCIS carefully matches your name with your application name and later with your passport and other official documents during the interview process.

Lawyer's Note

If you have received the notification of winning but you've failed to apply for the visa within one year, you would normally lose your chance of applying for visa. There is however, one exception that many attorneys or applicants overlook; As explained above and in the INA Act 2003, if the applicant can prove within two years of notification of winning that the reason for such miss was not beyond his/her control, the visa availability maybe reopened for the applicant:

Side Note
Federal Code of Regulation provides the Application Process as follows:

INA: ACT 203
...
(g) Lists. - For purposes of carrying out the Secretary's responsibilities in the orderly administration of this section, the Secretary of State may make reasonable estimates of the anticipated numbers of visas to be issued during any quarter of any fiscal year within each of the categories under subsections (a), (b), and (c) and to rely upon such estimates in authorizing the issuance of visas. The Secretary of State shall terminate the registration of any alien who fails to apply for an immigrant visa within one year following notification to the alien of the availability of such visa, but the Secretary shall reinstate the registration of any such alien who establishes within 2 years following the date of notification of the availability of such visa that such failure to apply was due to circumstances beyond the alien's control.

"...The Secretary of State shall terminate the registration of any alien who fails to apply for an immigrant visa within one year following notification to the alien of the availability of such visa, but the Secretary shall reinstate

the registration of any such alien who establishes within 2 years following the date of notification of the availability of such visa that such failure to apply was due to circumstances beyond the alien's control.

If you have such a case, it is recommended to consult with an attorney familiar with this matter.

-Visit "Getting Technical" for more information

Table 5-1 Selected Immigration Code

F. CHANGE OF STATUS SINCE SUBMISSION OF APPLICATION

If your status has changed since the time you applied for the Lottery application (e.g. you married, divorced, have a new son or daughter, etc.), USCIS will accept the new status, assuming that it does not make you ineligible to receive the visa.

Note: if USCIS discovers that you purposely changed your status just to benefit the other person from getting a visa to the United States, note that your application too will be tossed out, and your name added to the in the fraudulent applicants list. Remember that the United States visa is not an easy one to get so USCIS takes a very careful look at how your application is completed. Their job is to make sure the right people get the right visa and no one cheats the system.

Example 1: Mona is 22 years old and she likes to participate in the Green Card Lottery drawing. She sends in her application and lists only herself in the application. A couple months later she gets engaged and later marries Arman. During the drawing she is notified that she is selected for the Lottery Green Card. Mona and Ahmad are both qualified to apply for Green Card now because the status changed "after" she submitted the application, "not before" Same rule applies if they have a new child, etc.

Copyright © 2011 - GreenCard123.Com by UNorth® - All Rights Reserved

Example 2: Jonathan and Mary file for the Visa Lottery application. Mary was pregnant and she gives a birth to Sam Jr. shortly after. Approximately six months later, they are notified that their name is selected as a possible visa recipient. In addition to Jonathan and Mary who initially filed their application, Sam Jr. is also now eligible applicant because the new Status is recognized by the USCIS.

Example 3: Armin has filed his application for Green Card lottery. Later he is notified by USCIS that he has won the Lottery and can apply for the Green Card. His long-time friend, Sarah, has always been dreaming to come to United States. Knowing that if Armin's status changed after sending application, his spouse would still be qualified, Armin and Sarah decide to marry so that Sarah can also get Green Card during the process and they can divorce later once everything is done. Once all the documents are sent and Armin and Sara are interviewed at the US Consulate, Consulate questions them about their marriage and they fail to answer as expected of a married couple - . The Consulate becomes suspicious and think that the their marriage is fraudulent, made for immigration purposes and refers them for further investigation. They are asked to bring their family picture prior to the marriage. They did not plan to marry prior to that date so they cannot furnish the Consulate with such a photo request. The Consulate concludes that their marriage was fraudulent for the purpose of getting Green Card and so they are both disqualified. They will also be placed in a black-list which means if they apply in the future; the Consulate will take an extremely detailed look at their application and most likely will deny their application in the future.

G. APPLYING FROM AXIS-OF-EVIL COUNTRIES

If you are born in one of the countries on high terror-alert (e.g. Sudan, Iran, etc.) time may become even more important. Although all applicants for Visa Lottery need to pass a background check which would take quite some time, applicants from the high terror-alert countries may take even more time to process. If your name is selected in the drawing you must apply as quickly as possible to make sure you won't be backlogged.

Bottom line, you must be actually issued a visa by September 30th of the year you apply for (DV2011 application visas must be received by Sep 30, 2011; DV2012 must be received by Sep 30, 2012).

Over 2 million applicants were rejected in 2008 for incorrectly entering or falsifying information!

Copyright © 2011 - GreenCard123.Com by UNorth® - All Rights Reserved

THIS PAGE WAS INTENTIONALLY LEFT BLANK

Copyright © 2011 – GreenCard123.Com by UNorth® – All Rights Reserved

6. APPLYING FOR THE GREEN CARD

ROADMAP TO PREMANENT RESIDENCY VIA VISA LOTTERY:

I. Visa Lottery Information ✔
II. Register for Visa Lottery ✔
III. Checking Status and Winning ✔
IV. Getting your green card ✔
V. Entering the United States
    a. Prepare the Green Card Forms
    b. Interview at the Embassy/Consulate (or USCIS Service Center in case you are in the United States)
VI. Now that you have your green card

A. WHAT IS A GREEN CARD

You may not realize it but the Green Card is not green at all! A United States Permanent Resident Card, also known as a Green Card (due to the color of earlier versions), is an identification card attesting to the permanent resident status of an alien in the United States of America. The Green Card serves as proof that its holder, a Lawful Permanent Resident (LPR), has been officially granted immigration benefits, which include permission to reside and take employment in the USA. The holder must maintain permanent resident status, and can be removed from the US if certain conditions of this status are not met.

Green Cards were formerly issued by the Immigration and Naturalization Service (INS). During a re-organization process, that agency was absorbed into and replaced by the Bureau of Citizenship and Immigration Services (BCIS), a part of the Department of Homeland Security (DHS). Shortly after that re-organization, BCIS was renamed U.S. Citizenship and Immigration Services (USCIS), which still retains the responsibility for issuing Green Cards.

An example of new and old version of the United States Permanent Resident Card is shown in figure below:

B. SPOUSE AND CHILDREN

Assuming that you've followed the steps in all previous sections and included your spouse and children under 21 in the Diversity Visa application, they'll be allowed to apply for Green Card together with you once you are notified as a winner. Your children under 21 must remain married until they arrive in the United States or otherwise they'll lose their eligibility for Green Card.

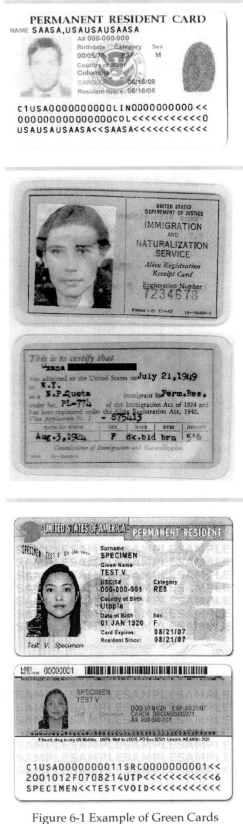

Figure 6-1 Example of Green Cards issued by USCIS

Copyright © 2011 - GreenCard123.Com by UNorth® - All Rights Reserved

C. CHANGE IN STATUS (AFTER VISA LOTTERY APPLICATION)

Of course things can happen in the life that would change some of the information that you originally submitted, such as

- Marriage (Including your new spouse's children)
- Divorce
- Separation
- Newborn baby
- Children under 21 years of age marries (and is considered independent)
- Adoption
- Death

D. CHANGES THAT MAKES A PERSON ELIGIBLE

Marriage, newborn child, and adoption are the changes that would provide immigration benefits for the new eligible person. For example, if after submission of your Visa Lottery application, you marry or you have a new child, your spouse or child also becomes eligible even though their name was not on the original Visa Lottery application.

Example: John, 25 years of old applies for Visa Lottery. After couple months he meets Linda and they immediately fall in love and marry. A couple months later John is informed that his Visa Lottery application is a winner! John and his new wife can now apply for a Green Card and enter United States together.

1) **Marriage after submitting the Diversity application:** If you marry after submitting your application, your new spouse is also eligible to receive a Green Card. To reduce the fraud, immigration officer/counselor would require additional documentation to ensure the marriage was not based on the Green Card (fraud).

2) **New child born:** If your new child is born during the processing time, he/she will also be allowed to apply for a Green Card. You simply need to provide the documentation and application for the new born.

3) **Child turning 21:** If your child is turning 21 after submitting your application for Diversity Visa, technically and for the purpose of Green Card, he/she is considered independent. However, law does provide some protection that allows you to subtract the days between the date you received your winning notification letter, and the date you were first eligible to apply for Diversity Visa from the age of your child. Sounds confusing? See the example below

Example: John and Mary have a daughter named Rose. The Diversity Visa Lottery program opened on October 01, 2010. They apply for Diversity Visa application on November 20, 2010. Rose's birthday is December 10, 1989 (meaning that she will turn 21 in March 20, 2010). Later John is notified as winner of lottery on May 30, 2011 and they apply for Green Card with interview date of August 10, 2011.

Technically, by August 10, 2011 when they are all at the interview, Rose is already 21 (143 days to be exact). However, the law allows the duration between October 01, 2010 (the application availability date) and winner notification letter date (May 30, 2011) be deducted from her age, or 241 days. That would put her about 3 months prior to becoming ineligible and thus the application is approved for John, Mary, and Rose.

If the above numbers don't work for you unfortunately, your child is considered independent and is not eligible to receive a Green Card. The parents however are still eligible to receive Green Card.

Copyright © 2011 - GreenCard123.Com by UNorth® - All Rights Reserved

4) **Forgot to include your spouse/children:** If you forgot to include your spouse (unless legally separated) and children on your Diversity Visa application, they will not be allowed to apply for the Green Card, and you will also be disqualified for falsifying your application. If this applies to you, contact an attorney immediately.

Note that as mentioned previously, submission of falsified information is ground for inadmissibility. This strict rule applies, even after you are admitted to the United States or worse even if you become a United States citizen down the road. If it is proven that you submitted incorrect information for the purpose of gaining immigration benefits, you can be denied admission to the United States, be deported or the government can revoke your residency or citizenship status.

Example: Mark applied for the Visa Green Card Lottery. A couple months later, Mark is informed that he is indeed a winner of the Green Card Lottery. One of his old friends, Sarah, had always dreamed of entering United States but was never successful in obtaining one. Mark knows that if he marries Sarah, they both can get their Green Cards.

E. CHANGES THAT MAKES A PERSON INELIGIBLE:

Divorce, Death, and marriage of a child under 21 years old are among changes that can potentially disqualify an applicant.

If the primary applicant on the Visa Lottery is deceased, the whole Lottery application is cancelled even though spouse would have been eligible if the person did not die.

Example: Robert and Mary apply for Visa Lottery

application, as Robert being the primary applicant. After few months Robert becomes extremely ill and unfortunately passes away after a couple of weeks. The following month, Mary receives a notice that they are the winners of the Visa Lottery application. However, since the primary applicant on the Visa Lottery application no longer lives, Mary is also ineligible.

Consult a Lawyer!

If you encounter a situation that the primary applicant is deceased, it is recommended that you consult a lawyer to see if any other remedy is available to you.

F. HOW TO APPLY FOR GREEN CARD ONCE YOU'RE CALLED AS WINNER

The process is slightly different whether you are applying outside of United States or from inside (or Adjustment of Status).

1) **For those applying outside the US:**
Once you are selected as a lottery winner, you'll be sent a set of forms and document requests (Packet 3) that must be returned as early as possible. Once those documents are returned, you'll be sent another set of documents (Packet 4) along with appointment letter that must be taken to the Consulate/Embassy selected along with the documentation requested. Once you attend the interview and assuming that all documentation was correct and acceptable, you'll be issued a visa. This visa allows you to apply to enter the United States at the US border (e.g. Airport). Once inspected at the airport, you'll receive Green Card stamp in your passport and later you'll receive your Green Card in the mail. You must complete the process by September 30th.

Copyright © 2011 - GreenCard123.Com by UNorth® - All Rights Reserved

2) For those applying Inside the US:

Once you are selected as a Lottery winner, you'll be sent your winner Lottery notification. You apply for Adjustment of Status, thereby changing your status from your current visa (e.g. student, etc.) to Permanent Resident via Diversity Lottery. Once your AOS application is sent and reviewed by USCIS, you'll receive an interview letter and biometric exam and once your application is approved, you'll receive your Green Card via mail. You must complete the processing by September 30th.

As indicated above, the process of applying for your Green Card whether or not you currently reside in the United States is more or less the same. However, internal applicants have a slight advantage in that they can appeal the denial application, and they are not inspected by the ICE officer at the airport, since they are already in the United States. At the same time, the Embassy/Consulate is known to process Diversity Visa applications slightly faster than USCIS.

If you are currently in the United States but frequently travelling outside, you chose to have a consulate handle your application instead of USCIS.

Do I need an attorney?

Do I need an attorney? Good question. The answer depends on you. If you believe you have a good understanding of the process and none of the inadmissible items apply to you, and have all the documentations readily available, you should be able to go through the process by yourself. However, if you are planning to apply for waivers or some of your documents are missing, it is highly recommended that you consult with an attorney to make sure you won't be hitting any roadblock down the road. In addition, attorney consultation may help to reduce the time by giving you the information you need.

Timing is critical at this step. You must get all the documentations ready as soon as possible and submit them so that you have a better chance of completing the process by September 30th.

Attorneys Make Mistakes Too!

Of course, attorneys do make mistakes; lots of them! Although it may not happen as often but their mistakes can delay your visa as well, which is not what you need. Try to review the information prior to attorney submission and perform thorough research when trying to find the attorney.

G. FOR THOSE APPLYING OUTSIDE THE UNITED STATES

Once your name is drawn as winner of the Lottery, you'll receive your winner notification letter, and set of documents and forms (DS-230 Part I).

Process: Diversity Visa process is categorized under "Immigrant Visa" and thus the process is very similar to other types of permanent visa requests. In Diversity Visa cases, the applicant (winner) will receive, along with the winning notification letter, a set of forms and instructions called Packet 3. This packet normally contains:

- Instruction for Immigrant Visa applicants (Checklist)
- Immigration Form , DS230-Part 1
- Medical exam instruction
- Medical exam form
- Photograph requirement

    Do not send any document to the Embassy/Consulate unless instructed when and where to deliver the documents.

Sample filled DS230-Part I is provided in Appendix I. To complete DS230-Part I, you will need the following information and documents:

Copyright © 2011 - GreenCard123.Com by UNorth® - All Rights Reserved

- ☐ Educational history
- ☐ Birth certificate information
- ☐ Marriage certificate/ information
- ☐ Photographs
- ☐ Previous addresses
- ☐ Parent information (name, address, etc)

Checklist for Preparing form to

- ☐ DS Form 230 Part I
- ☐ Affidavit of support
- ☐ Lottery winner notification
- ☐ Lottery registration page
- ☐ Two passport photographs

Don't Send Originals

Do Not send any original evidence (E.g. proof of education, etc); send copies. You'll need to present these in person during the interview process

Once the above forms are received by the consulate, you'll be scheduled for a visa interview. The Consulate will send you an appointment letter along with more set of instructions, called Packet 4, approximately one month in advance. It is not possible to predict when your interview will be scheduled since it may depend on the priority date for your visa category and country. However, you may continue to check Visa Bulletin publication by Secretary of State (Available electronically at travel.state.gov -- also explained in detail in Appendix IV).

Packet 4 contains set of documents and evidences that you must prepare, as soon as possible, and take with you to the interview. Unless otherwise instructed by the consulate, DO NOT MAIL PACKET 4. The documents requested are primarily to establish the fact that you are who you are claiming to be, and present evidence for your education, qualifications, family, military service, and record checks. Generally, you want to be as prepared as possible since any lack of documentation or inefficiencies may cause denial of your visa application or schedule for another interview, and especially in Diversity Visa, time is one of the essential factors as you want to complete your visa prior to the September 30th deadline and any delay in processing your visa may jeopardize the completion on time.

Medical Test: is one of the mandatory steps for any type of Immigrant Visa, including Diversity Lottery. You'll need record of your vaccinations, and you must take those to the designated USCIS-approved doctor. A list of medical

Copyright © 2011 - GreenCard123.Com by UNorth® - All Rights Reserved

doctors will be provided to you along with your application but also available on the USCIS website http://www.uscis.gov/civilsurgeons . Only an approved USCIS doctor has authority to certify your medical test. At the end of the test, you'll be given a sealed envelope that must not be opened, except by the Immigration Officer. If you are concerned whether or not your medical test had any problem, ask the doctor.

No Vaccination Records?

If you do not find your vaccination record, no worries! Medical doctors are well aware that some individuals may not be able to locate their long-time-ago documents. A workaround to this loss would be to get revaccinated at the doctor's office and you'll have new records! This normally causes an extra charge but if your vaccination records are not retrievable or not acceptable by doctor would be your only chance.

In addition, some individuals may need an x-ray for your TB test. X-ray may take few days to be examined and thus you'll need to try to get your medical certificate in advance of the interview. Don't wait until last minute or small issues like this may easily jeopardize your interview process.

Affidavit of Support: One of the other documents you need is called "Affidavit of Support." it basically is an indicator that whether or not you may potentially become a public charge for the Government of United States. If it seems likely that you do become a public charge, you'll most certainly not be getting your visa approved. If you do not have sufficient income to support yourself based on the USCIS guidelines, you may ask a friend or relative in the United States to sign the affidavit for you and basically

sponsor you. This is a legally binding responsibility that in case you become public chart, USCIS can force the sponsor to pay for your life support. There are two versions of the Affidavit of support: long and short; fortunately, Diversity Visa lottery requires the short version only.

DS-230 Part 2 has more detail regarding what may potentially disqualify you to receive the visa (e.g. inadmissible). In addition, it goes over your background for the same reason.

Birth Certificates: You'll need the original copies along with certified English Translation. It is understandable that in some countries, small typos inside the birth certificate may exist. Consulate officers are expert in their field and understand the difference between Government Typos and falsified document!

Marriage Certificate, Divorce, Death, and Adoption Certificates: Depending on your status, you do require to show evidence. For instance, if you are married, your official marriage certificate along with translated copy is needed. If you were divorce previously, you'll need to present your divorce certificate(s) along with translation copy. If your husband/wife or other relevant relative has died, you'll need to present the death certificate along with the translated copies.

Translation Service

It is highly recommended that you or someone you know read the translated copies prior to the interview to make sure they are translated properly. It has happened quite often that translation services may have typo themselves and/or make a mistake during translation. Again, you want to make sure everything is as prepared and complete as possible prior to the interview

Copyright © 2011 - GreenCard123.Com by UNorth® - All Rights Reserved

Military Service Record: If you've previously served in Military, makes sure to include your military service information and discharge info, if applicable. You'll also need translated copy of documents, if applicable.

Fees: Refer to your packet information regarding the fees and payment method. You can also find this information from USCIS website for latest fee information. Since the fees change quite often, it is not provided in the Book.

Proof of Education: As you may recall, the minimum requirement to participate in the Visa Lottery program is High School diploma. Although during the registration there is no step to validate this information, once won, you will be required to prove that you are qualified for what you claimed. The Consulate officer will compare your responses to the information submitted in the application. Proof of Education is one of the mandatory steps for Diversity Visa lottery. Make sure to include official records along with translated copy during the interview process.

Police Report: Each applicant aged 16 years or older must submit a police certificate. The applicant must submit police certificates that meet the following guidelines. The police certificate must:

- Cover the entire period of the applicant's residence in that area
- Be issued by the appropriate police authority
- Include all arrests, the reason for the arrest(s), and the disposition of each case of which there is a record.

How to obtain a police certificate?

- Determine from which countries an applicant is required to obtain police certificates. The table below will assist in determining from

where an applicant must obtain police certificates.
- Contact the appropriate police authorities. Selecting the appropriate country from the Reciprocity by Country page will provide you with additional information on how to obtain a police certificate.

Countries Exempt from Police Report

As of 2011, police certificate is not required for the following countries:

Afghanistan	Malaysia
Angola	Mexico
Azerbaijan	Mongolia
Bangladesh	Nepal
Bulgaria	Nicaragua
Cambodia	Pakistan
Chad	Saudi Arabia
Colombia	Sierra Leone
Costa Rica	Somalia
Equatorial Guinea	Sri Lanka
Ghana	Sudan
Guatemala	Syria
Haiti	Tajikistan
Honduras	Thailand
Indonesia	Turkey
Iran	USA
Iraq	Uzbekistan
Kazakhstan	Venezuela
Laos	Vietnam
Libya	

In addition to the list above, present and former residents of the United States should NOT obtain any police certificates covering their residence in the U.S.

Police Report and Time

Note that depending on your country of origin requesting and receiving police report may take some time. It is therefore highly recommended that you request for this as soon as you get your consular letter so that there will be enough time to gather your documents together.

Copyright © 2011 - GreenCard123.Com by UNorth® - All Rights Reserved

IF the applicant...	AND...	THEN the applicant needs a police certificate from...
is living in their country of nationality at their current residence for more than 6 months	is 16 years old or older	The police authorities of that locality.
lived in a different part of their country of nationality for more than 6 months	was 16 years or older at that time	The police authorities of that locality.
lived in a different country for more than 12 months	was 16 years or older at that time	The police authorities of that locality.
was arrested for any reason, regardless of how long they lived there	was any age at that time	The police authorities of that locality.

Source: http://travel.state.gov/

Here is a checklist of what is generally required in Packet 4:

- DS-230 Part 2
- Appointment letter
- Two color photos of each applicant
- Birth certificates
- Marriage certificates, if applicable
- Divorce certificates, if applicable
- Death certificates, if applicable
- Adoption information, if applicable
- Finger prints, if requested
- Military service records
- Affidavit of support form i-134
- Police report
- Photos: two photographs, color
- Medical exam
- Fees
- Police certificate
- Proof of education
- Valid passport

Passport Validity

Make sure your passport has at least 6 months validity available. The reason would be that after you initial interview, if you are eligible for the visa, the visa will be stamped in your passport with validity. When you arrive at the border, your passport must still be valid, along with the visa stamp, so you need at the minimum 6 months validity for the passport. If your passport is expiring within one year, it is recommended that you apply for renewal and have the visa be stamped in your new passport instead.

Fees: And of course, there are fees related to Diversity Visa. In fact, the actual cost of Diversity Visa program is recuperated from the winners of the lottery (not participants). Fee details will be provided in your information packet. For latest fee schedule visit USCIS Website http://www.uscis.gov

As of 2010 the visa fees are:

Fee	Cost
Visa Fee	$355
Diversity Visa Fee	$375
Security	$45

H. FOR THOSE APPLYING INSIDE THE UNITED STATES

Once your name is drawn as winner of lottery, you'll receive your winner notification letter, and set of documents and forms.

Your winning letter notification shows your case number (aka Rank number), your name, and address. Your case (Rank) number indicates your position on the list of winners. Recall that every year, 50,000 visas are available but approximately 100,000 winners are notified. In addition, the visa allocation number includes family of the winner, if any. In other words, family of 3, will take 3 out of allocated visa numbers.

Copyright © 2011 - GreenCard123.Com by UNorth® - All Rights Reserved

Example: John and Mary are married. They have a son (5 years old) and a daughter (17 years old). John applied for Diversity Visa Lottery in 2009 and in 2010 he was notified that he is a potential winner with rank number 88,123 (88,123rd). Since John had included Mary and their son and daughter in the application when they registered for visa lottery, they'll apply as a family to the consulate. If they're issued a visa, they'll take four out of 50,000 allocated visa numbers and thus available visas would be reduced to 49,996.

Don't think of your rank number as a guarantee that you will be issued a visa. Besides the number, many other factors influence your availability of visa. For example, even though your rank number may be at the bottom portion (e.g. > 75,000), you'll still go through the process and most likely will be issued a visa, assuming that your documentation and other visa issuance requirements are met. This is because even though there is 50,000 maximum visa available worldwide, there is a per-country quota of 3,500. That means that maximum visas available for each country cannot exceed 3,500 yearly. In addition, many people will be disqualified or would change their mind in the process so while the actual number of visa recipients stays around 50,000 almost all the winners will eventually be eligible to apply. That being said, you must apply as early as possible to increase your chances of completing your application for visa on time.

Do I need an attorney?

Do I need an attorney? Good question. The answer depends on you. If you believe you have a good understanding of the process and none of the inadmissible items apply to you, and have all the documentations readily available, you should be able to go through the process by yourself. However, if you are planning to apply for waivers or some of your documents are missing, it is highly recommended that you consult with an attorney to make sure you won't be hitting any roadblock down the road. In addition, attorney consultation may help to reduce the time by giving you the information you need.

Attorneys Make Mistakes Too!

Of course, attorneys do make mistakes; lots of them! Although it may not happen as often but their mistakes can delay your visa as well, which is not what you need. Try to review the information prior to attorney submission and perform thorough research when trying to find the attorney.

Process: Diversity Visa process is categorized under "Immigrant Visa" and thus the process is very similar to other types of permanent visa requests. In Diversity Visa cases, the applicant (winner) will receive, along with the winning notification letter, a set of forms and instructions. This packet normally contains:

- Instructions for adjustment of status (checklist)
- Immigration forms
- Medical exam instruction
- Medical exam form
- Photograph requirement

In general, the process is very similar to applying from abroad. However, you do have an edge by applying inside the United States. First of all, you may have appeal rights in case your application is denied, and second, since you are already in the United States, you do not need to be further inspected by border officers (ICE).

Process of applying inside the US is known as Adjustment of Status or AOS. In other words, you are not applying for a fresh visa, but rather changing your status from non-immigrant to immigrant so instead of a visa form, you'll need to file the I-485 (Adjustment of Status).

Copyright © 2011 - GreenCard123.Com by UNorth® - All Rights Reserved

What if I'm out of Status?

If you are currently "out of status" (e.g. illegal aliens, or people who overstayed their visa), you may not be eligible for Diversity Visa and may be punished by having to leave United States for extended period of time before being admitted back to US. If you are currently residing in the US without a valid visa, there are certain exceptions that you may be able to take advantage of; consult an attorney before submitting any form to USCIS.

E ORGANIZED!

USCIS officers receive very large number of applications on a daily basis. Organizing your paperwork ensures that the officer can easily find the documents that he/she is looking for and therefore making the application process for him less painful. If the officer cannot find a document in your application, he/she has to issue a letter called RFE or return your application, thus try to be as organized as possible to get the best response. Imagine that you are an USCIS officer and a clean, organized application comes at your desk, compared to an unorganized, messy and unreadable application; which one you prefer to work on?

To make it professional, you may draft a cover letter similar to the one below and attach it to the front of your package:

Dear Sir/Madam:

Enclosed please find my I-485 packet for John Smith. Since this is a Diversity Visa Application and highly time-sensitive, I would highly appreciate if it can be processed as early as possible. I have organized the packet as follows:

- *Check # 1000 for the amount of $1000*
- *Form I-485*
- *Form G-325*
- *Copy of my current passport - John Smith*
- *Copy of my Wife's Passport – Jane Smith*
- *Copy and Translation of my Birth Certificate - John Smith*

Once the above forms are received by the USCIS, you'll be scheduled for a visa interview at one of the USCIS Service Centers. First, you'll receive a confirmation receipt of your submission along with your application (receipt) number.

You'll receive a set of instructions along with your interview date and biometric appointment if applicable. Although it is not possible to predict when you'll receive your interview letter and when it will be scheduled, it certainly depends on your priority date for your visa category and country, and your rank number. However, you may continue to check Visa Bulletin publication by Secretary of State (Available electronically at travel.state.gov -- also explained in detail in Appendix IV).

This Packet contains set of documents and evidences that you must prepare, as soon as possible, and take with you to the interview. Unless otherwise instructed by the consulate, DO NOT MAIL THE FORMS, unless specifically instructed by USCIS. The documents requested are primarily to establish the fact that you are who you are claiming to be, and present evidence for your education, qualifications, family, military service, and record checks. Generally, you want to be as prepared as possible since any lack of documentation or inefficiencies may cause denial of your visa application or schedule for another interview, and especially for the Diversity Visa, time is one of the essential factors as you want to complete your visa process prior to the September 30th deadline and any delay in processing your visa may jeopardize the completion on time.

Copyright © 2011 - GreenCard123.Com by UNorth® - All Rights Reserved

Checklist for preparing form to USCIS:

- ☐ Adjustment of Status (AOS) I-485 along with the filing fee (check USCIS website for latest filing fees and exclusions)
- ☐ Biographical information - Form I-325A
- ☐ Affidavit of Support - Form I-134
- ☐ Lottery winner notification
- ☐ Lottery registration page
- ☐ Two passport photographs
  Optional:
- ☐ Work Permit - Form I-765

Evidences/Documents:

- ☐ Your winning letter, of course!
- ☐ Your passport. Although you normally need to send copy of the main pages and the page that current I-94 stamp is in, it is recommended that you attach a copy of all pages in your passport.
- ☐ Marriage and/or divorce documents. (Translation is required if not in English language)
- ☐ Education/degree documents or work experience document (e.g. letter from your previous employer, offer letter, paystub, etc)
- ☐ Birth Certificate for applicant and accompanying relatives (e.g. spouse and children). (Translation is required if not in English language)
- ☐ Medical exam results in sealed envelope, for the applicant and accompanying relatives. Do not open the envelope or you'll have to do it all over again!
- ☐ Photographs of the applicants and accompanying relatives (e.g. spouse and children). These photographs need to comply with the US standard for passport pictures Write your Full name, Date of Birth, and A number (if applicable) on the back of each photograph lightly.

Others Forms, if applicable (These are not common)

- ☐ Advance Parole - Form I-131 (For applicants that have a necessity to go outside of the United States while their Green Card application is being processed)

- ☐ Supplement A for I-485 Adjustment of Status (For Aliens who entered the United States without inspection, remained in the United States past the period of admission, worked unlawfully, or are otherwise ineligible for adjustment of status under section 245(c) of the Act must submit this form along with Form I-485, Application to Register Permanent Residence or Adjust Status.)

Note: *Make a full exact copy of everything you submit to USCIS.*

Don't Send Originals: *Except for the Medical Certificate (that's in sealed envelope), Do Not send any original evidence (E.g. proof of education, etc); send copies. You'll need to present the original documents in person during the interview process*

Medical Test: is one of the mandatory steps for any type of Immigrant Visa, including Diversity Lottery. You'll need record of your vaccinations, and you must take those to the designated USCIS-approved doctor. A list of medical doctors will be provided to you along with your application but also available on the USCIS website http://www.uscis.gov/civilsurgeons . Only an approved USCIS doctor has authority to certify your medical test. At the end of the test, you'll be given a sealed envelope that must not be opened, except by the Immigration Officer. If you are concerned whether or not your medical test had any problem, ask the doctor.

No Vaccination Records?

If you do not find your vaccination record, no worries! Medical doctors are well aware that some individuals may not be able to locate their long-time-ago documents. A workaround to this loss would be to get revaccinated at the doctor's office and you'll have new records! This normally causes an extra charge but if your vaccination records are not retrievable or not acceptable by doctor would be your only chance.

Copyright © 2011 - GreenCard123.Com by UNorth® - All Rights Reserved

In addition, some individuals may need an x-ray for your TB test. X-ray may take few days to be examined and thus you'll need to try to get your medical certificate in advance of the interview. Don't wait until last minute or small issues like this may easily jeopardize your interview process.

Affidavit of Support: One of the other documents you need is called "Affidavit of Support." it basically is an indicator that whether or not you may potentially become a public charge for the Government of United States. If it seems likely that you do become a public charge, you'll most certainly not be getting your visa approved. If you do not have sufficient income to support yourself based on the USCIS guidelines, you may ask a friend or relative in the United States to sign the affidavit for you and basically sponsor you. This is a legally binding responsibility that in case you become public chart, USCIS can force the sponsor to pay for your life support. There are two versions of the Affidavit of support: long and short; fortunately, Diversity Visa lottery requires the short version only.

Birth Certificates: You'll need the original copies along with certified English Translation. It is understandable that in <u>some countries</u>, small typos inside the birth certificate may exist. Consulate officers are expert in their field and understand the difference between Government Typos and falsified document!

Marriage Certificate, Divorce, Death, and Adoption Certificates: Depending on your status, you do require to show evidence. For instance, if you are married, your official marriage certificate along with translated copy is needed. If you were divorce previously, you'll need to present your divorce certificate(s) along with translation copy. If your husband/wife or other relevant relative has died, you'll need to

present the death certificate along with the translated copies.

Translation Service

It is highly recommended that you or someone you know read the translated copies prior to the interview to make sure they are translated properly. It has happened quite often that translation services may have typo themselves and/or make a mistake during translation. Again, you want to make sure everything is as prepared and complete as possible prior to the interview.

Military Service Record: If you've previously served in Military, makes sure to include your military service information and discharge info, if applicable. You'll also need translated copy of documents, if applicable.

Fees: Refer to your packet information regarding the fees and payment method. You can also find this information from USCIS website for latest fee information. Since the fees change quite often, it is not provided in the Book.

Proof of Education: As you may recall, the minimum requirement to participate in the Visa Lottery program is High School diploma. Although during the registration there is no step to validate this information, once won, you will be required to prove that you are qualified for what you claimed. The Consulate officer will compare your responses to the information submitted in the application. Proof of Education is one of the mandatory steps for Diversity Visa lottery. Make sure to include official records along with translated copy during the interview process.

Police Report: Each applicant aged 16 years or older must submit a police certificate. The applicant must submit police certificates that

Copyright © 2011 - GreenCard123.Com by UNorth® - All Rights Reserved

meet the following guidelines. The police certificate must:

- Cover the entire period of the applicant's residence in that area
- Be issued by the appropriate police authority
- Include all arrests, the reason for the arrest(s), and the disposition of each case of which there is a record.
- How to obtain a police certificate
- Determine from which countries an applicant is required to obtain police certificates. The table below will assist in determining from where an applicant must obtain police certificates.

Contact the appropriate police authorities. Selecting the appropriate country from the Reciprocity by Country page will provide you with additional information on how to obtain a police certificate.

Countries Exempt from Police Report

As of 2010, police certificate is not required for the following countries:

Afghanistan	Malaysia
Angola	Mexico
Azerbaijan	Mongolia
Bangladesh	Nepal
Bulgaria	Nicaragua
Cambodia	Pakistan
Chad	Saudi Arabia
Colombia	Sierra Leone
Costa Rica	Somalia
Equatorial Guinea	Sri Lanka
Ghana	Sudan
Guatemala	Syria
Haiti	Tajikistan
Honduras	Thailand
Indonesia	Turkey
Iran	USA
Iraq	Uzbekistan
Kazakhstan	Venezuela
Laos	Vietnam
Libya	

In addition to the list above, present and former residents of the United States should NOT obtain any police certificates covering their residence in the U.S.

Police Report and Time

Note that depending on your country of origin requesting and receiving police report may take some time. It is therefore highly recommended that you request for this as soon as you get your consular letter so that there will be enough time to gather your documents together.

IF the applicant...	AND...	THEN the applicant needs a police certificate from...
is living in their country of nationality at their current residence for more than 6 months	is 16 years old or older	the police authorities of that locality.
lived in a different part of their country of nationality for more than 6 months	was 16 years or older at that time	the police authorities of that locality.
lived in a different country for more than 12 months	was 16 years or older at that time	the police authorities of that locality.
was arrested for any reason, regardless of how long they lived there	was any age at that time	the police authorities of that locality.

Source: http://travel.state.gov/

Copyright © 2011 - GreenCard123.Com by UNorth® - All Rights Reserved

Here is a checklist of what is generally required in Adjustment of Status:

☐ Your winning letter, of course!
☐ Biometrics application g-325
☐ Affidavit of support i-134
☐ Filing fee
☐ Optional: i-485a if you are overstaying
☐ Optional: i-765 if you are applying for work-permit
☐ Optional: if you are applying for social security card
☐ I-94 form/card (received upon entry to united states)
☐ All documents received from KCC and Consulate regarding the lottery application. Most importantly, official notice of winner, and lottery registration
☐ Birth certificates
☐ Marriage certificates, if applicable
☐ Divorce certificates, if applicable
☐ Death certificates, if applicable
☐ Adoption information, if applicable
☐ Finger prints, if requested
☐ Military service records
☐ Affidavit of support form i-134
☐ Police report
☐ Photos: two photographs, color.
☐ Medical exam
☐ Fees
☐ Police certificate
☐ Proof of education
☐ Valid Passport

Fees: And of course, there are fees related to Diversity Visa. In fact, the actual cost of Diversity Visa program is recuperated from the winners of the lottery (not participants). Fee details will be provided in your Packet information. For latest fee schedule visit USCIS Website http://www.uscis.gov

As of 2010 the Visa fees are as follows:

Fee	Cost
• Visa Fee	$355
• Diversity Visa Fee	$375
• Security	$45

Fee Tips:
- If a filing fee is required with your immigration form or application, attach it to the top of the application package and mail it all together
- Never send cash for immigration fees- USCIS accepts money orders, cashier's check or personal check for payment of fees
- Always write your full name, your number and form number in the memo area of your check
- How do I bind my package?
- Make sure your check is signed and dated correctly
- Submit a separate check or cashier's check or money order for each application you are sending , OR, attach a paper with description of how you calculated your fees
- Do not overpay USCIS or underpay. In either case it may severely delay your case and other headaches you do not want to deal with
- If part of your application requires fingerprinting, you must also include a check for the finger printing fee

Once you've submitted your application, you'll receive what is called as NOA1 (Notification of Application), commonly known as the receipt of your application which includes your application number, the confirmation that you have paid the application and approximate wait time of your application. See Figure 6-2 for sample Receipt Notice.

While USCIS is reviewing your application, the officer may approve your application or issue an RFE (Request for Evidence) if a documentation is missing or confusing. Once the officer issues a RFE, your application will be placed on-hold until a response is received and thus it is crucial to try your best to submit the correct and complete information the first time

Copyright © 2011 - GreenCard123.Com by UNorth® - All Rights Reserved

to prevent RFE being issued. If you receive an RFE, either send in the documentation requested immediately or consult an attorney if the item in question is doubtful or documentation requested is not available).

If your application is approved, however, you may receive Biographic Fingerprint and/or the interview letter (depending on when the previous fingerprinting was conducted). See Figure 6-3 for Sample Interview Notice.

Copyright © 2011 – GreenCard123.Com by UNorth® – All Rights Reserved

Department of Homeland Security
U.S. Citizenship and Immigration Services

I-797C, Notice of Action

THE UNITED STATES OF AMERICA

RECEIPT NUMBER		CASE TYPE I290B
RECEIVED DATE	PRIORITY DATE	PETITIONER
NOTICE DATE	PAGE 1 of 1	

Notice Type: Receipt Notice

Amount received: $

Receipt notice - If any of the above information is incorrect, call customer service immediately.

Processing time - Processing times vary by kind of case.
- You can check our current processing time for this kind of case on our website at **uscis.gov**.
- On our website you can also sign up to get free e-mail updates as we complete key processing steps on this case.
- Most of the time your case is pending the processing status will not change because we will be working on others filed earlier.
- We will notify you by mail when we make a decision on this case, or if we need something from you. If you move while this case is pending, call customer service when you move.
- Processing times can change. If you don't get a decision or update from us within our current processing time, check our website or call for an update.

If you have questions, check our website or call customer service. Please save this notice, and have it with you if you contact us about this case.

Notice to all customers with a pending I-130 petition - USCIS is now processing Form I-130, Petition for Alien Relative, as a visa number becomes available. Filing and approval of an I-130 relative petition is only the first step in helping a relative immigrate to the United States. Eligible family members must wait until there is a visa number available before they can apply for an immigrant visa or adjustment of status to a lawful permanent resident. This process will allow USCIS to concentrate resources first on cases where visas are actually available. This process should not delay the ability of one's relative to apply for an immigrant visa or adjustment of status. Refer to **www.state.gov/travel** <http://www.state.gov/travel> to determine current visa availability dates. For more information, please visit our website at www.uscis.gov or contact us at 1-800-375-5283.

If this receipt is for an I-485, or I-698 application
USCIS WILL SCHEDULE YOUR BIOMETRICS APPOINTMENT. You will be receiving a biometrics appointment notice with a specific time, date and place where you will have your fingerprints and/or photos taken. You MUST wait for your biometrics appointment notice prior to going to the ASC for biometrics processing. This I-797 receipt notice is NOT your biometrics appointment notice and should not be taken to an ASC for biometrics processing.

WHAT TO BRING TO YOUR BIOMETRICS APPOINTMENT.
Please bring your biometrics appointment letter (with specific time, date and place where you will have your fingerprints and/or photo taken) AND your photo identification to your biometrics appointment.
Acceptable kinds of photo identification are:
- a passport or national photo identification issued by your country,
- a drivers license,
- a military photo identification, or
- a state - issued photo identification card.

Always remember to call customer service if you move while your case is pending. If you have a pending I-130 relative petition, also call customer service if you should decide to withdraw your petition or if you become a U.S. citizen.

Please see the additional information on the back. You will be notified separately about any other cases you filed.

Form I-797C (Rev. 01/31/05) N

Figure 6-2 - Notice of Action, Receipt

Copyright © 2011 - GreenCard123.Com by UNorth® - All Rights Reserved

Department of Homeland Security
U.S. Citizenship and Immigration Services

I-797C, Notice of Action

THE UNITED STATES OF AMERICA

REQUEST FOR APPLICANT TO APPEAR FOR INITIAL INTERVIEW			NOTICE DATE November 30, 2009
CASE TYPE FORM I-485, APPLICATION TO REGISTER PERMANENT RESIDENCE OR ADJUST STATUS			A# ▆▆▆▆▆▆
APPLICATION NUMBER ▆▆▆▆▆▆	RECEIVED DATE October 26, 2009	PRIORITY DATE October 26, 2009	PAGE 1 of 1

You are hereby notified to appear for the interview appointment, as scheduled below, for the completion of your Application to Register Permanent Residence or Adjust Status (Form I-485) and any supporting applications or petitions. *Failure to appear for this interview and/or failure to bring the below listed items will result in the denial of your application. (8 CFR 103.2(b)(13))*

Who should come with you?

- ☐ If your eligibility is based on your marriage, your husband or wife must come with you to the interview.
- ☐ If you do not speak English fluently, you should bring an interpreter.
- ☐ Your attorney or authorized representative may come with you to the interview.
- ☐ If your eligibility is based on a parent/child relationship and the child is a minor, the petitioning parent and the child must appear for the interview.

*NOTE: Every adult (over 18 years of age) who comes to the interview must bring Government-issued photo identification, such as a driver's license or ID card, in order to enter the building and to verify his/her identity at the time of the interview. You do not need to bring your children unless otherwise instructed. Please be on time, but do not arrive more than 45 minutes early. We may record or videotape your interview.

YOU MUST BRING THE FOLLOWING ITEMS WITH YOU: (Please use as a checklist to prepare for your interview)

- ☐ This Interview Notice and your Government issued photo identification.
- ☐ A completed medical examination (Form I-693) and vaccination supplement in a sealed envelope (unless already submitted).
- ☐ A completed Affidavit(s) of Support (Form I-864) with all required evidence, including the following, for each of your sponsors (unless already submitted):
  - ☐ Federal Income Tax returns and W-2's, or certified IRS printouts, for the most recent tax year;
  - ☐ Letters from each current employer, verifying current rate of pay and average weekly hours, and pay stubs for the past 2 months;
  - ☐ Evidence of your sponsor's and/or co-sponsor's United States Citizenship or Lawful Permanent Resident status.
- ☐ All documentation establishing your eligibility for Lawful Permanent Resident status.
- ☐ Any immigration-related documentation ever issued to you, including any Employment Authorization Document (EAD) and any Authorization for Advance Parole (Form I-512).
- ☐ All travel documents used to enter the United States, including Passports, Advance Parole documents (I-512) and I-94s (Arrival/Departure Document).
- ☐ Your Birth Certificate.
- ☐ Your petitioner's Birth Certificate and your petitioner's evidence of United States Citizenship or Lawful Permanent Resident Status.
- ☐ If you have children, bring a Birth Certificate for each of your children.
- ☐ If your eligibility is based on your marriage, in addition to your spouse coming to the interview with you, bring:
  - ☐ A certified copy of your Marriage Document issued by the appropriate civil authority.
  - ☐ Your spouse's Birth Certificate and your spouse's evidence of United States Citizenship or Lawful Permanent Resident status;
  - ☐ If either you or your spouse were ever married before, all divorce decrees/death certificates for each prior marriage/former spouse;
  - ☐ Birth Certificates for all children of this marriage, and custody papers for your children and for your spouse's children not living with you;
- ☐ Supporting evidence of your relationship, such as copies of any documentation regarding joint assets or liabilities you and your spouse may have together. This may include: tax returns, bank statements, insurance documents (car, life, health), property documents (car, house, etc.), rental agreements, utility bills, credit cards, contracts, leases, photos, correspondence and/or any other documents you feel may substantiate your relationship.
- ☐ Original and copy of each supporting document that you submitted with your application. Otherwise, we may keep your originals for our records.
- ☐ If you have ever been arrested, bring the related Police Report and the original or certified Final Court Disposition for each arrest, even if the charges have been dismissed or expunged. If no court record is available, bring a letter from the court with jurisdiction indicating this.
- ☐ A certified English translation for each foreign language document. The translator must certify that s/he is fluent in both languages, and that the translation in its entirety is complete and accurate.

YOU MUST APPEAR FOR THIS INTERVIEW. If an emergency, such as your own illness or a close relative's hospitalization, prevents you from appearing, call the U.S. Citizenship and Immigration Services (USCIS) National Customer Service Center at 1-800-375-5283 as soon as possible. Please be advised that rescheduling will delay processing of application/petition, and may require some steps to be repeated. It may also affect your eligibility for other immigration benefits while this application is pending.

If you have questions, please call the USCIS National Customer Service Center at 1-800-375-5283 (hearing impaired TDD service is 1-800-767-1833).

PLEASE COME TO: U.S. Citizenship and Immigration Services 1887 MONTEREY ROAD 2ND FLR ROOM 200 SAN JOSE CA 95112	ON: Tuesday, January 05, 2010 AT: 02:00 PM
9	APPLICANT COPY

Form I-797C (Rev. 01/31/05) N

Figure 6-3 Notice of Action, Interview

Copyright © 2011 - GreenCard123.Com by UNorth® - All Rights Reserved

7. INTERVIEW AND GET YOUR VISA, OR ADJUST STATUS

ROADMAP TO PREMANENT RESIDENCY VIA VISA LOTTERY:

- I. Visa Lottery Information ✔
- II. Register for Visa Lottery ✔
- III. Checking Status and Winning ✔
- IV. Getting your green card
   - **a.** Prepare the Green Card Forms
   - **b. Interview at the Embassy/Consulate (or USCIS Service Center in case you are in the United States)**
   - **c. Receive Your Visa/Adjustment of Status**
- **V. Entering the United States**
- VI. Now that you have your green card

Interview at Consulate or USCIS Office

Whether you are applying abroad or inside the United States, you'll be called for an in-person interview for your Diversity Visa. This is primarily to go over your documents, make sure you are who you are claiming to be, and clarify questions that consulate/immigration officer may have in your application. If you are applying outside of United States, your interview will be at the designated Embassy/Consulate at your home country (unless no embassy is available in your country, or you've chosen a different country), and if you are applying inside the United States, your interview will be at one of the USCIS Service centers.

Green Card Lottery winners who have sent their duly filled forms along with the required photos are selected and will be called for interview as of October 1. The lower case numbers will be called first and the interviews will continue in ascending order until the visa limit has been reached or when the program close date of September 30 is reached, whichever comes first. Before you go to the interview, you must carefully read the instructions on the web site of The United States Consular office in your home country or any United States of America Embassy nearest to you to ensure that you bring all documents and fees with you so that you meet the requirements.

I. IMPORTANCE OF BEING TRUTHFUL

Although generally having your documents and evidences in order is most important thing you can do for your interview session, providing untruthful information during your interview or on your application is the fastest way to get your visa application denied. Even if you are issued a visa, or more, if many years down the road you are even a US Citizen, and US government discovers that you purposely provided incorrect information to get your Green Card (e.g. would have made you otherwise ineligible), you may be prosecuted and/or deported.

J. ENGLISH PROFICIENCY

Considering that you are migrating to an English-speaking country, it is expected that you be able to have a general knowledge of speaking and understanding the English Language. However, depending on your country of origin, there may be a local-language interviewee available in the USCIS Center or the US Consulate. For example, if you are applying from France, there is a great chance that the US Consulate in France is able to talk in French as well as English.

If your English is not at the basic level of being able to interview, you may provide the consulate with a letter, explaining your situation and the documents that you provided. This helps the interviewer to go through your documents and only ask the necessary questions.

...
Dear Consulate.

I, John Smith, along with my wife, Jane Smith, and our two years old daughter, Rob Smith, are selected as the winner of the Diversity Visa Lottery and are applying for the immigrant visa to the United States. I am providing the following documents requested as part of my Visa Interview:
1.   Form DC230
2.   Affidavit of Support
3.   ...

My Information is as follows:
Name: John Smith
Date of Birth:
Address:
My Rank Number:

...

Regards,
John Smith

Copyright © 2011 - GreenCard123.Com by UNorth® - All Rights Reserved

If you are applying from inside the United States your interview will be conducted at the USCIS Service Center where you may bring an attorney along.

K. RESCHEDULING THE GREEN CARD INTERVIEW

If you want to reschedule your interview you can write an e-mail to U.S. Citizenship and US immigration Services or handover a requesting letter to the United States Consular officer in your home country or any United States of America Embassy nearest you on a working day.

Furthermore, you should be aware that when rescheduling a new interview date other applicants will be interviewed and given visas ahead of you. If there are no visas left the day of your rescheduled interview appointment, due to the U.S. Government reached the 55,000 Visa limit your new interview date will go useless and your interview will be canceled and you will lose your chance of getting a Green Card.

L. LOCATION OF YOUR INTERVIEW

If you are applying from inside the United States your interview will be at one of the USCIS Service Centers near you, and if you are applying from outside of the United States, your interview will be at the US Consulate/Embassy in your country (or another country near you if no Consulate is available in your country).

M. WHAT TO BRING TO THE INTERVIEW

Unless you're advised otherwise, the list below is the minimum you have to take with yourself to the Interview

- ☐ **Police clearance record** according to the United States Consular officer in your home country or

any United States of America Embassy nearest to you
- ☐ **Medical certificate** as per the United States Consular officer in your home country or any United States of America Embassy nearest to you
- ☐ Copy of the application that you submitted to USCIS or Consulate, if any
- ☐ Original of all the documentations related
- ☐ Original passport
- ☐ Other government official documents such as Identification Card, Driver's License, Advance Parole, or Social Security Card if available
- ☐ **Fee:** (for outside of US Applicants) Be ready to pay three non refundable fees for the visa and Green Card processing according to the U.S. Government's Instructions. As of 2010, the fee structure is as follows:
  - ☐ Immigrant visa application processing fee (Form DS-230) (for each person), US$355.00 or equivalent in local currency if accepted
  - ☐ Green Card Lottery surcharge for immigrant visa application (for each person): US$375.00
  - ☐ Immigrant visa security surcharge, for all Green Card applicants: US$45.00

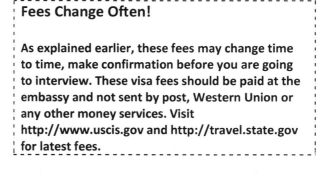

Fees Change Often!

As explained earlier, these fees may change time to time, make confirmation before you are going to interview. These visa fees should be paid at the embassy and not sent by post, Western Union or any other money services. Visit http://www.uscis.gov and http://travel.state.gov for latest fees.

N. CHANGE IN STATUS SINCE FILING FOR GREEN CARD

If you have a newborn baby after submission of the Green Card application, you need to take the following with you to the interview at the United States Consulate:

- Birth certificate of the newborn baby
- Photograph
- A refilled form DC-230 with the baby information (not required but recommended)

Copyright © 2011 - GreenCard123.Com by UNorth® - All Rights Reserved

O. INTERVIEW TIPS THAT CAN SAVE YOUR LIFE

Be Prepared: Whether or not you prepared your application review your application prior to the interview. If any part of your application requires explanation (e.g. committed a crime or a part of documentation missing due to information not available), prepare your answer in advance.

Get a Checklist: It's highly recommended that prior to the interview, prepare a checklist or use one in the book to prepare the requirements for your Interview. As the interview date gets closer, you may have less time and potentially be more stressful and may overlook a document. By preparing a checklist, you make sure all needed documents are in one place.

Be Truthful: It cannot be emphasized enough that your truthfulness is one of the key reasons that can give you or take the visa away from you. Remember that United States has extensive database of background histories and your application will be checked prior to grant of visa. If any of the information is not accurate you may be caught.

Answer Precisely: An officer would generally ask you specific questions and is interested in a precise answer to those questions. Provide as much information as needed, but just enough to cover the question; if you provide more information than needed, you may bring another irrelevant question to the officer's mind.

Translation Problem?

Sure, English may not be your primary language. Fortunately, in most US embassies, consular official are fluent in the local language as well.

Example: During the interview, the officer asks Ron about his previous marriage and when it was ended. Ron answers the date and also goes over what caused the divorce and that his ex-wife had filed a lawsuit against him prior to marriage, etc. Officer becomes interested on the details of the lawsuit and may ask Ron for additional information now that was originally not necessary.

Bring all original documents. If you are picky and want to bring more documentation that is needed, feel free, but separate those documents from those that are required and if you are asked, provide the rest.

Bring all US Immigration documents. If you were previously admitted to United States or currently residing in the US, bring your paperwork in case you are asked.

Be organized: Organize your application. Use a folder, tab, separator or similar method to organize your documents.

P. IF YOUR FAIL OR YOU'RE MISSING A DOCUMENT

It Pays to Be Prepared

Unless the officer finds a ground of inadmissibility that cannot be waived (e.g. drug offense, money laundering, etc), you may be either asked to provide additional information or to reapply. However, due to the time sensitiveness of the Diversity Visa, it is highly recommended that you do your best to complete the requirements on your first shot.

Note: If your case falls under any of the inadmissibility grounds, it is highly recommended that you consult with an experienced attorney.

Copyright © 2011 - GreenCard123.Com by UNorth® - All Rights Reserved

Office Having a Bad Day?

If you believe you have provided everything needed but officer is not cooperating, you may ask for the supervisor. You normally can also request a written explanation. However, use caution since if you get on the wrong track with the officer, and then apply again he/she may be the one interviewing you next time too! Try to be polite and use phrases like "Is it possible if I could check this with the supervisor as well" instead of being insulting, "You are nonsense. Give me the supervisor".

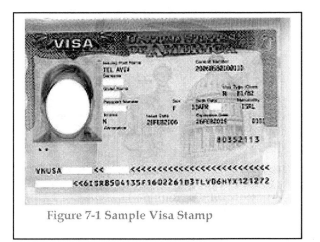

Figure 7-1 Sample Visa Stamp

Q. RECEIVING YOUR VISA

For applicants outside of the United States, assuming that your had prepared all the needed documents and your Interview proceeded successfully, you'll receive a stamp in your passport that indicates you're approved to travel to the United States. This stamp is called Visa.

For those inside the United States, you already had received a Visa from your previous entrance in non-immigrant visa status and your information is already recorded in the I-94 or I94W, which serves as the official document authorizing the alien's stay in the United States in a particular non-immigrant visa status and for a particular period of time. You may skip to the next chapter.

A sample of Visa is shown in the figure below. Visa has various sections, including the date of issuance, the date of expiration (typically 180 days after issuance), your picture, and where it was issued. It also has encrypted numbers and identification information for the CBP officer in the Airport and USCIS.

R. WHAT IS A VISA

As briefly explained in Chapter 1, contrary to a popular misconception, a U.S. visa does not authorize the alien's entry to the United States, nor does it authorize the alien's stay in the U.S. under a particular status. This may seem odd at first, considering all the hassle that you've been through with the preparation, expenses, interviews, medical tests, etc. but a U.S. visa only serves as a preliminary permission given to the alien to travel to the United States to seek admission to the United States at a designated port of entry (e.g. Airport). The final admission to the United States under a particular status and for a particular period of time is made at the port of entry by a CBP officer. CBP officer (aka Border Patrol, CBP, abbreviated for Customs Border Protection -- See Glossary) has to say whether or not they want you to enter the United States. If they determine that you've provided false information and perhaps got through the system up to this point, they can easily turn you back and you do not have any right to appeal; it would be as easy as turning back and going back to your country.

A visa is only issued by the Department of State, also known as Embassy/Consulate located outside of the United States itself. This makes sense because you only need a Visa to apply for entry at the US borders. Once you are inside the United States, you need permission to stay. USCIS does not issue visas

Copyright © 2011 - GreenCard123.Com by UNorth® - All Rights Reserved

but can extend your permission to stay (I-94) or adjust your status. If you exit the country and want to come back to US, you need a valid visa (issued by an embassy) or advance parole (issued by USCIS).

How many visas are issued every year?

In case you wondered, United States government issued 6.6 million visas to foreign nationals visiting the United States and to 470,000 immigrants in 2008 alone.

Copyright © 2011 – GreenCard123.Com by UNorth® – All Rights Reserved

8. ENTERING UNITED STATES AND RECEIVING YOUR GREEN CARD

ROADMAP TO PREMANENT RESIDENCY VIA VISA LOTTERY:

    I.   Visa Lottery Information ✔
   II.   Register for Visa Lottery ✔
  III.   Checking Status and Winning ✔
  IV.   Getting your green card ✔
   V.   Entering the United States
        a.   Entering United States prior to Visa Expiration
        b.   Wait for the actual Green Card to arrive in the mail
  VI.   Now that you have your green card

> ### Congratulations on coming this far. Hooray!
>
> **If you are already in the United States,** your only step is to wait for your Green Card to arrive in the mail (assuming that the USCIS officer did not find any grounds of inadmissibility in your application and has approved your LPR status). You may skip to next section.
>
> **If you are outside of the United States,** however, you are only few steps away from reaching your dreams and receiving your Permanent Resident Card. These are the steps :
>
> 1) Receive your visa (DONE!)
> 2) Book your travel to United States
> 3) Fill-in Custom's declaration and
> 4) Be inspected by the ICE and CBP officers
> 5) Enter United States
> 6) Receive your Green Card in the Mail

A. RECEIVE YOUR VISA (DONE!)

You've already had the visa stamp in your passport, along with a sealed package that you are supposed to hand over to the BCP officer at the airport (or point of entry if you are not travelling via Airplane). Review the information or potential typos in your passport and if you find any, inform the consulate/embassy immediately. As odd as this may seem, typing errors happen quite often and it is your responsibility to catch and report them or otherwise you may have a problem while entering the United States.

B. BOOK YOUR TRAVEL TO THE UNITED STATES

We let this one step be your responsibility. Book your travel in a way that the date you are entering into the United States is not past the visa entrance deadline (typically within 6 months of visa issuance). It is highly recommended to plan your flight well in advance so as to have enough time to prepare and in case of any change you can come up with another plan. You must also think of the possibility of airplane delay and other factors and with all these considered, plan your trip.

PROTECTING YOUR TRAVEL DOCUMENTS

Be careful with your travel documents. There have been numerous cases that after receiving their visa and ticket, the identification documents of the person is stolen. You may want to use a front-side carrier or store your passport and Consulate's sealed-envelope in a safe place.

Best practices for protecting your passport and other travel documents:

- Make a copy of your passport and leave it with someone you trust
- Make a second copy to carry with you when you arrive at your destination
- During transit, keep your passport with you at all times
- Never lay your passport down on a table or counter. It can be forgotten
- Keep your passport in the hotel safe and not in your room
- Report a lost or stolen passport immediately

C. RESTRICTED ITEMS

United States has very strict rules about what can or cannot be brought into the United States from its borders. These rules may greatly differ from what your local country allows. Here is the list of CBP restriction along with exceptions, if any:

- **Absinthe** (Alcohol)
- **Alcoholic Beverages:** In addition to U.S. laws, the laws of the state in which you first arrive in the United States will govern the amount of alcohol you may bring with you, and whether you need a license. If you plan to bring alcoholic

Copyright © 2011 - GreenCard123.Com by UNorth® - All Rights Reserved

beverages with you, before you depart, you should contact the state's applicable alcoholic beverage control board to determine what you need to do to comply with that state's laws and regulations.

- **Automobiles:** Automobiles imported into the United States must meet the fuel-emission requirements of the Environmental Protection Agency and the safety, bumper, and theft prevention standards of the U.S. Department of Transportation. Trying to import a car that doesn't meet all the requirements can be difficult. Please see the importing a Motor Vehicle page for more information
- **Biologicals**
- **Ceramic Tableware:** Although ceramic tableware is not prohibited or restricted, you should know that such tableware made in foreign countries may contain dangerous levels of lead in the glaze, which can seep into foods and beverages. The U.S. Food and Drug Administration recommends that if you buy ceramic tableware abroad - especially in Mexico, China, Hong Kong or India - you have it tested for lead release when you return, or use it for decorative purposes only.
- **Cultural Artifacts and Cultural Property**
- **Defense Articles** or Items with Military or Proliferation Applications
- **Dog and Cat Fur:** It is illegal in the United States to import, export, distribute, transport, manufacture or sell products containing dog or cat fur in the United States. As of November 9, 2000, the Dog and Cat Protection Act of 2000 calls for the seizure and forfeiture of each item containing dog or cat fur.

  The Act provides that any person who violates any provision may be assessed a civil penalty of not more than $10,000 for each separate knowing and intentional violation, $5,000 for each separate gross negligent violation, or $3,000 for each separate negligent violation.
- **Drug Paraphernalia:** It is illegal to bring drug paraphernalia into the United States unless prescribed for authentic medical conditions such as diabetes. CBP will seize any illegal drug paraphernalia. The Law prohibits the importation, exportation, manufacture, sale or transportation of drug paraphernalia. If you are

convicted of any of these offenses, you will be subject to fines and imprisonment.

- **Firearms**
- **Fish and Wildlife**
- **Food Products (Prepared):** You may bring bakery items and certain cheeses into the United States. The APHIS Web site features a Travelers Tips section and Game and Hunting Trophies section that offers extensive information about bringing food and other products into the U.S. Many prepared foods are admissible. However, bush meat made from African wildlife and almost anything containing meat products, such as bouillon, soup mixes, etc., is not admissible. As a general rule, condiments, vinegars, oils, packaged spices, honey, coffee and tea are admissible. Because rice can often harbor insects, it is best to avoid bringing it into the United States. Some imported foods are also subject to requirements of the U.S. Food and Drug Administration.
- **Fruits and Vegetables:** Bringing fruits and vegetables depends on a number of factors. For instance, consider the apple you bought at the foreign airport just before boarding and then did not eat. Whether or not CBP will allow the apple into the United States depends on where you got it and where you are going after you arrive in the United States. The same would be true for Mediterranean tomatoes. Such factors are important because fresh fruits and vegetables can introduce plant pests or diseases into the United States.

One good example of problems imported fruits and vegetables can cause is the Mediterranean fruit fly outbreak during the 1980s. The outbreak cost the state of California and the federal government approximately $100 million to get rid of this pest. The cause of the outbreak was one traveler who brought home one contaminated piece of fruit. It is best not to bring fresh fruits or vegetables into the United States. However, if you plan to, contact either CBP or check the Permits section on the USDA-APHIS Web site for a general approved list on items that need a permit.

Copyright © 2011 - GreenCard123.Com by UNorth® - All Rights Reserved

Penalty for Failing to Declare

The civil penalty for failing to declare agricultural items at U.S. ports of entry will cost first time offenders $300. The penalty for the second violation goes up to $500. To avoid receiving a penalty declare all agricultural items and present them to Customs and Border Protection for inspection so that an agriculture specialist can determine if it is admissible.

- **Game and Hunting Trophies**
- **Gold** (prohibited if brought from certain countries: Cuba, Iran, Burma (Myanmar) and most of Sudan)
- **Haitian animal hide drums**
- **Meats, Livestock and Poultry** (You may not import fresh, dried or canned meats or meat products from most foreign countries into the United States. Also, you may not import food products that have been prepared with meat.)
- **Medication:** Rule of thumb: When you go abroad, take the medicines you will need, no more, no less. Narcotics and certain other drugs with a high potential for abuse - Rohypnol, GHB and Fen-Phen, to name a few - may not be brought into the United States, and there are severe penalties for trying to do so. If you need medicines that contain potentially addictive drugs or narcotics (e.g., some cough medicines, tranquilizers, sleeping pills, antidepressants or stimulants), do the following:

  o Declare all drugs, medicinal, and similar products to the appropriate CBP official;
  o Carry such substances in their original containers;
  o Carry only the quantity of such substances that a person with that condition (e.g., chronic pain) would normally carry for his/her personal use; and
  o Carry a prescription or written statement from your physician that the substances are being used under a doctor's supervision and that they are necessary for your physical well being while traveling.

- **Merchandise from Embargoed Countries:** Generally, you may not bring in any merchandise

from Cuba, Iran, Burma (Myanmar) or most of Sudan.

Exceptions: You may, however, bring from any of these countries information and informational materials - books, magazines, films, posters, photographs, microfilms, tapes, CDs, records, works of art, etc. Blank tapes and blank CDs are not informational materials.

  o Allowed importations of merchandise from Iran include foodstuffs intended for human consumption, carpets and other textile floor coverings, and gifts of up to $100 (U.S.) in value.
  o Allowed importations of merchandise from Sudan include gifts of up to $100 (U.S.) in value.
  o Importations of merchandise from Sudan are generally allowed if acquired directly from these parts of Sudan: Southern Sudan, Southern Kordofan/Nuba Mountains State, Blue Nile State,

- **Pets:** If you plan to take your pet abroad or import one on your return, please review a copy of the CBP brochure Pets and Wildlife. You should also check with state, county and local authorities to learn if their restrictions and prohibitions on pets are stricter than federal requirements.
- **Plants and Seeds :** Some plants, cuttings, seeds that are capable of propagation, unprocessed plant products and certain endangered species are allowed into the United States but require import permits and other documents; some are prohibited entirely. Threatened or endangered species that are permitted must have export permits from the country of origin.
- **Soil:** Soil is considered the loose surface material of the earth in which plants, trees, and scrubs grow. In most cases, the soil consists of disintegrated rock with a mixture of organic material and soluble salts. Soil is prohibited entry unless accompanied by an import permit. Soil must be declared and the permit must be verified.
- **Textiles and Clothing:** In general, there is no limit to how much fabric and clothing you can bring back as long as it is for your personal use or as gifts. If you have exceeded your personal exemption, you may have to pay duty on the items. Unaccompanied personal shipments (packages that are mailed or shipped), however, may be subject to limitations on amount.

Copyright © 2011 - GreenCard123.Com by UNorth® - All Rights Reserved

Trademarked and Copyrighted Articles: CBP enforces laws relating to the protection of trademarks and copyrights. Articles that infringe a federally registered trademark or copyright or copyright protected by the Berne Convention for the Protection of Literary and Artistic Works are subject to detention and/ or seizure. Infringing articles may consist of articles that use a protected right without the authorization of the trademark or copyright owner or articles that copy or simulate a protected right. However, travelers arriving in the United States may be permitted an exemption and allowed to import one article of each type, which must accompany the person, bearing a counterfeit, confusingly similar or restricted gray market trademark, provided that the article is for personal use and is not for sale.

Visit CBP website at http://www.cbp.gov for updated list and additional and updated information

D. FILLING-IN CUSTOM'S DECLARATION CBP 6095B AND I-94

Just before your arrival into the US Airport (or port of entry if not travelling with Airplane), you'll be given two sets of forms:

The first form is the **"Custom's Declaration"** form CBP 6059B that records information about you and what you are bringing into the United States so that the BCP officer can examine it. The second form is **I-94** which is your information and Arrival/Departure Record. The good news is that as the instruction states, as an immigrant (Alien with immigrant Visa), you do not need to fill-in I-94 form since all your paper work are in the sealed envelope that you'll be handing over to the officer shortly.

Instruction for filling Customs Declaration

How to Fill CBP 6095BForm

Use CAPITAL letters. If you have typos in your form, simply ask for another form instead

1. Print your last name. Print your first name. Print the first letter of your middle name
2. Print your date of birth in the appropriate day/month/year boxes
3. Print the number of family members traveling with you (do not include yourself)

4. Print your current street address in the United States. If you are staying at a hotel, include the hotel's name and street address. Print the city and the state in the appropriate boxes

Figure 8-2 CBP Declaration Form

Copyright © 2011 – GreenCard123.Com by UNorth® - All Rights Reserved

5. Print the name of the country that issued your passport

6. Print your passport number

7. Print the name of the country where you currently live

8. Print the name of the country(ies) that you visited on your trip prior to arriving in the United States

9. If traveling by airline, print the airline's name and flight number. If traveling by vessel (ship), print the vessel's name

10. Mark an X in the Yes or No box. Are you traveling on a business (work-related) trip?
    - For the purpose of Diversity Visa Lottery, you are not considered to be on a business trip so you would answer No to this question

11. Mark an X in the Yes or No box. Are you bringing with you:

    a. Fruits, plants, food, or insects?
    b. Meats, animals, or animal/wildlife products?
    c. Disease agents, cell cultures, or snails?
    d. Soil or have you visited a farm/ranch/pasture outside the United States?

12. Mark an X in the Yes or No box. Have you or any family members traveling with you been in close proximity of (such as touching or handling) livestock outside the United States?

13. Mark an X in the Yes or No box. Are you or any family members traveling with you bringing $10,000 or more in U.S. dollars or foreign equivalent in any form into the United States?

    - Read definition of monetary instruments on the reverse side of the form.

Examples: coins, cash, personal or cashier's check, traveler's checks, money orders, stocks, bonds.
If yes, your must complete the Customs Form 4790. *Form http://www.irs.gov/pub/irs-prior/f4790--2002.pdf* - See (Figure 8-3)

You can bring as much cash as you want

It is perfectly legal to bring cash or other money instruments of any amount to the United States. However, if you are physically moving currencies or cash equivalents, the government needs to know more about it to ensure it has nothing to do with money laundering practices and is not the proceeds of criminal organizations.

As the form refers to, the above rule is only for physical moving of money or money instruments. In other words if you transfer your funds electronically you do not fall into this category. See Figure 8-3 for sample filled form

Bank Secrecy Act

The Bank Secrecy Act of 1970 (or BSA, or otherwise known as the Currency and Foreign Transactions Reporting Act) requires financial institutions in the United States to assist U.S. government agencies to detect and prevent money laundering. Specifically, the act requires financial institutions to keep records of cash purchases of negotiable instruments, and file reports of cash purchases of these negotiable instruments of $10,000 or more (daily aggregate amount), and to report suspicious activity that might signify money laundering, tax evasion, or other criminal activities. Many banks will no longer sell negotiable instruments when purchased with cash, requiring the purchase to be withdrawn from an account at that institution. BSA was passed by the Congress of the United States in 1970. The BSA is sometimes referred to as an "anti-money laundering" law ("AML") or jointly as "BSA/AML". Several anti-money laundering acts, including provisions in title III of the USA PATRIOT Act, have been enacted up to the present to amend the BSA. (See 31 USC 5311-5330 and 31 CFR 103.) From: Wikipedia, the free encyclopedia

Copyright © 2011 - GreenCard123.Com by UNorth® - All Rights Reserved

(U.S. Customs Use Only)		DEPARTMENT OF THE TREASURY UNITED STATES CUSTOMS SERVICE REPORT OF INTERNATIONAL TRANSPORTATION OF CURRENCY OR MONETARY INSTRUMENTS	OMB No. 1506-0014 ►This form is to be filed with the United States Customs Service ►For Paperwork Reduction Act Notice and Privacy Act Notice, see back of form.

Control No.

31 U.S.C. 5316; 31 CFR 103.23 and 103.27
► Please type or print.

Part I FOR A PERSON DEPARTING FROM OR ENTERING THE UNITED STATES, OR A PERSON SHIPPING, MAILING, OR RECEIVING CURRENCY OR MONETARY INSTRUMENTS. (IF ACTING FOR ANYONE ELSE, ALSO COMPLETE PART II BELOW.)

1. NAME (Last or family, first, and middle) SMITH, JOHN	2. IDENTIFICATION NO. (See instructions) PASSPORT 0000000000102	3. DATE OF BIRTH (Mo./Day/Yr.) 10 20 1970
4. PERMANENT ADDRESS IN UNITED STATES OR ABROAD 123 FIRST ST, WASHINGTON, DC 10001		5.YOUR COUNTRY OR COUNTRIES OF CITIZENSHIP FRANCE
6. ADDRESS WHILE IN THE UNITED STATES 123 FIRST ST, WASHINGTON, DC 10001		7. PASSPORT NO. & COUNTRY 0000000000102 FRANCE
8. U.S. VISA DATE 01/01/2011	9. PLACE UNITED STATES VISA WAS ISSUED PARIS, FRANCE	10. IMMIGRATION ALIEN NO. (If any) N/A

11. IF CURRENCY OR MONETARY INSTRUMENT IS ACCOMPANIED BY A PERSON, COMPLETE 11a **OR** 11b

A. EXPORTED FROM THE UNITED STATES		B. IMPORTED INTO THE UNITED STATES	
Departed From: (U.S. Port /City in U.S.) N/A	Arrived At: (Foreign City/Country) N/A	Departed From: (Foreign City/Country) PARIS, FRANCE	Arrived At: (City in U.S.) WASHINGTON, DC

12. IF CURRENCY OR MONETARY INSTRUMENT WAS MAILED OR OTHERWISE SHIPPED, COMPLETE 12a THROUGH 12f

12a. DATE SHIPPED (Mo./Day/Yr.)	12b. DATE RECEIVED (Mo./Day/Yr.)	12c. METHOD OF SHIPMENT (e.g., U.S. Mail, Public Carrier, etc.) N/A	12d. NAME OF CARRIER

12e. SHIPPED TO (Name and Address)
N/A

12f. RECEIVED FROM (Name and Address)
N/A

Part II INFORMATION ABOUT PERSON(S) OR BUSINESS ON WHOSE BEHALF IMPORTATION OR EXPORTATION WAS CONDUCTED

13. NAME (Last or family, first, and middle or Business Name)
SMITH, JOHN

14. PERMANENT ADDRESS IN THE UNITED STATES OR ABROAD
123 FIRST ST, WASHINGTON, DC 10001

15. TYPE OF BUSINESS ACTIVITY, OCCUPATION, OR PROFESSION COMPUTER ENGINEER	15a. IS THE BUSINESS A BANK? ☐ YES ☑ NO

Part III CURRENCY AND MONETARY INSTRUMENT INFORMATION (SEE INSTRUCTIONS ON REVERSE)(To be completed by everyone)

16. TYPE AND AMOUNT OF CURRENCY/MONETARY INSTRUMENTS			17. IF OTHER THAN U.S. CURRENCY IS INVOLVED, PLEASE COMPLETE BLOCKS A AND B. ☐
Currency and Coins	☑ ►	$ 15,000	A. Currency Name EURO
Other Monetary Instruments (Specify type, issuing entity and date, and serial or other identifying number.)	☐ ►	$	
(TOTAL)	☐ ►	$ 15,000	B. Country FRANCE

Part IV SIGNATURE OF PERSON COMPLETING THIS REPORT

Under penalties of perjury, I declare that I have examined this report, and to the best of my knowledge and belief it is true, correct and complete.

18. NAME AND TITLE (Print) JOHN SMITH	19. SIGNATURE	20. DATE OF REPORT 01/01/2011

U.S. CUSTOMS USE ONLY			COUNT VERIFIED Yes No	VOLUNTARY REPORT Yes No
DATE	AIRLINE/FLIGHT/VESSEL	LICENSE PLATE STATE/COUNTRY | NUMBER	INSPECTOR (Name and Badge Number)	

Cat. No. 42005H

Customs Form 4790 (04/00)

8-3 Report of International Transportation of Currency or Monetary Instruments

Copyright © 2011 - GreenCard123.Com by UNorth® - All Rights Reserved

Continued information for form CBP

14. Mark an X in the Yes or No box. Are you or any family members traveling with you bringing commercial merchandise into the United States?

> **Examples:** *all articles intended to be sold or left in the United States, samples used for soliciting orders, or goods that are not considered personal effects.*

15. If you are a U.S. resident, print the total value of all goods (including commercial merchandise) you or any family members traveling with you have purchased or acquired abroad (including gifts for someone else, but not items mailed to the United States) and are bringing into the United States.

> **Note:** *U.S. residents are normally entitled to a duty-free exemption of $800 on items accompanying them*

If you are a visitor (non-U.S. Resident), print the total value of all goods (including commercial merchandise) you or any family members traveling with you are bringing into the United States and will remain in the United States.
Note: Visitors (non-U.S. Residents) are normally entitled to an exemption of $100.

Declare all articles on this form. For gifts, please indicate the retail value. Use the reverse side of this form if additional space is needed to list the items you will declare.

The U.S. Customs officer will determine duty. Duty will be assessed at the current rate on the first $1,000 above the exemption.

- Read the notice on the reverse side of the form.
- Sign the form and print the date.
- Keep the complete form with you and hand it to the CBP inspector when you approach the Customs and Border Protection area.

- Controlled substances, obscene articles, and toxic substances are generally prohibited entry.

E. BE INSPECTED BY THE CBP OFFICERS

As explained earlier, various government agencies work hand-in-hand to complete processing of your Visa and entrance to the United States. So far you've been dealing with the USCIS that selected you as the winner, and Department of State in which issued your visa. The process of entering the United States from one of the points of entries, are handled by CBP (Customs and Borders Protection).
CBP's primary mission is preventing terrorists and terrorist weapons from entering the United States, but also responsible for apprehending individuals attempting to enter the United States illegally, stemming the flow of illegal drugs and similar tasks.

Once you enter the United States and at your point of entry (POE), you will need to present your identification documents, Immigration documents, along with the forms you filled in the plane to the officer.

The officer is generally responsible to determine:

- You are who you are claiming to be
- You don't possess any danger to the United States
- You do not possess any illegal object (e.g. drugs, etc.)

Important Tips

- Be polite to the officer and present the documents to him
- If any question asked, be direct and answer exactly the question asked; you should give enough answer to cover the question and at the same time no need to add extra piece of information that can complicate your case
- If something doesn't go right, No matter what the situation, stay calm. Remember that, although

Copyright © 2011 - GreenCard123.Com by UNorth® - All Rights Reserved

exercised very rarely, the officer has the power to have you turn back and go home without any right to object so it is to your benefit to work with them to resolve the situation
- You may also ask for a supervisor, but again, stay calm throughout the process

Although you may occasionally encounter an officer that steps out of the line, don't take the questions personal; remember that the officers handle thousands of people in a very short period of time and they like get over with your d arrives.

On your way to the exit doors of the airport and into the United States, you also have to go through the baggage screening. Depending on the country of origin and content of the Custom Declaration, you may be asked to have your baggage inspected either via electronic machines or even hand screening. Again, be polite and answer the questions properly. If the officer identifies an item that is restricted, may ask you further questions or may not allow you to take the item with you. Unfortunately, you do not have much choice here but try to explain to the officer the purpose and the reason you are carrying such item.

Example: Rob carries allergy medicine with him all the time. Since he suffers from severe allergy reactions, his doctor prescribed him to take 2 tables each time, 5 times a day and since he is not sure when he can find a doctor to get a refill in the US, he takes 1 month of the medication with him. During the baggage screening, an officer notices that he has a large amount of this medicine with him. The officer asks Rob the reason and after Rob provides the information and shows the doctor prescription, officer understands that it's for personal use (than sale) and lets him take the medication with him.

Example: Ali from Middle East is bringing different spices and herbals with him for himself and various relatives in the US. When asked by the officer why

case as much as you do. At the same time, due to the large number of fraudulent visas, drug issues, and illegal entries, their main duty is to protect the United States borders.

The officer will record your entry, compare your passport information with the content of the sealed envelope, will review the lottery winning letter and stamp your passport. This stamp will serve as your temporary Green Card (permission to stay in the United States) until your actual permanent   resident   car

---

he is bringing all these spices, he gets frustrated and screams at the officer instead of answering the question. The officer goes through the list of species in detail and since the amount is large assumes that Ali has brought them for resell and thus does not allow him to take them with him.

F. ENTER THE UNITED STATES

Yes, Yes! You are finally here. Congratulations for completing your mission! Pat yourself on the back!

While you are still relaxing and enjoying from all the work you've done, you can mark some items in your To Do List as completed and add some more. Here are some general things that after you enter Untied States need to happen:

- Getting your Social Security Number
- Opening a bank account
- Getting your driver's license
- Getting your work permit

G. RECEIVE YOUR GREEN CARD

You have completed your journey! You should receive your Green Card in the mail in few weeks at the address in your application. If you do not receive your Green Card, you may schedule a time with an Infopass officer at the USCIS center near you.

Copyright © 2011 - GreenCard123.Com by UNorth® - All Rights Reserved

THIS PAGE WAS INTENTIONALLY LEFT BLANK

Copyright © 2011 – GreenCard123.Com by UNorth® – All Rights Reserved

9. NOW THAT YOU HAVE YOUR GREEN CARD

ROADMAP TO PREMANENT RESIDENCY VIA VISA LOTTERY:

   I.   Visa Lottery Information ✔
   II. Register for Visa Lottery ✔
   III. Checking Status and Winning ✔
   IV. Getting your green card ✔
   V. Entering the United States ✔
   VI. **Now that you have your green card**
      a. **Your rights and responsibilities**
      b. **Social Security Number and Other Benefits**
      c. **Become a US Citizen**

> **Hooray! You are now a Permanent Resident!**
>
> **Congratulations for coming this far. You are now officially a United States Permanent Resident, with a Green Card!**

The privilege of being a Permanent Resident privilege provides you with certain benefits that non-residents don't possess. These include:

- ❑ Permission to Work in the United States
- ❑ Ability to enter and live in the United States as often as you wish. You are no longer considered a visa holder and don't need to get permission from an Embassy or Point of Entry (border) every time you enter the United States.
- ❑ Can sponsor spouse and family to United States
- ❑ Receive Social Security benefits (upon retirement)
- ❑ Paying local (resident) fee for schools, colleges, and universities
- ❑ Eligible for Educational Financial Aid
- ❑ And eligible to apply for United States citizenship after five years
- ❑ Your rights as Permanent Resident is same as an American Born or a US Citizen (with some exceptions)
- ❑ You may legally own property and firearms
- ❑ Other tax Benefits that only Green Card Holders and US Citizens can take advantage of.

Green Cards were formerly issued by the Immigration and Naturalization Service (INS). During a re-organization process, that agency was absorbed into and replaced by the Bureau of Citizenship and Immigration Services (BCIS), part of the Department of Homeland Security (DHS). Shortly after that re-organization, BCIS was renamed the U.S. Citizenship and Immigration Services (USCIS), which still retains the responsibility of issuing Green Cards.

A. GREEN CARD EXPIRATION

Your Green Card normally expires in 10 years and you will need to renew your card. This does not mean that you have to go through the whole process of applying for it again. You just need to inform USCIS that you would like to renew your permanent resident status.

As a Green Card, holder you are assumed to be staying in the United States majority of your time. If you stay outside of the United States for a long time, you may lose your permanent residency privileges and you will need to go through the whole application process again.

Note: If your intention is to visit the United States on a short-term basis, don't bother going through the Green Card process. The purpose of becoming a Permanent Resident is to have your place of residence in the United States.

B. ABANDONMENT OR LOSS OF PERMANENT RESIDENT STATUS

There are two basic ways that your permanent residency can end: Voluntarily an Involuntarily:

- o **Voluntary Abandonment:**
  A Green Card holder may abandon permanent residence by filing appropriate forms and filing at a US Embassy or Consulate.

- o **Involuntarily Abandonment:**
  Even though you possess permanent residency status, you can still be deported from the United States and your Green Card be revoked if you are convicted of a crime. Crimes that can deport you are similar to those conditions that make someone inadmissible to the United States and include but not limited to:

  - Committing a criminal act that makes a person removable from the United States

Copyright © 2011 - GreenCard123.Com by UNorth® - All Rights Reserved

- Moving to another country to live there permanently, staying outside the USA for more than 365 days (without getting a re-entry permit before leaving)
- Not filing your Income Tax
- Drug offences
- Felonies
- Engaging in sabotaging the government
- Terrorist activities
- Engaging in or attempting to transport anyone to the United States illegally
- Money laundering activities

In addition to the criminal offenses above, if USCIS discovers that you provided falsified information for the purpose of receiving immigration benefits (e.g. lied in your application to make yourself eligible for Green Card when you were otherwise ineligible), at any point, even if you become a US Citizen, can revoke your Green Card status and deport you back.

A person who loses permanent residence status is immediately removable from the United States and must leave the country as soon as possible or face deportation and removal. In some cases the person may be banned from entering the country for three or seven years, or even permanently.

Failure to Renew

The failure to renew the permanent resident card does not result in the loss of status, except in the case of conditional permanent residents for some types of visa (not applicable to Diversity Visa Lottery).

C. YOUR RIGHTS AND RESPONSIBILITIES AS A PERMANENT RESIDENT

Obviously good things don't come for free and Permanent Residency is not an exception either. To keep your permanent residency in the United States you have certain rights responsibilities. These include:

- **Residing in the United States:** As a Permanent Resident, you do have certain rights and responsibilities that ensure your continued residency status in the United States. As the name refers, a Permanent Resident is expected to stay most of the time in the United States. This of it as US is your home now; In other words, if you need to be out of the United States for more than a year, you need to get permission from USCIS or otherwise risk losing your residency status. This permission is called "Re-Entry" permit and can extend your stay by up to two years outside of the United States.
- **Filing Income Tax:** As a resident of the United States, you are also expected to file your annual income tax reporting your income (including foreign income) and pay tax. Your tax status will change from non-resident to resident and though you may be paying higher taxes, you'll be taking advantage of the tax benefits, tax cuts and tax credits. You'll be paying State and Federal Taxes on your income every year (not on the money that you already have).
- **Military Duty:** As a resident of the United States, you are also expected to defend your country in case of need. All males between age of 18 and 26 need to be registered in what is called Selective Service. This organization is in charge of drafting individuals if a war requires additional individuals to participate (more than available military personnel). As a permanent resident, you may have an option to exclude yourself from selective service but doing so will waive your eligibility to become a US Citizen down the road.

D. SOCIAL SECURITY NUMBER

The Social Security Number is your primary identification number in the United States. If you have been previously in the United States, you probably are already aware and may possess a Social Security Number. It is a 9 digit number in this format 111-22-3333 and issued to U.S. citizens, permanent residents, and temporary (working) residents. A Social Security Number is

Copyright © 2011 - GreenCard123.Com by UNorth® - All Rights Reserved

important because you need it to get a job, collect Social Security benefits and receive some other government services. Many other businesses, such as banks and credit companies, also ask for your number.

Common places that use Social Security Number:
- Banks to open an account or identify you
- Working, for employer to hire you and check your background
- Insurance, to identify you
- Department of Motor Vehicles, to check your residency and issue your identification and driver license
- Government, to check your background
- Loans, and credit card companies
- Social Security Administration to track your Social Security (Retirement) benefits
- IRS to collect and track your taxes and identify you

That being said, your social security number is an important piece of information. You should do your best to protect this number and don't just give it away to anyone asking for it. Make sure you provide it only to secure places that you trust.

If you lose your Social Security card, you may request a replacement. There is a limit to the number of replacement Social Security cards you may receive to 3 per calendar year and 10 in a lifetime.

Visit Social Security website at http://www.ssa.gov for latest forms, Social Security office near you and the required documentation to issue a Social Security Card to you.

If you already have a Social Security card, you may visit a Social Security office near you to update your residency status. You will need to bring your passport and or your Permanent Resident card.

E. CHANGE IN ADDRESS

As a permanent resident, USCIS would still need to have your location on-file. If you move or change your (mailing) address, you should notify USCIS within ten days of your move. To change your address, you may do so simply online or via a form available at the USCIS website. Visit http://www.uscis.gov/addresschange for latest updates and information.

F. BENEFITING FROM IMMIGRATION BENEFITS FOR RELATIVES

As a permanent resident, you are eligible to request (officially known as filing a petition) for close relative to also migrate to the United States. For example your wife, and parents. Although in the case of Diversity Visa your spouse and children have already benefited from receiving their permanent residency, if you did not have a spouse and after you receive your Green Card you get married to a foreigner, you may file a petition for him or her. Keep in mind that Permanent Residents have lower priority compared to relatives of the US Citizen when it comes to applying for a visa for relatives. This priority is known as quota and depending on the country that you were from originally; there may be a backlog, even more than 10 years. This is due to the fact that there is a numerical limit on the Visas available on annual basis, similar to the Diversity Visa that has a 50,000 visa limit.

G. BECOME A US CITIZEN

Permanent residency is a great privilege. If you enjoy being in the United States, you may also consider to become a United States citizen and enjoy the benefits available in the US to the fullest level.

Copyright © 2011 - GreenCard123.Com by UNorth® - All Rights Reserved

H. PATH TO U.S. CITIZENSHIP

A lawful permanent resident can apply for United States citizenship, or naturalization, after five years of residency. Lawful permanent residents may submit their applications for naturalization as much as 90 days before meeting the residency requirement. Citizens are entitled to more rights (and obligations) than permanent residents (who are still classified as aliens in this respect). Certain conditions that may put a permanent resident in deportation proceedings do not apply to U.S. citizens. Once the US Government accepts your application to become a U.S. citizen, the process is called Naturalization.

I. ADVANTAGES OF BECOMING U.S. CITIZEN

Whether you are originally born in the US, or you become naturalized, you have certain benefits. Some of these benefits are already included in the permanent residency benefits and some are not:

- **The Right to Vote:** Having a right to vote is the greatest privilege that a US Citizen can gain. As unimportant that this may seem to some, consider that in the United States history there has been numerous occasion that a law, proposition, or a public official was chosen by one vote. That one vote made the difference:
  - In 1980, Idaho became a state by margin of one vote
  - In 1867, Alaska purchase vote was won by one vote

- **Freedom to live and work in the United States** is perhaps the biggest benefit of U.S. citizenship and legal residency. There are many jobs, opportunities, and educational opportunities. Some immigrants see citizenship as a way of locking in economic gains that they have made as legal residents.

- **Government support when traveling is a privilege.** While traveling abroad, if a person is arrested or detained by foreign authorities, there is the chance that the U.S. government might intervene on their behalf.[6] For example, an American citizen named William E. Petty, who was jailed by authorities in France in 1854, petitioned U.S. authorities to intervene on his behalf.

- **Access to services provided by the federal government,** such as income support, has been cited as a benefit of citizenship

- **Benefits for Athletes:** Citizens can compete as athletes for the United States Olympics team; President Reagan with Olympian Mary Lou Retton in 1987

- **Increased ability to sponsor relatives living abroad is a benefit** which allows an immigrant to extend an open hand to relatives living abroad

- **Less fear of government is a benefit.** Citizens have greatly reduced need to fear being deported.[6] While there are millions of persons living illegally in the nation, deportations are expensive, time-consuming procedures, and the general pattern is for government to avoid having to deport people unless there are specific and powerful reasons.

- **Other benefits.** The USCIS sometimes honors the achievements of naturalized U.S. citizens. The 'Outstanding American by Choice Award' was created by the USCIS to recognize the outstanding achievements of naturalized U.S. citizens, and past recipients include author Elie Wiesel who won the Nobel Peace Prize; Indra K. Nooyi who is CEO of PepsiCo; John Shalikashvili who was Chairman of the Joint Chiefs of Staff; and others.[17] Further, citizenship status can affect which country an athlete can compete as a member of in competitions such as the Olympics.

J. HISTORY OF CITIZENSHIP IN THE UNITED STATES

Citizenship began in colonial times as an active relation between people working cooperatively to solve municipal problems and participating actively in democratic decision-making, such as in New England Town Hall meetings. A variety of forces changed this relation during the nation's history; an underlying factor was a

Copyright © 2011 - GreenCard123.Com by UNorth® - All Rights Reserved

push for economic success which in turn caused people to avoid participating in local government. Citizenship became less defined by participation in politics and more defined as a legal relation with accompanying rights and privileges. While the realm of civic participation in the public sphere has shrunk, the citizenship franchise has been expanded to include not just propertied white adult men but African-American men and adult women. Citizenship offers a chance to participate in a dynamic economic marketplace.

Copyright © 2011 - GreenCard123.Com by UNorth® - All Rights Reserved

APPENDIX

I. SAMPLE FORMS AND PROCEDURES

Although we have provided sample forms here for you, USCIS changes forms frequently. The best place to get immigration and naturalization a form is the USCIS website itself. Depending whether you're applying from inside the United States or outside, different forms are required; refer to your USCIS letter for information on which form you need to fill.

Note the following:

> **Filling in forms requires a PDF reader application such as Adobe PDF or other compatible applications.**

- ❑ Only get the forms from USCIS website itself. This way you are certain that the latest version of the form is obtained
- ❑ There is no fee to retrieve a form
- ❑ Although not related to the Diversity Visa forms, some of the other USCIS forms can be completed online
- ❑ USCIS Website is available 24 hours a day, 7 days a week, and 365 days a year!
- ❑ If your computer supports, you may fill-in the forms on your computer and print*; using the computer-filled forms. This enables you to produce a clean-professional form similar to those that attorneys create for their client (Instead of handwriting the information in the form)
- ❑ If you are living in the United States, you may request the forms be mailed to you by contacting USCIS directly or visiting the USCIS service center near you.
- ❑ If you are living outside of the United States, most of the forms are available at your nearest US Embassy/consulate.
- ❑ Always make a copy of the submitted or mailed form for your reference

Copyright © 2011 - GreenCard123.Com by UNorth® - All Rights Reserved

U.S. Department of State

OMB APPROVAL NO. 1405-0015
EXPIRES: 02/29/2012
ESTIMATED BURDEN: 1 HOUR*
(See Page 2)

APPLICATION FOR IMMIGRANT VISA AND ALIEN REGISTRATION

PART I - BIOGRAPHIC DATA

Instructions: Complete one copy of this form for yourself and each member of your family, regardless of age, who will immigrate with you. Please print or type your answers to all questions. Mark questions that are **Not Applicable** with **"N/A"**. If there is insufficient room on the form, answer on a separate sheet using the same numbers that appear on the form. **Attach any additional sheets to this form.**

Warning: Any false statement or concealment of a material fact may result in your permanent exclusion from the United States. This form *(DS-230 Part I)* is the first of two parts. This part, together with Form DS-230 Part II, constitutes the complete Application for **Immigrant Visa and Alien Registration.**

1. Family Name	First Name	Middle Name
SMITH	JOHN	M

2. Other Names Used or Aliases *(If married woman, give maiden name)*
N/A

3. Full Name in Native Alphabet *(If Roman letters not used)*
JOHN M. SMITH

4. Date of Birth *(mm-dd-yyyy)*	5. Age	6. Place of Birth *(City or Town)*	*(Province)*	*(Country)*
10-20-1970	45	PARIS	PARIS	FRANCE

7. Nationality *(If dual national, give both.)*	8. Gender	9. Marital Status
FRANCE	☐ Female ☒ Male	☐ Single *(Never Married)* ☒ Married ☐ Widowed ☐ Divorced ☐ Separated Including my present marriage, I have been married ___1___ times.

10. Permanent address in the United States where you intend to live, if known *(street address including ZIP code)*. Include the name of a person who currently lives there.	11. Address in the United States where you want your Permanent Resident Card *(Green Card)* mailed, if different from address in item #10 *(include the name of a person who currently lives there)*.
MR. GEORGE WILSON 234 FIRST ST WASHINGTON, DC 10000	C/O: MR. GEORGE WILSON 234 FIRST ST WASHINGTON, DC 10000
Telephone number (111) 222-3333	Telephone number (111) 222-3333

12. Present Occupation	13. Present Address *(Street Address) (City or Town) (Province) (Country)*
	2. AVENUE GABRIEL, PARIS, FRANCE 75016
COMPUTER ENGINEER	Telephone Number *(Home)* (33) 1 22 3344 55 ǀ Telephone Number *(Office)* (33) 1 22 3344 55 ǀ Email Address johnsmith@example.com

14. Spouse's Maiden or Family Name	First Name	Middle Name
SMITH	JANE	

15. Date *(mm-dd-yyyy)* and Place of Birth of Spouse
12-10-1973   ACCOUNTANT

16. Address of Spouse *(If different from your own)*	17. Spouse's Occupation
-SAME AS ABOVE-	04-15-1992
	18. Date of Marriage *(mm-dd-yyyy)* 04-15-1992

19. Father's Family Name	First Name	Middle Name
SMITH	GABRIEL	

20. Father's Date of Birth *(mm-dd-yyyy)*	21. Place of Birth	22. Current Address	23. If Deceased, Give Year of Death
05-05-1945	PARIS, FRANCE	3. AVENUE GABRIEL, PARIS, FRANC	

24. Mother's Family Name at Birth	First Name	Middle Name
10-03-1950	PARIS, FRANCE	

25. Mother's Date of Birth *(mm-dd-yyyy)*	26. Place of Birth	27. Current Address	28. If Deceased, Give Year of Death
10-03-1950	PARIS, FRANCE	3. AVENUE GABRIEL, PARIS,FRANCE	

DS-230 Part I
02-2010

This Form May be Obtained Free at Consular Offices of the United States of America
Previous Editions Obsolete

Page 1 of 4

Copyright © 2011 - GreenCard123.Com by UNorth® - All Rights Reserved

29. List Names, Dates and Places of Birth, and Addresses of **ALL** Children.

Name	Date (mm-dd-yyyy)	Place of Birth	Address (If different from your own)
SMITH, ROBERT JR.	01-10-1994	PARIS, FRANCE	-SAME AS ABOVE-
SMITH, SARAH	03-18-1996	PARIS, FRANCE	-SAME AS ABOVE-

30. List below all places you have lived for at least six months since reaching the age of 16, including places in your country of nationality. Begin with your present residence.

City or Town	Province	Country	From/To (mm-yyyy) or "Present"	
PARIS	FRANCE	FRANCE	10-1970	PRESENT

31a. Person(s) named in 14 and 29 who will accompany you to the United States now.

JANE SMITH / ROBERT JR. SMITH / SARAH SMITH

31b. Person(s) named in 14 and 29 who will follow you to the United States at a later date.

N/A

32. List below all employment for the last ten years.

Employer	Location	Job Title	From/To (mm-yyyy) or "Present"	
IBM CORPORATION	PARIS, FRANCE	COMPUTER SPECIALIST	02-2005	PRESENT
XYZ SOFTWARE	PARIS, FRANCE	DESKTOP TECHNICIAN	06-2002	02-2005
PARIS UNIVERSITY OF TECH	PARIS, FRANCE	CUSTOMER SERVICE	04-2000	08-2000

In what occupation do you intend to work in the United States?

33. List below all educational institutions attended.

School and Location	From/To (mm-yyyy)		Course of Study	Degree or Diploma
PARIS UNIVERSITY OF TECHNOLOGY	04-1997	02-2002	COMPUTER SCIENCE	BACHELOR SCIEN
PARIS COLLEGE	03-1993	03-1994	ACCOUNTING	CERTIFICATE
PARIS HIGH SCHOOL	09-1985	09-1989	N/A	H.S. DIPLOMA
PARIS MIDDLE AND ELEMENTRY SCHOOL	09-1978	09-1985	N/A	N/A

Languages spoken or read_____ FRENCH, ENGLISH

Professional associations to which you belong _____ N/A

34. Previous Military Service ☐ Yes ☒ No

Branch _____ N/A _____ Dates of Service (mm-dd-yyyy) _____

Rank/Position _____ Military Speciality/Occupation _____

35. List dates of all previous visits to or residence in the United States. (If never, write "never") Give type of visa status, if known. Give DHS "A" number if any.

From/To (mm-yyyy)		Location	Type of Visa	"A" Number (If known)
08-1998	11-1998	LOS ANGELES, CA	VISITOR VISA	N/A

Signature of Applicant	Date (mm-dd-yyyy)
/JOHN M. SMITH/	08-09-2011

Privacy Act and Paperwork Reduction Act Statements

The information asked for on this form is requested pursuant to Section 222 of the Immigration and Nationality Act. The U.S. Department of State uses the facts you provide on this form primarily to determine your classification and eligibility for a U.S. immigrant visa. Individuals who fail to submit this form or who do not provide all the requested information may be denied a U.S. immigrant visa. If you are issued an immigrant visa and are subsequently admitted to the United States as an immigrant, the Department of Homeland Security will use the information on this form to issue you a Permanent Resident Card, and, if you so indicate, the Social Security Administration will use the information to issue you a social security number and card.

*Public reporting burden for this collection of information is estimated to average 1 hour per response, including time required for searching existing data sources, gathering the necessary documentation, providing the information and/or documents required, and reviewing the final collection. You do not have to supply this information unless this collection displays a currently valid OMB control number. If you have comments on the accuracy of this burden estimate and/or recommendations for reducing it, please send them to: A/GIS/DIR, Room 2400 SA-22, U.S. Department of State, Washington, DC 20522-2202

DS-230 Part I

Page 2 of 4

Copyright © 2011 - GreenCard123.Com by UNorth® - All Rights Reserved

U.S. Department of State

APPLICATION FOR IMMIGRANT VISA AND ALIEN REGISTRATION

OMB APPROVAL NO. 1405-0015
EXPIRES: 02/29/2012
ESTIMATED BURDEN: 1 HOUR*

PART II - SWORN STATEMENT

Instructions: Complete one copy of this form for yourself and each member of your family, regardless of age, who will immigrate with you. Please print or type your answers to all questions. Mark questions that are **Not Applicable** with **"N/A"**. If there is insufficient room on the form, answer on a separate sheet using the same numbers that appear on the form. Attach any additional sheets to this form. The fee should be paid in United States dollars or local currency equivalent, or by bank draft.

Warning: Any false statement or concealment of a material fact may result in your permanent exclusion from the United States. Even if you are issued an immigrant visa and are subsequently admitted to the United States, providing false information on this form could be grounds for your prosecution and/or deportation.

This form *(DS-230 Part II)*, together with Form DS-230 Part I, constitutes the complete Application for Immigrant Visa and Alien Registration.

36. Family Name	First Name	Middle Name
SMITH	JOHN	M.

37. Other Names Used or Aliases *(If married woman, give maiden name)*

N/A

38. Full Name in Native Alphabet *(If Roman letters not used)*

JOHN M. SMITH

39. Name and Address of Petitioner	Telephone number
-SAME-	(33) 1 22 3344 55
	Email Address johnsmith@example.com

40. United States laws governing the issuance of visas require each applicant to state whether or not he or she is a member of any class of individuals excluded from admission into the United States. The excludable classes are described below in general terms. You should read carefully the following list and answer **Yes** or **No** to each category. The answers you give will assist the consular officer to reach a decision on your eligibility to receive a visa.

Except as Otherwise Provided by Law, Aliens Within the Following Classifications are Ineligible to Receive a Visa. Do Any of the Following Classes Apply to You?

a. An alien who has a communicable disease of public health significance; who has failed to present documentation of having received vaccinations in accordance with U.S. law; who has or has had a physical or mental disorder that poses or is likely to pose a threat to the safety or welfare of the alien or others; or who is a drug abuser or addict. ☐ Yes ☒ No

b. An alien convicted of, or who admits having committed, a crime involving moral turpitude or violation of any law relating to a controlled substance or who is the spouse, son or daughter of such a trafficker who knowingly has benefited from the trafficking activities in the past five years; who has been convicted of 2 or more offenses for which the aggregate sentences were 5 years or more; who is coming to the United States to engage in prostitution or commercialized vice or who has engaged in prostitution or procuring within the past 10 years; who is or has been an illicit trafficker in any controlled substance; who has committed a serious criminal offense in the United States and who has asserted immunity from prosecution; who, while serving as a foreign government official, was responsible for or directly carried out particularly severe violations of religious freedom; or whom the President has identified as a person who plays a significant role in a severe form of trafficking in persons, who otherwise has knowingly aided, abetted, assisted or colluded with such a trafficker in severe forms of trafficking in persons, or who is the spouse, son or daughter of such a trafficker who knowingly has benefited from the trafficking activities within the past five years. ☐ Yes ☒ No

c. An alien who seeks to enter the United States to engage in espionage, sabotage, export control violations, terrorist activities, the overthrow of the Government of the United States or other unlawful activity; who is a member of or affiliated with the Communist or other totalitarian party; who participated, engaged or ordered genocide, torture, or extrajudicial killings; or who is a member or representative of a terrorist organization as currently designated by the U.S. Secretary of State. ☐ Yes ☒ No

d. An alien who is likely to become a public charge. ☐ Yes ☒ No

e. An alien who seeks to enter for the purpose of performing skilled or unskilled labor who has not been certified by the Secretary of Labor; who is a graduate of a foreign medical school seeking to perform medical services who has not passed the NBME exam or its equivalent; or who is a health care worker seeking to perform such work without a certificate from the CGFNS or from an equivalent approved independent credentialing organization. ☐ Yes ☒ No

f. An alien who failed to attend a hearing on deportation or inadmissibility within the last 5 years; who seeks or has sought a visa, entry into the United States, or any immigration benefit by fraud or misrepresentation; who knowingly assisted any other alien to enter or try to enter the United States in violation of law; who, after November 30, 1996, attended in student (F) visa status a U.S. public elementary school or who attended a U.S. public secondary school without reimbursing the school; or who is subject to a civil penalty under INA 274C. ☐ Yes ☒ No

Privacy Act and Paperwork Reduction Act Statements

The information asked for on this form is requested pursuant to Section 222 of the Immigration and Nationality Act. The U.S. Department of State uses the facts you provide on this form primarily to determine your classification and eligibility for a U.S. immigrant visa. Individuals who fail to submit this form or who do not provide all the requested information may be denied a U.S. immigrant visa. If you are issued an immigrant visa and are subsequently admitted to the United States as an immigrant, the Department of Homeland Security will use the information on this form to issue you a Permanent Resident Card, and, if you so indicate, the Social Security Administration will use the information to issue you a social security number and card.

*Public reporting burden for this collection of information is estimated to average 1 hour per response, including time required for searching existing data sources, gathering the necessary documentation, providing the information and/or documents required, and reviewing the final collection. You do not have to supply this information unless this collection displays a currently valid OMB control number. If you have comments on the accuracy of this burden estimate and/or recommendations for reducing it, please send them to: A/GIS/DIR, Room 2400 SA-22, U.S. Department of State, Washington, DC 20522-2202

DS-230 Part II   Previous Editions Obsolete   Page 3 of 4

Copyright © 2011 – GreenCard123.Com by UNorth® – All Rights Reserved

g. An alien who is permanently ineligible for U.S. citizenship; or who departed the United States to evade military service in time of war.	☐ Yes	☒ No
h. An alien who was previously ordered removed within the last 5 years or ordered removed a second time within the last 20 years; who was previously unlawfully present and ordered removed within the last 10 years or ordered removed a second time within the last 20 years; who was convicted of an aggravated felony and ordered removed; who was previously unlawfully present in the United States for more than 180 days but less than one year who voluntarily departed within the last 3 years; or who was unlawfully present for more than one year or an aggregate of one year within the last 10 years.	☐ Yes	☒ No
i. An alien who is coming to the United States to practice polygamy; who withholds custody of a U.S. citizen child outside the United States from a person granted legal custody by a U.S. court or intentionally assists another person to do so; who has voted in the United States in violation of any law or regulation; or who renounced U.S. citizenship to avoid taxation.	☐ Yes	☒ No
j. An alien who is a former exchange visitor who has not fulfilled the 2-year foreign residence requirement.	☐ Yes	☒ No
k. An alien determined by the Attorney General to have knowingly made a frivolous application for asylum.	☐ Yes	☒ No
l. An alien who has ordered, carried out or materially assisted in extrajudicial and political killings and other acts of violence against the Haitian people; who has directly or indirectly assisted or supported any of the groups in Colombia known as FARC, ELN, or AUC; who through abuse of a governmental or political position has converted for personal gain, confiscated or expropriated property in Cuba, a claim to which is owned by a national of the United States, has trafficked in such property or has been complicit in such conversion, has committed similar acts in another country, or is the spouse, minor child or agent of an alien who has committed such acts; who has been directly involved in the establishment or enforcement of population controls forcing a woman to undergo an abortion against her free choice or a man or a woman to undergo sterilization against his or her free choice; or who has disclosed or trafficked in confidential U.S. business information obtained in connection with U.S. participation in the Chemical Weapons Convention or is the spouse, minor child or agent of such a person.	☐ Yes	☒ No

41. Have you ever been charged, arrested or convicted of any offense or crime? *(If answer is Yes, please explain)* N/A	☐ Yes	☒ No

42. Have you ever been refused admission to the United States at a port-of-entry? *(If answer is Yes, please explain)*	☐ Yes	☒ No

43a. Have you ever applied for a Social Security Number *(SSN)*? ☐ Yes ☒ No Give the number _____ Would you like to receive a replacement card? (You must answer YES to question 43b. to receive a card.) ☐ Yes ☒ No Do you want the Social Security Administration to assign you a SSN and issue a card? (You must answer YES to question 43b. to receive a number and a card.) ☒ Yes ☐ No	43b. **Consent to Disclosure:** I authorize disclosure of information from this form to the Department of Homeland Security *(DHS)*, the Social Security Administration *(SSA)*, such other U.S. Government agencies as may be required for the purpose of assigning me an SSN and issuing me a Social Security card, and I authorize the SSA to share my SSN with the INS. ☒ Yes ☐ No The applicant's response does not limit or restrict the Government's ability to obtain his or her SSN, or other information on this form, for enforcement or other purposes as authorized by law.

44. Were you assisted in completing this application?   ☐ Yes   ☐ No *(If answer is Yes, give name and address of person assisting you, indicating whether relative, friend, travel agent, attorney, or other)* N/A

DO NOT WRITE BELOW THE FOLLOWING LINE
The consular officer will assist you in answering Item 45.
DO NOT SIGN this form until instructed to do so by the consular officer

45. I claim to be:

☐ A Family-Sponsored Immigrant
☐ An Employment-Based Immigrant
☐ A Diversity Immigrant
☐ A Special Category *(Specify)* _____
   (Returning resident, Hong Kong, Tibetan, Private Legislation, etc.)

☐ I derive foreign state chargeability under Sec. 202(b) through my _____

☐ Preference _____

☐ Numerical limitation _____
(foreign state)

I understand that I am required to surrender my visa to the **United States Immigration Officer** at the place where I apply to enter the United States, and that the possession of a visa does not entitle me to enter the United States if at that time I am found to be inadmissible under the immigration laws.

I understand that any willfully false or misleading statement or willful concealment of a material fact made by me herein may subject me to permanent exclusion from the United States and, if I am admitted to the United States, may subject me to criminal prosecution and/or deportation.

I, the undersigned applicant for a United States immigrant visa, do solemnly swear *(or affirm)* that all statements which appear in this application, consisting of Form DS-230 Part I and Part II combined, have been made by me, including the answers to Items 1 through 45 inclusive, and that they are true and complete to the best of my knowledge and belief. I do further swear *(or affirm)* that, if admitted into the United States, I will not engage in activities which would be prejudicial to the public interest, or endanger the welfare, safety, or security of the United States; in activities which would be prohibited by the laws of the United States relating to espionage, sabotage, public disorder, or in other activities subversive to the national security; in any activity a purpose of which is the opposition to or the control, or overthrow of, the Government of the United States, by force, violence, or other unconstitutional means.

I understand that completion of this form by persons required by law to register with the Selective Service System *(males 18 through 25 years of age)* constitutes such registration in accordance with the Military Selective Service Act.

_____
Signature of Applicant

Subscribed and sworn to before me this _____ day of _____ _____ at: _____

_____
Consular Officer

Copyright © 2011 - GreenCard123.Com by UNorth® - All Rights Reserved

U.S. Department of State
SUPPLEMENTAL REGISTRATION FOR
THE DIVERSITY IMMIGRANT VISA PROGRAM

OMB APPROVAL NO. 1405-0098
EXPIRATION DATE: 12/31/2006
ESTIMATED BURDEN: 30 MINUTES
*See Page 2

INSTRUCTIONS

The following is a supplemental registration form for the Diversity Immigrant Visa Program under Section 203(c) of the Immigration and Nationality Act.

Clearly print or type all answers in the English language. Answer all questions.

Using the enclosed self-adhesive return address label, immediately send this form along with Form DS-230 to: Diversity Immigrant Visa Program, Kentucky Consular Center, 3505 N. Highway 25W, Williamsburg, KY 40769. Failure to follow instructions will disqualify your application.

You will be notified by mail of your appointment date, therefore the answer to question No. 3 must be accurate.

1. NAME *(Last, First, MI)*

    SMITH   JOHN   M

2. RANK ORDER NUMBER *(Case number on envelope)*

    2011EU00099999

3. CURRENT MAILING ADDRESS *(Address at which you receive your mail. Give any change of mailing address here.)*

    2, AVENUE GABRIEL
    PARIS, FRANCE 75016

    Telephone Number   (33) 1 22 3344 55

4. NAME OF UNITED STATES CONSULAR OFFICE WHERE YOU WOULD LIKE TO PROCESS YOUR APPLICATION
    This will usually be the consular office nearest the place you live. However, please note that some U. S. Embassies and Consulates do not process immigrant visas. If you are not sure whether the U.S. Embassy or Consulate nearest you processes immigrant visas, or if you do not know which is the U.S. Embassy or Consulate nearest you, please list the city and country where you live. If you live in the United States and plan to adjust status with the Bureau of Citizenship and Immigration Services in the U.S., please list "BCIS"; if you live in the United States but you intend to return abroad to be interviewed, please list the U.S. Embassy or Consulate that processes immigrant visas for the area where you lived before you came to the United States.

    PARIS, FRANCE

5. THE COUNTRY YOU LISTED AS YOUR NATIVE COUNTRY ON YOUR DIVERSITY VISA PROGRAM APPLICATION
    In most cases, this will be the country where you were born. You may also claim the country of birth of your husband or wife. In addition, you may claim the country of birth of either of your parents, if neither of your parents lived in, or was born in, the country where you were born.

    FRANCE

6. EDUCATION
    a. Check the highest level of education completed.

    ☐ High School, No Degree   ☐ High School Diploma   ☐ Vocational School

    ☐ College, No Degree   ☑ University Degree   ☐ Advanced Degree

    ☐ Other _____

    b. Names and addresses of all schools, colleges, and universities attended *(include trade and vocational schools)*:

NAME OF EDUCATIONAL INSTITUTION	FROM *(mm-yyyy)*	TO *(mm-yyyy)*	DEGREE(S) OR CERTIFICATE(S) RECEIVED
PARIS UNIVERSITY OF TECHNOLOGY	04-1997	02-2002	BACHELOR OF SCIENCE
PARIS COLLEGE	03-1993	03-1994	ACCOUNTING CERTIFICATE
PARIS HIGH SCHOOL	09-1985	09-1989	HIGHSCHOOL DIPLOMA
PARIS MIDDLE AND ELEMENTRY SCHOOL	09-1978	09-1985	N/A
N/A			

DSP-122
12-2003

Page 1 of 2

Copyright © 2011 – GreenCard123.Com by UNorth® – All Rights Reserved

7. WORK EXPERIENCE

a. Within the last 5 years, I have worked at least 2 years in a job that requires at least 2 years of training or experience:

☑ Yes   ☐ No

b. Occupation - If you answered "yes" to question 7a, give the job title and describe the type of work you did. Be as specific as possible.

COMPUTER SPECIALIST (ONE JOB CODE 15-1031.00)

c. Names and addresses of your employers during the past 5 years in the work you described above, and the dates *(beginning and ending months and years)* you worked for each.

NAME OF EMPLOYER	ADDRESS	FROM *(mm-yyyy)* ..	TO *(mm-yyyy)*
IBM CORPORATION	5, AVENUE GABRIEL	02-2005	PRESENT

SIGNED STATEMENT

I certify that only one application was or has been submitted by me or on my behalf for this immigrant visa registration. I further certify that I have read and understand all the questions set forth above and that the answers I have furnished on this form are true and correct to the best of my knowledge and belief. I understand that any false or misleading statement may result in the refusal of a visa or denial of entry into the United States.

/JOHN M. SMITH/	08-09-2011
Signature of Applicant	Date *(mm-dd-yyyy)*

PRIVACY ACT AND PAPERWORK REDUCTION ACT STATEMENTS

The information asked for on this form is requested pursuant to Section 222 of the Immigration and Nationality Act. The U.S. Department of State uses the facts you provide on this form primarily to determine your eligibility for a U.S. immigrant visa. Individuals who fail to submit this form or who do not provide all the requested information may be denied a U.S. immigrant visa. If you are issued an immigrant visa and are subsequently admitted to the United States as an immigrant, the Bureau of Citizenship and Immigration Services will use the information on this form to issue you a Permanent Resident Card, and, if you so indicate, the Social Security Administration will use the information to issue you a social security number and card.

*Public reporting burden for this collection of information is estimated to average 30 minutes per response, including time required for searching existing data sources, gathering the necessary data, providing the information required, and reviewing the final collection. In accordance with 5 CFR 1320 5(b), persons are not required to respond to the collection of this information unless this form displays a currently valid OMB control number. Send comments on the accuracy of this estimate of the burden and recommendations for reducing it to the U.S. Department of State, A/RPS/DIR, 1800 G Street (Suite 2400), NW, Washington, DC 20522.

DO NOT WRITE IN THIS SPACE - FOR OFFICIAL USE ONLY

Occupation Code:_____

DSP-122

Copyright © 2011 – GreenCard123.Com by UNorth® - All Rights Reserved

OMB No. 1615-0023; Expires 12/31/2010

Form I-485, Application to Register
Permanent Residence or Adjust Status

Department of Homeland Security
U.S. Citizenship and Immigration Services

START HERE - Type or Print (Use black ink)

For USCIS Use Only

Part 1. Information About You

Family Name (Last Name)	Given Name (First Name)	Middle Name
JOHN		SMITH

Address - Street Number and Name — Apt. #

123 FIRST STREET

C/O (in care of)

City	State	Zip Code
WASHINGTON	DC	10001

Date of Birth (mm/dd/yyyy)	Country of Birth
10/20/1970	FRANCE

Country of Citizenship/Nationality	U.S. Social Security # (if any)	A # (if any)
FRANCE		000-000-000

Date of Last Arrival (mm/dd/yyyy)	I-94 #
01/05/2010	003023094 09

Current USCIS Status	Expires on (mm/dd/yyyy)
VALID / H1	01/05/2012

For USCIS Use Only

Returned

Receipt

Resubmitted

Reloc Sent

Reloc Rec'd

Applicant Interviewed

Part 2. Application Type (Check one)

I am applying for an adjustment to permanent resident status because:

a. ☐ An immigrant petition giving me an immediately available immigrant visa number that has been approved. (Attach a copy of the approval notice, or a relative, special immigrant juvenile, or special immigrant military visa petition filed with this application that will give you an immediately available visa number, if approved.)

b. ☐ My spouse or parent applied for adjustment of status or was granted lawful permanent residence in an immigrant visa category that allows derivative status for spouses and children.

c. ☐ I entered as a K-1 fiancé(e) of a U.S. citizen whom I married within 90 days of entry, or I am the K-2 child of such a fiancé(e). (Attach a copy of the fiancé(e) petition approval notice and the marriage certificate.)

d. ☐ I was granted asylum or derivative asylum status as the spouse or child of a person granted asylum and am eligible for adjustment.

e. ☐ I am a native or citizen of Cuba admitted or paroled into the United States after January 1, 1959, and thereafter have been physically present in the United States for at least 1 year.

f. ☐ I am the husband, wife, or minor unmarried child of a Cuban described above in **(e),** and I am residing with that person, and was admitted or paroled into the United States after January 1, 1959, and thereafter have been physically present in the United States for at least 1 year.

g. ☐ I have continuously resided in the United States since before January 1, 1972.

h. ☒ Other basis of eligibility. Explain (for example, I was admitted as a refugee, my status has not been terminated, and I have been physically present in the United States for 1 year after admission). If additional space is needed, see **Page 2** of the instructions. DV-2012 SELECTEE

I am already a permanent resident and am applying to have the date I was granted permanent residence adjusted to the date I originally arrived in the United States as a nonimmigrant or parolee, or as of May 2, 1964, whichever date is later, and: (Check one)

i. ☐ I am a native or citizen of Cuba and meet the description in **(e)** above.

j. ☐ I am the husband, wife, or minor unmarried child of a Cuban and meet the description in **(f)** above.

Section of Law
☐ Sec. 209(a), INA
☐ Sec. 209(b), INA
☐ Sec. 13, Act of 9/11/57
☐ Sec. 245, INA
☐ Sec. 249, INA
☐ Sec. 1 Act of 11/2/66
☐ Sec. 2 Act of 11/2/66
☐ Other

Country Chargeable

Eligibility Under Sec. 245
☐ Approved Visa Petition
☐ Dependent of Principal Alien
☐ Special Immigrant
☐ Other

Preference

Action Block

To be Completed by
Attorney or Representative, if any
☐ Fill in box if Form G-28 is attached to represent the applicant.

VOLAG #

ATTY State License #

Form I-485 (Rev. 07/15/10) Y

Copyright © 2011 – GreenCard123.Com by UNorth® – All Rights Reserved

Part 3. Processing Information

A. City/Town/Village of Birth

PARIS

Current Occupation

COMPUTER ENGINEER

Your Mother's First Name

SARAH

Your Father's First Name

GABRIEL

Give your name exactly as it appears on your Form I-94, Arrival-Departure Record

JOHN M. SMITH

Place of Last Entry Into the United States *(City/State)*

WASHINGTON, DC

In what status did you last enter? *(Visitor, student, exchange visitor, crewman, temporary worker, without inspection, etc.)*

TEMPORARY WORKER

Were you inspected by a U.S. Immigration Officer?   Yes ☒   No ☐

Nonimmigrant Visa Number

VS00000000000000000000001

Consulate Where Visa Was Issued

PARIS, FRANCE

Date Visa Issued *(mm/dd/yyyy)*

10/01/2009

Gender   ☒ Male   ☐ Female

Marital Status   ☒ Married   ☐ Single   ☐ Divorced   ☐ Widowed

Have you ever applied for permanent resident status in the U.S.?   ☐ Yes *(If "Yes" give date and place of filing and final disposition.)*   ☒ No

N/A

B. List your present spouse and all of your children (include adult sons and daughters). (If you have none, write "None." If additional space is needed, see **Page 2** of the instructions.)

Family Name *(Last Name)*	Given Name *(First Name)*	Middle Initial	Date of Birth *(mm/dd/yyyy)*
SMITH	JANE		10/10/1973
Country of Birth	Relationship	A # *(if any)*	Applying with you?
CHINA	SPOUSE	000-000-000	Yes ☒ No ☐
Family Name *(Last Name)*	Given Name *(First Name)*	Middle Initial	Date of Birth *(mm/dd/yyyy)*
SMITH	ROBERT	JR	01/10/1994
Country of Birth	Relationship	A # *(if any)*	Applying with you?
FRANCE	CHILD (SON)	000-000-000	Yes ☒ No ☐
Family Name *(Last Name)*	Given Name *(First Name)*	Middle Initial	Date of Birth *(mm/dd/yyyy)*
SMITH	SARAH		03/18/1996
Country of Birth	Relationship	A # *(if any)*	Applying with you?
FRANCE	CHILD (DAUGHTER)	000-000-000	Yes ☒ No ☐
Family Name *(Last Name)*	Given Name *(First Name)*	Middle Initial	Date of Birth *(mm/dd/yyyy)*
N/A			
Country of Birth	Relationship	A # *(if any)*	Applying with you?
			Yes ☐ No ☐
Family Name *(Last Name)*	Given Name *(First Name)*	Middle Initial	Date of Birth *(mm/dd/yyyy)*
Country of Birth	Relationship	A # *(if any)*	Applying with you?
			Yes ☐ No ☐

Form I-485 (Rev. 07/15/10) Y Page 2

Copyright © 2011 - GreenCard123.Com by UNorth® - All Rights Reserved

Part 3. Processing Information *(Continued)*

C. List your present and past membership in or affiliation with every organization, association, fund, foundation, party, club, society, or similar group in the United States or in other places since your 16th birthday. Include **any military service** in this part. If none, write "None." Include the name of each organization, location, nature, and dates of membership. If additional space is needed, attach a separate sheet of paper. Continuation pages must be submitted according to the guidelines provided on **Page 2** of the instructions under "What Are the General Filing Instructions?"

Name of Organization	Location and Nature	Date of Membership From	Date of Membership To
CHILD FOUNDATION	PARIS, FRANCE - FUNDRAISING FOR CHILDREN, AFFILICATION WITH UNICEF	01/01/2001	10/01/2009
N/A			

Answer the following questions. (If your answer is **"Yes"** to any question, explain on a separate piece of paper. Continuation pages must be submitted according to the guidelines provided on **Page 2** of the instructions under "What Are the General Filing Instructions?" Information about documentation that must be include with your application is also provide in this section.) Answering **"Yes"** does not necessarily mean that you are not entitled to adjust status or register for permanent residence.

1. Have you **EVER**, in or outside the United States:

   a. Knowingly committed any crime of moral turpitude or a drug-related offense for which you have not been arrested?　　Yes ☐　No ☒

   b. Been arrested, cited, charged, indicted, convicted, fined, or imprisoned for breaking or violating any law or ordinance, excluding traffic violations?　　Yes ☐　No ☒

   c. Been the beneficiary of a pardon, amnesty, rehabilitation decree, other act of clemency, or similar action?　　Yes ☐　No ☒

   d. Exercised diplomatic immunity to avoid prosecution for a criminal offense in the United States?　　Yes ☐　No ☒

2. Have you received public assistance in the United States from any source, including the U.S. Government or any State, county, city, or municipality (other than emergency medical treatment), or are you likely to receive public assistance in the future?　　Yes ☐　No ☒

3. Have you **EVER**:

   a. Within the past 10 years been a prostitute or procured anyone for prostitution, or intend to engage in such activities in the future?　　Yes ☐　No ☒

   b. Engaged in any unlawful commercialized vice, including, but not limited to, illegal gambling?　　Yes ☐　No ☒

   c. Knowingly encouraged, induced, assisted, abetted, or aided any alien to try to enter the United States illegally?　　Yes ☐　No ☒

   d. Illicitly trafficked in any controlled substance, or knowingly assisted, abetted, or colluded in the illicit trafficking of any controlled substance?　　Yes ☐　No ☒

4. Have you **EVER** engaged in, conspired to engage in, or do you intend to engage in, or have you ever solicited membership or funds for, or have you through any means ever assisted or provided any type of material support to any person or organization that has ever engaged or conspired to engage in sabotage, kidnapping, political assassination, hijacking, or any other form of terrorist activity?　　Yes ☐　No ☒

Form I-485 (Rev. 07/15/10) Y Page 3

Copyright © 2011 - GreenCard123.Com by UNorth® - All Rights Reserved

Part 3. Processing Information *(Continued)*

5. Do you intend to engage in the United States in:

    a. Espionage?   Yes ☐   No ☒

    b. Any activity a purpose of which is opposition to, or the control or overthrow of, the Government of the United States, by force, violence, or other unlawful means?   Yes ☐   No ☒

    c. Any activity to violate or evade any law prohibiting the export from the United States of goods, technology, or sensitive information?   Yes ☐   No ☒

6. Have you **EVER** been a member of, or in any way affiliated with, the Communist Party or any other totalitarian party?   Yes ☐   No ☒

7. Did you, during the period from March 23, 1933, to May 8, 1945, in association with either the Nazi Government of Germany or any organization or government associated or allied with the Nazi Government of Germany, ever order, incite, assist, or otherwise participate in the persecution of any person because of race, religion, national origin, or political opinion?   Yes ☐   No ☒

8. Have you **EVER** been deported from the United States, or removed from the United States at government expense, excluded within the past year, or are you now in exclusion, deportation, removal, or rescission proceedings?   Yes ☐   No ☒

9. Are you under a final order of civil penalty for violating section 274C of the Immigration and Nationality Act for use of fraudulent documents or have you, by fraud or willful misrepresentation of a material fact, ever sought to procure, or procured, a visa, other documentation, entry into the United States, or any immigration benefit?   Yes ☐   No ☒

10. Have you **EVER** left the United States to avoid being drafted into the U.S. Armed Forces?   Yes ☐   No ☒

11. Have you **EVER** been a J nonimmigrant exchange visitor who was subject to the 2-year foreign residence requirement and have not yet complied with that requirement or obtained a waiver?   Yes ☐   No ☒

12. Are you now withholding custody of a U.S. citizen child outside the United States from a person granted custody of the child?   Yes ☐   No ☒

13. Do you plan to practice polygamy in the United States?   Yes ☐   No ☒

14. Have you **EVER** ordered, incited, called for, committed, assisted, helped with, or otherwise participated in any of the following:

    a. Acts involving torture or genocide?   Yes ☐   No ☒

    b. Killing any person?   Yes ☐   No ☒

    c. Intentionally and severely injuring any person?   Yes ☐   No ☒

    d. Engaging in any kind of sexual contact or relations with any person who was being forced or threatened?   Yes ☐   No ☒

    e. Limiting or denying any person's ability to exercise religious beliefs?   Yes ☐   No ☒

15. Have you **EVER**:

    a. Served in, been a member of, assisted in, or participated in any military unit, paramilitary unit, police unit, self-defense unit, vigilante unit, rebel group, guerrilla group, militia, or insurgent organization?   Yes ☐   No ☒

    b. Served in any prison, jail, prison camp, detention facility, labor camp, or any other situation that involved detaining persons?   Yes ☐   No ☒

16. Have you **EVER** been a member of, assisted in, or participated in any group, unit, or organization of any kind in which you or other persons used any type of weapon against any person or threatened to do so?   Yes ☐   No ☒

Form I-485 (Rev. 07/15/10) Y Page 4

Copyright © 2011 – GreenCard123.Com by UNorth® – All Rights Reserved

Part 3. Processing Information *(Continued)*

17. Have you **EVER** assisted or participated in selling or providing weapons to any person who to your knowledge used them against another person, or in transporting weapons to any person who to your knowledge used them against another person? Yes ☐ No ☒

18. Have you **EVER** received any type of military, paramilitary, or weapons training? Yes ☐ No ☒

Part 4. Accommodations for Individuals With Disabilities and/or Impairments *(See **Page 10** of the instructions before completing this section.)*

Are you requesting an accommodation because of your disability(ies) and/or impairment(s)? Yes ☐ No ☒

If you answered "Yes," check any applicable box:

☐ **a.** I am deaf or hard of hearing and request the following accommodation(s) (if requesting a sign-language interpreter, indicate which language (e.g., American Sign Language)):

> N/A

☐ **b.** I am blind or sight-impaired and request the following accommodation(s):

> N/A

☐ **c.** I have another type of disability and/or impairment (describe the nature of your disability(ies) and/or impairment(s) and accommodation(s) you are requesting):

> N/A

Part 5. Signature *(Read the information on penalties on **Page 10** of the instructions before completing this section. You must file this application while in the United States.)*

Your Registration With U.S. Citizenship and Immigration Services

"I understand and acknowledge that, under section 262 of the Immigration and Nationality Act (INA), as an alien who has been or will be in the United States for more than 30 days, I am required to register with U.S. Citizenship and Immigration Services (USCIS). I understand and acknowledge that, under section 265 of the INA, I am required to provide USCIS with my current address and written notice of any change of address within **10** days of the change. I understand and acknowledge that USCIS will use the most recent address that I provide to USCIS, on any form containing these acknowledgements, for all purposes, including the service of a Notice to Appear should it be necessary for USCIS to initiate removal proceedings against me. I understand and acknowledge that if I change my address without providing written notice to USCIS, I will be held responsible for any communications sent to me at the most recent address that I provided to USCIS. I further understand and acknowledge that, if removal proceedings are initiated against me and I fail to attend any hearing, including an initial hearing based on service of the Notice to Appear at the most recent address that I provided to USCIS or as otherwise provided by law, I may be ordered removed in my absence, arrested, and removed from the United States."

Selective Service Registration

The following applies to you if you are a male at least 18 years of age, but not yet 26 years of age, who is required to register with the Selective Service System: "I understand that my filing Form I-485 with U.S. Citizenship and Immigration Services (USCIS) authorizes USCIS to provide certain registration information to the Selective Service System in accordance with the Military Selective Service Act. Upon USCIS acceptance of my application, I authorize USCIS to transmit to the Selective Service System my name, current address, Social Security Number, date of birth, and the date I filed the application for the purpose of recording my Selective Service registration as of the filing date. If, however, USCIS does not accept my application, I further understand that, if so required, I am responsible for registering with the Selective Service by other means, provided I have not yet reached 26 years of age."

Form I-485 (Rev. 07/15/10) Y Page 5

Copyright © 2011 - GreenCard123.Com by UNorth® - All Rights Reserved

Part 5. Signature *(Continued)*

Applicant's Statement *(Check one)*

☒ I can read and understand English, and I have read and understand each and every question and instruction on this form, as well as my answer to each question.

☐ Each and every question and instruction on this form, as well as my answer to each question, has been read to me in the _____ language, a language in which I am fluent, by the person named in **Interpreter's Statement and Signature**. I understand each and every question and instruction on this form, as well as my answer to each question.

I certify, under penalty of perjury under the laws of the United States of America, that the information provided with this application is all true and correct. I certify also that I have not withheld any information that would affect the outcome of this application.

I authorize the release of any information from my records that U.S. Citizenship and Immigration Services (USCIS) needs to determine eligibility for the benefit I am seeking.

Signature *(Applicant)*	Print Your Full Name	Date *(mm/dd/yyyy)*	Daytime Phone Number *(include area code)*
	/JOHN M. SMITH/	08/09/11	(111)222-3333

NOTE: *If you do not completely fill out this form or fail to submit required documents listed in the instructions, you may not be found eligible for the requested benefit, and this application may be denied.*

Interpreter's Statement and Signature

I certify that I am fluent in English and the below-mentioned language.

Language Used *(language in which applicant is fluent)*

I further certify that I have read each and every question and instruction on this form, as well as the answer to each question, to this applicant in the above-mentioned language, and the applicant has understood each and every instruction and question on the form, as well as the answer to each question.

Signature *(Interpreter)*	Print Your Full Name	Date *(mm/dd/yyyy)*	Phone Number *(include area code)*

Part 6. Signature of Person Preparing Form, If Other Than Above

I declare that I prepared this application at the request of the above applicant, and it is based on all information of which I have knowledge.

Signature	Print Your Full Name	Date *(mm/dd/yyyy)*	Phone Number *(include area code)*

Firm Name and Address	E-Mail Address *(if any)*

Form I-485 (Rev. 07/15/10) Y Page 6

Copyright © 2011 - GreenCard123.Com by UNorth® - All Rights Reserved

Department of Homeland Security
U.S. Citizenship and Immigration Services

OMB No. 1615-0008; Expires 06/30/2011

G-325A, Biographic Information

(Family Name)	(First Name)	(Middle Name)	☒ Male ☐ Female	Date of Birth (mm/dd/yyyy)	Citizenship/Nationality	File Number
SMITH	JOHN	M		10/20/1970	FRANCE	**A** 000-000-000

All Other Names Used (include names by previous marriages)	City and Country of Birth	U.S. Social Security # *(if any)*
N/A	PARIS, FRANCE	

	Family Name	First Name	Date of Birth (mm/dd/yyyy)	City, and Country of Birth (if known)	City and Country of Residence
Father	SMITH	GABRIEL	05/05/1945	PARIS, FRANCE	PARIS, FRANCE
Mother (Maiden Name)	JOHNSON	SARAH	10/03/1950	PARIS, FRANCE	PARIS, FRANCE

Current Husband or Wife (If none, so state) Family Name (For wife, give maiden name)	First Name	Date of Birth (mm/dd/yyyy)	City and Country of Birth	Date of Marriage	Place of Marriage
SMITH	JANE	10/10/1973	SHANGHAI, CHINA	04/15/1992	PARIS FRANCE

Former Husbands or Wives (If none, so state) Family Name (For wife, give maiden name)	First Name	Date of Birth (mm/dd/yyyy)	Date and Place of Marriage	Date and Place of Termination of Marriage
N/A				

Applicant's residence last five years. List present address first.

Street and Number	City	Province or State	Country	From Month	From Year	To Month	To Year
123 FIRST STREET	WASHINGTON	DC	UNITED STATES	JAN	2010	Present Time	
2, AVENUE GABRIEL	PARIS	PARIS	FRANCE	SEP	2000	DEC	2009

Applicant's last address outside the United States of more than 1 year.

Street and Number	City	Province or State	Country	From Month	From Year	To Month	To Year
2, AVENUE GABRIEL	PARIS	PARIS	FRANCE	SEP	2000	DEC	2009

Applicant's employment last five years. (If none, so state.) List present employment first.

Full Name and Address of Employer	Occupation (Specify)	From Month	From Year	To Month	To Year
ABC CORPORATION	COMPUTER ENGINEER	JAN	2010	Present Time	
IBM CORPORATION (PARIS, FRANCE)	COMPUTER SPECIALIST	FEB	2005	DEC	2009

Last occupation abroad if not shown above. (Include all information requested above.)

SAME AS ABOVE				

This form is submitted in connection with an application for:	Signature of Applicant	Date
☐ Naturalization ☐ Other (Specify): ☒ Status as Permanent Resident	/JOHN M. SMITH/	08/09/2⊞

If your native alphabet is in other than Roman letters, write your name in your native alphabet below:

Penalties: Severe penalties are provided by law for knowingly and willfully falsifying or concealing a material fact.

Applicant: Print your name and Alien Registration Number in the box outlined by heavy border below.

Complete This Box (Family Name)	(Given Name)	(Middle Name)	(Alien Registration Number)
SMITH	JOHN	M	**A** 000-000-000

Form G-325A (Rev. 06/12/09)Y

Copyright © 2011 - GreenCard123.Com by UNorth® - All Rights Reserved

---

Instructions

What Is the Purpose of This Form?

Complete this biographical information form and include it with the application or petition you are submitting to U.S. Citizenship and Immigration Services (USCIS).

USCIS will use the information you provide on this form to process your application or petition.

If you have any questions on how to complete the form, call our National Customer Service Center at **1-800-375-5283**.

Privacy Act Notice

We ask for the information on this form, and associated evidence, to determine if you have established eligibility for the immigration benefit for which you are filing. Our legal right to ask for this information can be found in the Immigration and Nationality Act, as amended. We may provide this information to other government agencies. Failure to provide this information, and any requested evidence, may delay a final decision or result in denial of your immigration benefit.

Paperwork Reduction Act

An agency may not conduct or sponsor an information collection and a person is not required to respond to a collection of information unless it displays a currently valid OMB control number. The public reporting burden for this collection of information is estimated at 15 minutes per response, including the time for reviewing instructions and completing and submitting the form. Send comments regarding this burden estimate or any other aspect of this collection of information, including suggestions for reducing this burden, to: U.S. Citizenship and Immigration Services, Regulatory Products Division, 111 Massachusetts Avenue, N.W., 3rd Floor, Suite 3008, Washington, DC 20529-2210. OMB No. 1615-0008. **Do not mail your application to this address.**

Form G-325A (Rev. 06/12/09)Y Page 2

Copyright © 2011 – GreenCard123.Com by UNorth® – All Rights Reserved

Department of Homeland Security
U.S. Citizenship and Immigration Services

OMB No. 1615-0014; Exp. 05/31/2011

Form I-134, Affidavit of Support

(Answer all items. Type or print in black ink.)

I, GEORGE WILSON residing at 234 FIRST ST

    (Name)   (Street Number and Name)

WASHINGTON   DC   10001 . 1111   UNITED STATES

   (City)   (State)   (Zip Code if in U.S.)   (Country)

certify under penalty of perjury under U.S. law, that:

1. I was born on 02/05/1965 in LOS ANGELES   CALIFORNIA   UNITED STATES

    (Date-*mm/dd/yyyy*)   (City)   (State)   (Country)

If you are not a U.S. citizen based on your birth in the United States, or a non-citizen U.S. national based on your birth in American Samoa (including Swains Island), answer the following as appropriate:

    a. If a U.S. citizen through naturalization, give Certificate of Naturalization number   INS02938308

    b. If a U.S. citizen through parent(s) or marriage, give Certificate of Citizenship number

    c. If U.S. citizenship was derived by some other method, attach a statement of explanation.

    d. If a Lawful Permanent Resident of the United States, give A-Number

    e. If a lawfully admitted nonimmigrant, give Form I-94, Arrival-Departure Record, number

2. I am 45 years of age and have resided in the United States since 02/05/1965

                                                              (Date-*mm/dd/yyyy*)

3. This affidavit is executed on behalf of the following person:

Name (Family Name)	(First Name)	(Middle Name)		Gender	Age
SMITH	JOHN	M		MALE	40

Citizen of (Country)		Marital Status	Relationship to Sponsor	
FRANCE		MARRIED	FRIEND	

Presently resides at (Street Number and Name)	(City)	(State)	(Country)
2, AVENUE GABRIEL	PARIS		UNITED STATES

Name of spouse and children accompanying or following to join person:

Spouse	Gender	Age	Child	Gender	Age
SMITH, JANE	FEMALE	37	SMITH, ROBERT JR	MALE	16
Child	Gender	Age	Child	Gender	Age
SMITH, SARAH	FEMALE	14	N/A		
Child	Gender	Age	Child	Gender	Age

4. This affidavit is made by me for the purpose of assuring the U.S. Government that the person(s) named in **item (3)** will not become a public charge in the United States.

5. I am willing and able to receive, maintain, and support the person(s) named in **item 3**. I am ready and willing to deposit a bond, if necessary, to guarantee that such person(s) will not become a public charge during his or her stay in the United States, or to guarantee that the above named person(s) will maintain his or her nonimmigrant status, if admitted temporarily, and will depart prior to the expiration of his or her authorized stay in the United States.

6. I understand that:

    a. Form I-134 is an "undertaking" under section 213 of the Immigration and Nationality Act, and I may be sued if the person(s) named in **item 3** becomes a public charge after admission to the United States;

    b. Form I-134 may be made available to any Federal, State, or local agency that may receive an application from the person(s) named in **item 3** for Food Stamps, Supplemental Security Income, or Temporary Assistance to Needy Families; and

    c. If the person(s) named in **item 3** does apply for Food Stamps, Supplemental Security Income, or Temporary Assistance for Needy Families, my own income and assets may be considered in deciding the person's application. How long my income and assets may be attributed to the person(s) named in **item 3** is determined under the statutes and rules governing each specific program.

Form I-134 (Rev. 05/21/10) Y

Copyright © 2011 – GreenCard123.Com by UNorth® – All Rights Reserved

7. I am employed as or engaged in the business of SOFTWARE DEVELOPMENT with INTERNATIONAL CORPORAT
(Type of Business)   (Name of Concern)

at 111 MAIN ST   LOS ANGELES   CA   10000 . 1000
(Street Number and Name)   (City)   (State)   (Zip Code)

I derive an annual income of: *(If self-employed, I have attached a copy of my last income tax return or report of commercial rating concern which I certify to be true and correct to the best of my knowledge and belief. See instructions for nature of evidence of net worth to be submitted.)* $ 130,000

I have on deposit in savings banks in the United States: $ 35,000

I have other personal property, the reasonable value of which is: $ 5,000

I have stocks and bonds with the following market value, as indicated on the attached list, which I certify to be true and correct to the best of my knowledge and belief: $ 25,000

I have life insurance in the sum of: $ 300,000

With a cash surrender value of: $ 300,000

I own real estate valued at: $

   With mortgage(s) or other encumbrance(s) thereon amounting to: $

   Which is located at: _____
     (Street Number and Name)   (City)   (State)   (Zip Code)

8. The following persons are dependent upon me for support: *(Check the box in the appropriate column to indicate whether the person named is **wholly** or **partially** dependent upon you for support.)*

Name of Person	Wholly Dependent	Partially Dependent	Age	Relationship to Me
N/A	☐	☐		
	☐	☐		
	☐	☐		

9. I have previously submitted affidavit(s) of support for the following person(s). If none, state "None".

Name of Person	Date submitted
N/A	

10. I have submitted a visa petition(s) to U.S. Citizenship and Immigration Services on behalf of the following person(s). If none, state "None".

Name of Person	Relationship	Date submitted
N/A		

11. I ☒ intend ☐ do not intend to make specific contributions to the support of the person(s) named in **item 3**.

(If you check "intend," indicate the exact nature and duration of the contributions. For example, if you intend to furnish room and board, state for how long and, if money, state the amount in U.S. dollars and whether it is to be given in a lump sum, weekly or monthly, and for how long.)

PROVIDE TEMPORARY RESIDENCE UNTIL A PLACE IS FOUND.

Oath or Affirmation of Sponsor

I acknowledge that I have read "Sponsor and Alien Liability" on Page 2 of the instructions for this form, and am aware of my responsibilities as a sponsor under the Social Security Act, as amended, and the Food Stamp Act, as amended.
I certify under penalty of perjury under United States law that I know the contents of this affidavit signed by me and that the statements are true and correct.

Signature of Sponsor _____ **Date** 08/09/2011

Form I-134 (Rev. 05/21/10) Y Page 2

Copyright © 2011 - GreenCard123.Com by UNorth® - All Rights Reserved

Department of Homeland Security
U.S. Citizenship and Immigration Services

OMB No. 1615-0007; Expires 09/30/11

AR-11, Alien's Change of Address Card

Name (Last in CAPS)	(First Name)	(Middle Name)	I am in the United States as a:
SMITH	JOHN	M	☐ Visitor ☒ Permanent Resident ☐ Student ☐ Other ___ (Specify)

Country of Citizenship	Date of Birth (mm/dd/yyyy)	Copy Number From Alien Card
FRANCE	10/20/1970	A 00000000

Present Address (Street or Rural Route)	(City or Post Office)	(State)	(Zip Code)
123 FIRST ST	WASHINGTON	DC	10001

(If the above address is temporary) I expect to remain there 1 Years 0 Months

Last Address (Street or Rural Route)	(City or Post Office)	(State)	(Zip Code)
111 MAIN ST	LOS ANGELES	CA	10001

I work for or attend school at: (Employer's Name or Name of School)

ABC CORPORATION

(Street Address or Rural Route)	(City or Post Office)	(State)	(Zip Code)
555 SECOND ST	WASHINGTON	DC	10001

Port of Entry Into U.S.	Date of Entry Into U.S. (mm/dd/yyyy)	If not a Permanent Resident, my stay in the U.S. expires on: (Date - mm/dd/yyyy)
WASHINGTON	01/05/2010	

Signature	Date (mm/dd/yyyy)	
/JOHN M. SMITH/	08/09/2011	

Form AR-11 (Rev. 10/06/08) Y

AR-11, Alien's Change of Address Card

This card is to be used by all aliens to report a change of address within ten days of such change.

The collection of this information is required by Section 265 of the Immigration and Nationality Act (8 U.S.C. 1305). The data is used by U.S. Citizenship and Immigration Services for statistical and record purposes and may be furnished to Federal, State, local and foreign law enforcement officials. Failure to report a change of address is punishable by fine or imprisonment and/or removal.

ADVISORY: This card is not evidence of identity, age, or status claimed.

Paperwork Reduction Act

An agency may not conduct or sponsor an information collection and a person is not required to respond to a collection of information unless it displays a currently valid OMB control number. The public reporting burden for this collection of information is estimated at five minutes per response, including the time for reviewing instructions and completing and submitting the form. Send comments regarding this burden estimate or any other aspect of this collection of information, including suggestions for reducing this burden, to: U.S. Citizenship and Immigration Services, Regulatory Management Division, 111 Massachusetts Avenue, N.W., 3rd Floor, Suite 3008, Washington, DC 20529. OMB No. 1615-0007. **Do not mail your application to this address.**

Mail Your Form to the Address Shown Below:

	For commercial overnight or fast freight
Department of Homeland Security U.S. Citizenship and Immigration Services Change of Address P.O. Box 7134 London, KY 40742-7134	**Department of Homeland Security** U.S. Citizenship and Immigration Services Change of Address 1084-I South Laurel Road London, KY 40742-7134

Copyright © 2011 - GreenCard123.Com by UNorth® - All Rights Reserved

USCIS Fee Schedule

Effective: July 30, 2007

USCIS fees change on July 30, 2007. This fee schedule applies if you file on or after that date. The fees listed below include both the filing fee and any required biometric fees.

Form #	Purpose	Fee
I 90	**Renew or replace your Permanent Resident Card (green card)**	
	If filing to renew your card within 30 days of turning 14	No fee
	All others where a fee is required: filing + biometric=	$ 370
I 102	**Replace or receive an I-94 Nonimmigrant Arrival-Departure Record**	$ 320
I 129	**Petition for Nonimmigrant Worker**	$ 320
	Note: Petitions for H-1B, H2B and L-1 workers must also include the supplemental fees and fraud prevention fees described on the form. Those fee amounts are unchanged.	
I 129F	**Fianceé Petition**	
	General fiancée petition:	$ 455
	For K-3 status based on an immigrant petition filed by the same U.S. citizen husband or wife:	No fee
I 130	**Relative Petition**	$ 355
I 131	**Reentry permit, refugee travel document or advance parole**	
	Reentry permit or refugee travel document	$ 305
	Advance Parole	$ 305
I 140	**Petition for an Immigrant Worker**	$ 475
I 191	**Permission to return to an unrelinquished domicile**	$ 545
I 192	**Advance permission to enter as a Nonimmigrant**	$ 545
I 193	**Waive passport and/or visa requirement to enter the U.S.**	$ 545
I 212	**Permission to reapply for Admission to the U.S. after deportation or removal**	$ 545
I 290B	**Appeal; Motion to Reopen or Reconsider**	$ 585
I 360	**Petition for AmerAsian, Widow(er) of U.S.C. or Special Immigrant**	
	For AmerAsian	No fee
	Self-petitioning battered or abused spouse, parent or child of a U.S. citizen or Permanent Resident	No fee
	Special Immigrant Juvenile	No fee
	All others	$ 375
I 485	**Adjust status and become a permanent resident while in the U.S.**	
	Applying based on your having been admitted to the U.S. as a refugee	No fee
	All other eligibility-	
	If under 14 and - filing with the I-485 application of at least one parent:	$ 600
	not filing with the I-485 application of at least one parent:	$ 930
	If 79 or older	$ 930
	All others: filing + biometric=	$ 1,010
	Note: The penalty fee, where it applies, is in addition to the above fees, and is unchanged.	
I 526	**Investor Petition**	$ 1,435
I 539	**Extend stay as Nonimmigrant or change Nonimmigrant status**	$ 300
I 589	**Asylum**	No fee
I 600A	**Advance processing for Orphan Petition -**	$750 (filing + biometric) for you + $ 80 biometric fee for each person 18 or older living with you
	Note: If you already have an approved I-600A that is about to expire, and have not yet filed your I-600 petition, you can receive one free extension of your I-600A by filing a new I-600A without fee before the first expires.	
I 600	**Orphan Petition** If based on an approved I-600A	No fee
	Otherwise	$750 (filing + biometric) for you + $ 80 biometric fee for each person 18 or older living with you
I 601	**Waive grounds of excludability**	$ 545
I 612	**Waive foreign residence requirement**	$ 545
I-730	**Refugee/Asylee Relative Petition**	No fee
I 751	**Remove conditions on your Permanent Resident status**	$ 545 (filing + biometric) for you + $80 biometric fee for each dependent you include in your application
I 765	**Employment Authorization /Employment Authorization Document (EAD)**	$ 340
I 821	**Temporary Protected Status (TPS) Program**	
	First time applicant If under 14 and not applying for an EAD	$ 50
	Otherwise: filing + biometric=	$ 130
	Renewal or re-registration: biometric=	$ 80
I 824	**Follow-up action on an approved application or petition**	$ 340

Continued on Back...

USCIS Fee Schedule

Effective: July 30, 2007

Form #	Purpose		Fee
I 829	**Remove conditions on Permanent Resident status (investor)**		$ 2,930 (filing + biometric) for you + $80 biometric fee for each dependent you include in your application
I 881	**NACARA — suspension of deportation or special rule**		
	Filed with USCIS - A base filing fee of $ 285 per person, with a base fee family cap of $ 570 for applications filed together by a husband, wife and unmarried children. Each applicant must also pay an $ 80 biometric fee.		
	Filed with the Immigration Court		$ 165
I 905	**Authorization for organization to issue certification to health care workers**		$ 230
I 907	**Premium processing fee**		$ 1,000
I 914	**For 'T ' nonimmigrant status**		No fee

U.S. Citizenship

Form #	Purpose		Fee
N 300	**To file Declaration of Intent to apply for U.S. Citizenship**		$ 235
N 336	**Request hearing on decision on naturalization application**		$ 605
N 400	**Naturalization (to become a U.S. citizen)**	Through service in the U.S. armed forces	No fee
		All others: filing + biometric=	$ 675
N 470	**Preserve residence for naturalization purposes**		$ 305
N 565	**Replace Naturalization/Citizenship Certificate**		$ 380
N 600 N 600K	**Recognition of U.S. citizenship**	for biological child	$ 460
		for adopted child	$ 420
N 644	**Posthumous citizenship**		No fee

Programs under the 1986 Legalization and Special Agricultural Worker (SAW) Programs

Form #	Purpose		Fee
I 687	**Become a Temporary Resident:** filing + biometric=		$ 790
I 690	**Waive grounds of Excludability**		$ 185
I 694	**Appeal**		$ 545
I 695	**Replace Temporary Resident Card or Employment Authorization Document:** filing + biometric=		$ 210
I 698	**Temporary Resident's application for permanent resident status**		
	Filed within 31 months after granted temporary residence: filing + biometric=		$ 1,450
	Filed later: filing + biometric=		$ 1,490
I 817	**Status under Family Unity Program**	If under 14	$ 440
		All others: filing + biometric=	$ 520

Please be sure you include the correct fee. Cases with the wrong fee will be rejected. Your payment must be in U.S. dollars. Checks and money orders must be from U.S. institutions. Do not mail cash. Checks are accepted subject to collection. Make your check out to "Department of Homeland Security" except that:

- If you are filing an I-881 with the Immigration Court make your payment out to "Department of Justice".
- If you live in Guam, make your payment out to "Treasurer, Guam".
- If you live in the U.S. Virgin Islands, make your payment out to "Commissioner of Finance of the Virgin Islands".

Please spell the name out completely. Do not use initials, such as DHS. Filing and biometric fees cannot be refunded. We may use electronic check conversion for the payment process. Our returned check fee is $30.

Fee waivers – USCIS has already waived fees for certain kinds of cases and circumstances. In certain other instances an applicant or petitioner who believes that they are financially unable to pay that fee even though others must pay that fee can apply for a fee waiver. Waiver requests can only be considered for the following forms – I-90; I-751; I-765; I-817; N-300; N-400; N-470; N-565; N-600; N-600k; the I-485 if adjustment of status if based on asylum status, on 'T' or 'U' nonimmigrant status, on an approved self-petitioning battered or abused spouse, parent or child of a U.S. citizen or Permanent Resident, or to whom the public charge provisions do not apply; and the I-290B and N-336 appeals and motions for the above forms. For more information about how to apply, and how to prove eligibility for a waiver, see our website or call us at 1-800-375-5283.

Copies of documents – If you are applying to renew or replace a card or USCIS document, and the instructions say to include your current one when you apply, then you must submit your actual card or document. For all other applications and petitions you can submit legible photocopies of documents such as a Naturalization Certificate, birth certificate, marriage certificate, divorce decree or Permanent Resident Card. Any copy must be a complete copy of the front and back. As we process your case we may ask you for the original for verification.

Adjustment applications and ancillary benefits – The new application fee for an I-485 is a package fee that includes associated EAD and advance parole applications. Thus, if you file an I-485 with the fee listed above, while you will still need to submit applications for an EAD and advance parole, you will not need to pay a separate fee so long as your adjustment application is pending. However, if you filed your I-485 before this fee change, to apply for or renew your EAD or advance parole, you must file a new application with the new fee for those applications.

Copyright © 2011 – GreenCard123.Com by UNorth® – All Rights Reserved

DEPARTMENT OF THE TREASURY
UNITED STATES CUSTOMS SERVICE

REPORT OF INTERNATIONAL TRANSPORTATION OF CURRENCY OR MONETARY INSTRUMENTS

OMB No. 1506-0014

▶ This form is to be filed with the United States Customs Service

▶ For Paperwork Reduction Act Notice and Privacy Act Notice, see back of form.

(U.S. Customs Use Only)

Control No.

31 U.S.C. 5316; 31 CFR 103.23 and 103.27
▶ **Please type or print.**

Part I FOR A PERSON DEPARTING FROM OR ENTERING THE UNITED STATES, OR A PERSON SHIPPING, MAILING, OR RECEIVING CURRENCY OR MONETARY INSTRUMENTS. (IF ACTING FOR ANYONE ELSE, ALSO COMPLETE PART II BELOW.)

| 1. NAME (Last or family, first, and middle) SMITH, JOHN | 2. IDENTIFICATION NO. (See instructions) PASSPORT 0000000000102 | 3. DATE OF BIRTH (Mo./Day/Yr.) 10 | 20 | 1970 |

4. PERMANENT ADDRESS IN UNITED STATES OR ABROAD
123 FIRST ST, WASHINGTON, DC 10001

5. YOUR COUNTRY OR COUNTRIES OF CITIZENSHIP
FRANCE

6. ADDRESS WHILE IN THE UNITED STATES
123 FIRST ST, WASHINGTON, DC 10001

7. PASSPORT NO. & COUNTRY
0000000000102 FRANCE

8. U.S. VISA DATE
01/01/2011

9. PLACE UNITED STATES VISA WAS ISSUED
PARIS, FRANCE

10. IMMIGRATION ALIEN NO. (If any)
N/A

11. IF CURRENCY OR MONETARY INSTRUMENT IS ACCOMPANIED BY A PERSON, COMPLETE 11a OR 11b

A. EXPORTED FROM THE UNITED STATES		B. IMPORTED INTO THE UNITED STATES	
Departed From: (U.S. Port /City in U.S.)	Arrived At: (Foreign City/Country)	Departed From: (Foreign City/Country)	Arrived At: (City in U.S.)
N/A	N/A	PARIS, FRANCE	WASHINGTON, DC

12. IF CURRENCY OR MONETARY INSTRUMENT WAS MAILED OR OTHERWISE SHIPPED, COMPLETE 12a THROUGH 12f

| 12a. DATE SHIPPED (Mo./Day/Yr.) | 12b. DATE RECEIVED (Mo./Day/Yr.) | 12c. METHOD OF SHIPMENT (e.g., U.S. Mail, Public Carrier, etc.) N/A | 12d. NAME OF CARRIER |

12e. SHIPPED TO (Name and Address)
N/A

12f. RECEIVED FROM (Name and Address)
N/A

Part II INFORMATION ABOUT PERSON(S) OR BUSINESS ON WHOSE BEHALF IMPORTATION OR EXPORTATION WAS CONDUCTED

13. NAME (Last or family, first, and middle or Business Name)
SMITH, JOHN

14. PERMANENT ADDRESS IN THE UNITED STATES OR ABROAD
123 FIRST ST, WASHINGTON, DC 10001

15. TYPE OF BUSINESS ACTIVITY, OCCUPATION, OR PROFESSION
COMPUTER ENGINEER

15a. IS THE BUSINESS A BANK?
☐ YES   ☑ NO

Part III CURRENCY AND MONETARY INSTRUMENT INFORMATION (SEE INSTRUCTIONS ON REVERSE) (To be completed by everyone)

16. TYPE AND AMOUNT OF CURRENCY/MONETARY INSTRUMENTS

			17. IF OTHER THAN U.S. CURRENCY IS INVOLVED, PLEASE COMPLETE BLOCKS A AND B.
Currency and Coins	☑	▶ $ 15,000	A. Currency Name
Other Monetary Instruments (Specify type, issuing entity and date, and serial or other identifying number.)	☐	▶ $	EURO
(TOTAL)	☐	▶ $ 15,000	B. Country FRANCE

Part IV SIGNATURE OF PERSON COMPLETING THIS REPORT

Under penalties of perjury, I declare that I have examined this report, and to the best of my knowledge and belief it is true, correct and complete.

| 18. NAME AND TITLE (Print) JOHN SMITH | 19. SIGNATURE | 20. DATE OF REPORT 01/01/2011 |

U.S. CUSTOMS USE ONLY		COUNT VERIFIED Yes No	VOLUNTARY REPORT Yes No
DATE	AIRLINE/FLIGHT/VESSEL	LICENSE PLATE	INSPECTOR (Name and Badge Number)
		STATE/COUNTRY NUMBER	

Cat. No. 42005H

Customs Form 4790 (04/00)

Copyright © 2011 - GreenCard123.Com by UNorth® - All Rights Reserved

GENERAL INSTRUCTIONS

This report is required by 31 U.S.C. 5316 and Treasury Department regulations (31 CFR 103).

Who Must File.-- **(1)** Each person who physically transports, mails, or ships, or causes to be physically transported, mailed, or shipped currency or other monetary instruments in an aggregate amount exceeding $10,000 at one time from the United States to any place outside the United States or into the United States from any place outside the United States, and **(2)** Each person who receives in the United States currency or other monetary instruments in an aggregate amount exceeding $10,000 at one time which have been transported, mailed, or shipped to the person from any place outside the United States.

A TRANSFER OF FUNDS THROUGH NORMAL BANKING PROCEDURES WHICH DOES NOT INVOLVE THE PHYSICAL TRANSPORTATION OF CURRENCY OR MONETARY INSTRUMENTS IS NOT REQUIRED TO BE REPORTED.

Exceptions.--In addition, reports are not required to be filed by: (1) a Federal Reserve bank, (2) a bank, a foreign bank, or a broker or dealer in securities in respect to currency or other monetary instruments mailed or shipped through the postal service or by common carrier, (3) a commercial bank or trust company organized under the laws of any State or of the United States with respect to overland shipments of currency or monetary instruments shipped to or received from an established customer maintaining a deposit relationship with the bank, in amounts which the bank may reasonably conclude do not exceed amounts commensurate with the customary conduct of the business, industry, or profession of the customer concerned, (4) a person who is not a citizen or resident of the United States in respect to currency or other monetary instruments mailed or shipped from abroad to a bank or broker or dealer in securities through the postal service or by common carrier, (5) a common carrier of passengers in respect to currency or other monetary instruments in the possession of its passengers, (6) a common carrier of goods in respect to shipments of currency or monetary instruments not declared to be such by the shipper, (7) a travelers' check issuer or its agent in respect to the transportation of travelers' checks prior to their delivery to selling agents for eventual sale to the public, (8) a person with a restrictively endorsed traveler's check that is in the collection and reconciliation process after the traveler's check has been negotiated, nor by (9) a person engaged as a business in the transportation of currency, monetary instruments and other commercial papers with respect to the transportation of currency or other monetary instruments overland between established offices of banks or brokers or dealers in securities and foreign persons.

WHEN AND WHERE TO FILE:

A. Recipients--Each person who receives currency or other monetary instruments in the United States shall file Form 4790, within 15 days after receipt of the currency or monetary instruments, with the Customs officer in charge at any port of entry or departure or by mail with the Commissioner of Customs, Attention: Currency Transportation Reports, Washington DC 20229.

B. Shippers or Mailers--If the currency or other monetary instrument does not accompany the person entering or departing the United States, Form 4790 may be filed by mail on or before the date of entry, departure, mailing, or shipping with the Commissioner of Customs, Attention: Currency Transportation Reports, Washington DC 20229.

C. Travelers--Travelers carrying currency or other monetary instruments with them shall file Form 4790 at the time of entry into the United States or at the time of departure from the United States with the Customs officer in charge at any Customs port of entry or departure.

An additional report of a particular transportation, mailing, or shipping of currency or the monetary instruments, is not required if a complete and truthful report has already been filed. However, no person otherwise required to file a report shall be excused from liability for failure to do so if, in fact, a complete and truthful report has not been filed. Forms may be obtained from any United States Customs Service office.

PENALTIES.-- Civil and criminal penalties, including under certain circumstances a fine of not more than $500,000 and imprisonment of not more than ten years, are provided for failure to file a report, filing a report containing a material omission or misstatement, or filing a false or fraudulent report. In addition, the currency or monetary instrument may be subject to seizure and forfeiture. See 31 U.S.C. 5321 and 31 CFR 103.47; 31 U.S.C. 5322 and 31 CFR 103.49; 31 U.S.C. 5317 and 31 CFR 103.48.

DEFINITIONS:

Bank--Each agent, agency, branch or office within the United States of any person doing business in one or more of the capacities listed: (1) a commercial bank or trust company organized under the laws of any State or of the United States; (2) a private bank; (3) a savings association, savings and loan association, and building and loan association organized under the laws of any State or of the United States; (4) an insured institution as defined in section 401 of the National Housing Act; (5) a savings bank, industrial bank or other thrift institution; (6) a credit union organized under the laws of any State or of the United States; and (7) any other organization chartered under the banking laws of any State and subject to the supervision of the bank supervisory authorities of a State other than a money service business; (8) a bank organized under foreign law; and (9) any national banking association or corporation acting under the provisions of section 25A of the Federal Reserve Act (12 U.S.C. Sections 611-632).

Foreign Bank--A bank organized under foreign law, or an agency, branch or office located outside the United States of a bank. The term does not include an agent, agency, branch or office within the United States of a bank organized under foreign law.

Broker or Dealer in Securities--A broker or dealer in securities, registered or required to be registered with the Securities and Exchange Commission under the Securities Exchange Act of 1934.

Identification Number--Individuals must enter their social security number, if any. However, aliens who do not have a social security number should enter passport or alien registration number. All others should enter their employer identification number.

Monetary Instruments-- (1) Coin or currency of the United States or of any other country, (2) traveler's checks in any form, (3) negotiable instruments (including checks, promissory notes, and money orders) in bearer form, endorsed without restriction, made out to a fictitious payee, or otherwise in such form that title thereto passes upon delivery, (4) incomplete instruments (including checks, promissory notes, and money orders) that are signed but on which the name of the payee has been omitted, and (5) securities or stock in bearer form or otherwise in such form that title thereto passes upon delivery. Monetary instruments do not include (i) checks or money orders made payable to the order of a named person which have not been endorsed or which bear restrictive endorsements, (ii) warehouse receipts, or (iii) bills of lading.

Person--An individual, a corporation, a partnership, a trust or estate, a joint stock company, and association, a syndicate, joint venture or other unincorporated organization or group, an Indian Tribe (as that term is defined in the Indian Gaming Regulatory Act), and all entities cognizable as legal personalties.

SPECIAL INSTRUCTIONS:

You should complete each line which applies to you. **Part I.--**Blocks 12a and 12b, enter the exact date you shipped or received currency or monetary instrument(s). **Part II--Block 13, provide the complete name of the shipper or recipient on whose behalf the exportation or importation was conducted. Part III.--**Block 23, specify type of instrument, issuing entity, and date, serial or other identifying number, and payee (if any). Block 17, if currency or monetary instruments of more than one country is involved, attach a list showing each type, country of origin and amount.

PRIVACY ACT AND PAPERWORK REDUCTION ACT NOTICE

Pursuant to the requirements of Public Law 93-579 (Privacy Act of 1974), notice is hereby given that the authority to collect information on Form 4790 in accordance with 5 U.S.C. 552a(e)(3) is Public Law 91-508; 31 U.S.C. 5316; 5 U.S.C. 301; Reorganization Plan No. 1 of 1950; Treasury Department No.165, revised, as amended; 31 CFR 103; and 44 U.S.C. 3501.

The principal purpose for collecting the information is to assure maintenance of reports or records where such reports or records have a high degree of usefulness in criminal, tax, or regulatory investigations or proceedings. The information collected may be provided to those officers and employees of the Customs Service and any other constituent unit of the Department of the Treasury who have a need for the records in the performance of their duties. The records may be referred to any other department or agency of the Federal Government upon the request of the head of such department or agency. The information collected may also be provided to appropriate state, local, and foreign criminal law enforcement and regulatory personnel in the performance of their official duties.

Disclosure of this information is mandatory pursuant to 31 U.S.C. 5316 and 31 CFR Part 103. Failure to provide all or any part of the requested information may subject the currency or monetary instruments to seizure and forfeiture, as well as subject the individual to civil and criminal liabilities.

Disclosure of the social security number is mandatory. The authority to collect this number is 31 U.S.C. 5316(b) and 31 CFR 103.27(d). The social security number will be used as a means to identify the individual who files the record.

An agency may not conduct or sponsor, and a person is not required to respond to, a collection of information unless it displays a currently valid OMB control number.

The collection of this information is mandatory pursuant to 31 U.S.C. 5316, of Title II of the Bank Secrecy Act, which is administered by Treasury's Financial Crimes Enforcement Network (FINCEN).

Statement Required by 5 CFR 1320.8(b)(3)(iii) : The estimated average burden associated with this collection of information is 11 minutes per respondent or recordkeeper depending on individual circumstances. Comments concerning the accuracy of this burden estimate and suggestions for reducing this burden should be directed to Financial Crimes Enforcement Center, 2070 Chain Bridge Road, Suite 200, Vienna, Virginia 22182. **DO NOT** send completed form(s) to this office.

Customs Form 4790 (04/00) (Back)

Copyright © 2011 – GreenCard123.Com by UNorth® – All Rights Reserved

U.S. DEPARTMENT of STATE

TRAVEL.STATE.GOV Ⓒ BUREAU OF CONSULAR AFFAIRS

INSTRUCTIONS FOR THE 2012 DIVERSITY IMMIGRANT VISA PROGRAM (DV-2012)

The congressionally mandated Diversity Immigrant Visa Program is administered on an annual basis by the Department of State and conducted under the terms of Section 203(c) of the Immigration and Nationality Act (INA). Section 131 of the Immigration Act of 1990 (Pub. L. 101-649) amended INA 203 and provides for a class of immigrants known as "diversity immigrants." Section 203(c) of the INA provides a maximum of 55,000 Diversity Visas (DVs) each fiscal year to be made available to persons from countries with low rates of immigration to the United States. For fiscal year 2012, 50,000 DVs will be available.

The annual DV program makes visas available to persons meeting simple, but strict, eligibility requirements. A computer-generated, random lottery drawing chooses selectees for DVs. The visas are distributed among six geographic regions, with a greater number of visas going to regions with lower rates of immigration, and with no visas going to nationals of countries sending more than 50,000 immigrants to the United States over the period of the past five years. Within each region, no single country may receive more than seven percent of the available DVs in any one year.

For DV-2012, natives of the following countries[1] are **not** eligible to apply because the countries sent a total of more than 50,000 immigrants to the United States in the previous five years:

> **BRAZIL, CANADA, CHINA (mainland-born), COLOMBIA, DOMINICAN REPUBLIC, ECUADOR, EL SALVADOR, GUATEMALA, HAITI, INDIA, JAMAICA, MEXICO, PAKISTAN, PERU, PHILIPPINES, POLAND, SOUTH KOREA, UNITED KINGDOM (except Northern Ireland) and its dependent territories, and VIETNAM.**
>
> Persons born in Hong Kong SAR, Macau SAR, and Taiwan are eligible.

For DV-2012, no countries have been added or removed from the previous year's list of eligible countries.

The Department of State implemented the electronic registration system beginning with DV-2005 in order to make the DV process more efficient and secure. The Department utilizes special technology and other means to identify those who commit fraud for the purposes of illegal immigration or those who submit multiple entries.

DV REGISTRATION PERIOD

Entries for the DV-2012 DV lottery must be submitted electronically between noon, Eastern Daylight Time (EDT) (GMT-4), Tuesday, October 5, 2010, and noon, Eastern Standard Time (EST) (GMT-5), Wednesday, November 3, 2010. Applicants may access the electronic DV Entry Form (E-DV) at www.dvlottery.state.gov during the registration period. Paper entries will not be accepted. Applicants are strongly encouraged not to wait until the last week of the registration period to enter. Heavy demand may result in website delays. No entries will be accepted after noon, EST, on November 3, 2010.

---

[1] The term "country" in this notice includes countries, economies, and other jurisdictions explicitly listed at the end of these instructions.

1

Copyright © 2011 – GreenCard123.Com by UNorth® – All Rights Reserved

REQUIREMENTS FOR ENTRY

- **To enter the DV lottery, you must be a native of one of the listed countries.** See List Of Countries By Region Whose Natives Qualify.

  Native of a country whose natives qualify: In most cases, this means the country in which you were born. However, there are two other ways you may be able to qualify. First, if you were born in a country whose natives are ineligible but your spouse was born in a country whose natives are eligible, you can claim your spouse's country of birth—provided that both you and your spouse are on the selected entry, are issued visas, and enter the United States simultaneously. Second, if you were born in a country whose natives are ineligible, but neither of your parents was born there or resided there at the time of your birth, you may claim nativity in one of your parents' countries of birth if it is a country whose natives qualify for the DV-2012 program.

- **To enter the lottery, you must meet either the education *or* work experience requirement of the DV program:** You must have either a high school education or its equivalent, defined as successful completion of a 12-year course of elementary and secondary education; OR two years of work experience within the past five years in an occupation requiring at least two years of training or experience to perform. The U.S. Department of Labor's O*Net OnLine database will be used to determine qualifying work experience. For more information about qualifying work experience, see Frequently Asked Question #13.

  If you cannot meet either of these requirements, you should NOT submit an entry to the DV program.

PROCEDURES FOR SUBMITTING AN ENTRY TO DV-2012

- **The Department of State will only accept completed E-DV entry forms submitted electronically at** www.dvlottery.state.gov **during** the registration period between noon, EDT (GMT-4), Tuesday, October 5, 2010 and noon, EST (GMT-5), Wednesday, November 3, 2010.
  - All entries by an individual will be disqualified if more than ONE entry for that individual is received, regardless of who submitted the entry. You may prepare and submit your own entry or have someone submit the entry for you.
  - A successfully registered entry will result in a confirmation screen containing your name and a unique confirmation number. You should print this confirmation screen for your records using the print function of your web browser and ensure that you retain your confirmation number. Starting May 1, 2011, you will be able to check the status of your DV-2012 entry by returning to www.dvlottery.state.gov Entry Status Check and entering your unique confirmation number and personal information. **Entry Status Check will be the sole means of informing you of your selection for DV-2012, providing instructions to you on how to proceed with your application, and notifying you of your appointment for your immigrant visa interview, so it is essential you retain your confirmation number.**
  - Paper entries will not be accepted.

- **It is very important that all required photographs be submitted.** Your entry will be disqualified if all required photographs are not submitted. Recent photographs of the following people must be submitted electronically with the E-DV entry form:
  - You
  - Your spouse
  - Each unmarried child under 21 years of age at the time of your electronic entry, including all natural children as well as all legally adopted children and stepchildren, even if a child no longer resides with you or you do not intend for a child to immigrate under the DV program.

  Failure to submit the required photographs for your spouse and each child listed will result in an incomplete entry to the E-DV system. The entry will not be accepted and must be resubmitted.

- A spouse or child who is already a U.S. citizen or a Lawful Permanent Resident will not require or be issued a DV visa. However, you should include all family members in your registration and photos of each person

2

Copyright © 2011 - GreenCard123.Com by UNorth® - All Rights Reserved

who will receive a DV visa. Group or family photographs will not be accepted; there must be a separate photograph for each family member.

Failure to enter the correct photograph of each individual into the E-DV system may result in disqualification of the principal applicant and refusal of all visas associated with the case at the time of the visa interview.

- Entries are subject to disqualification and visa refusal for cases in which the photographs are not recent or have been manipulated or fail to meet the specifications explained below.

Instructions for Submitting a Digital Photograph (Image)

A digital photograph (image) of you, your spouse, and each child must be submitted online with the E-DV entry form. The image file can be produced either by taking a new digital photograph or by scanning a photographic print with a digital scanner. The image file must adhere to the following compositional and technical specifications and can be produced in one of the following ways: taking a new digital image or using a digital scanner to scan a photograph. Entrants may test their photos for suitability through the photo validator link on the e-DV website before submitting their entries. The photo validator provides additional technical advice on photo composition, along with examples of acceptable and unacceptable photos.

Compositional Specifications: The submitted digital image must conform to the following compositional specifications or the entry will be disqualified.

- **Head Position**
  - The person being photographed must directly face the camera.
  - The head of the person should not be tilted up, down, or to the side.
  - The head height or facial region size (measured from the top of the head, including the hair, to the bottom of the chin) must be between 50 percent and 69 percent of the image's total height. The eye height (measured from the bottom of the image to the level of the eyes) should be between 56 percent and 69 percent of the image's height.

- **Background**
  - The person being photographed should be taken with the person in front of a neutral, light-colored background.
  - Dark or patterned backgrounds are not acceptable.

- **Focus**
  - The photograph must be in focus.

- **Decorative Items**
  - Photographs in which the person being photographed is wearing sunglasses or other items that detract from the face will not be accepted.

- **Head Coverings and Hats**
  - Photos of applicants wearing head coverings or hats are only acceptable if the head covering is worn for religious beliefs; even then, the head covering may not obscure any portion of the face of the applicant. Photographs of applicants with tribal or other headgear not specifically religious in nature will not be accepted; photographs of military, airline, or other personnel wearing hats will not be accepted.

Color photographs in 24-bit color depth are required. Color photographs may be downloaded from a camera to a file in the computer or they may be scanned onto a computer. If you are using a scanner, the settings must be for True Color or 24-bit color mode. See the additional scanning requirements below.

Technical Specifications
The submitted digital photograph must conform to the following specifications or the system will automatically reject the E-DV entry form and notify the sender.

- **Taking a New Digital Image.** If a new digital image is taken, it must meet the following specifications:

3

Copyright © 2011 - GreenCard123.Com by UNorth® - All Rights Reserved

Image File Format:	The image must be in the Joint Photographic Experts Group (JPEG) format.
Image File Size:	The maximum image file size is 240 kilobytes (240 KB).
Image Resolution and Dimensions:	Minimum acceptable dimensions are 600 pixels (width) x 600 pixels (height). Image pixel dimensions must be in a square aspect ratio (meaning the height must be equal to the width).
Image Color Depth:	image must be in color (24 bits per pixel). 24-bit black and white or 8-bit images will not be accepted.

- **Scanning a Submitted Photograph.** Before a photographic print is scanned, it must meet the compositional specifications listed above. If the photographic print meets the print color and compositional specifications, scan the print using the following scanner specifications:

Scanner Resolution:	Scanned at a resolution of at least 300 dots per inch (dpi).
Image File Format:	The image must be in the Joint Photographic Experts Group (JPEG) format.
Image File Size:	The maximum image file size is 240 kilobytes (240 KB).
Image Resolution:	600 by 600 pixels.
Image Color Depth:	24-bit color. [Note that black and white, monochrome, or grayscale images will not be accepted.]

INFORMATION REQUIRED FOR THE ELECTRONIC ENTRY

There is only one way to enter the DV-2012 lottery. You must submit the DS 5501, the Electronic Diversity Visa Entry Form (E-DV Entry Form), which is accessible only online at the EDV website www.dvlottery.state.gov. **Failure to complete the form in its entirety will disqualify the entry. Those who submit the E-DV entry will be asked to include the following information on the E-DV Entry Form.**

NOTE: The Department of State strongly encourages applicants to complete the entry form without the assistance of "Visa Consultants," "Visa Agents," or other individuals who offer to submit an entry on behalf of applicants. If you use the services of somebody else to complete your entry form, you should be present when the entry is prepared, and you should retain the confirmation page and your unique confirmation number. Facilitators may try to withhold confirmation numbers in order to make an unlawful demand for money in exchange for notification information that should have been directly available to you. Your confirmation number ensures that you can go to the E-DV website and receive notification of whether your entry has been selected through the Entry Status Check available from May 1, 2011 on the E-DV website www.dvlottery.state.gov. Entry Status Check will be the sole means of informing you of your selection for DV-2012, providing instructions to you on how to proceed with your application, and notifying you of the date and time of your appointment for your immigrant visa interview.

1. **FULL NAME** – Last/Family Name, First Name, Middle name
2. **DATE OF BIRTH** – Day, Month, Year
3. **GENDER** – Male or Female
4. **CITY WHERE YOU WERE BORN**
5. **COUNTRY WHERE YOU WERE BORN** – The name of the country should be that which is currently in use for the place where you were born.
6. **COUNTRY OF ELIGIBILITY OR CHARGEABILITY FOR THE DV PROGRAM** – Your country of eligibility will normally be the same as your country of birth. Your country of eligibility is **not** related to where you live. If you were born in a country that is not eligible for the DV program, please review the instructions to see if there is another option for country chargeability available for you. For additional information on chargeability, please review "Frequently Asked Question #1" of these instructions.

4

Copyright © 2011 - GreenCard123.Com by UNorth® - All Rights Reserved

7. **ENTRY PHOTOGRAPH(S)** – See the <u>technical information on photograph specifications</u>. Make sure you include photographs of your spouse and all your children, if applicable. See Frequently Asked Question #3.

8. **MAILING ADDRESS** – In Care Of, Address Line 1, Address Line 2, City/Town, District/Country/Province/State, Postal Code/Zip Code, and Country

9. **COUNTRY WHERE YOU LIVE TODAY**

10. **PHONE NUMBER (optional)**

11. **E-MAIL ADDRESS** – **provide an e-mail address to which you have direct access. You will NOT receive an official selection letter at this address. However, if your entry is selected and you respond to the notification of your selection through the Entry Status Check, you will receive follow-up communication from the Kentucky Consular Center (KCC) by e-mail notifying you that details of your immigrant visa interview are available on Entry Status Check.**

12. **WHAT IS THE HIGHEST LEVEL OF EDUCATION YOU HAVE ACHIEVED, AS OF TODAY?** You must indicate which **one** of the following represents your own highest level of educational achievement: (1) Primary school only, (2) High school, no degree, (3) High school degree, (4) Vocational school, (5) Some university courses, (6) University degree, (7) Some graduate level courses, (8) Master degree, (9) Some doctorate level courses, and (10) Doctorate degree

13. **MARITAL STATUS** – Unmarried, Married, Divorced, Widowed, or Legally Separated

14. **NUMBER OF CHILDREN** – Entries **MUST** include the name, date, and place of birth of your spouse and all natural children. Entries must also include all children legally adopted by you, and stepchildren who are unmarried and under the age of 21 on the date of your electronic entry , even if you are no longer legally married to the child's parent, and even if the spouse or child does not currently reside with you and/or will not immigrate with you. Note that married children and children 21 years or older are not eligible for the DV; however, U.S. law protects children from "aging out" in certain circumstances. If your electronic DV entry is made before your unmarried child turns 21, and the child turns 21 before visa issuance, he/she may be protected from aging out by the Child Status Protection Act and be treated as though he/she were under 21 for visa-processing purposes. **Failure to list all children who are eligible will result in disqualification of the principal applicant and refusal of all visas in the case at the time of the visa interview.** See <u>Frequently Asked Question #11</u>.

15. **SPOUSE INFORMATION** – Name, Date of Birth, Gender, City/Town of Birth, Country of Birth, and Photograph. **Failure to list your eligible spouse will result in disqualification of the principal applicant and refusal of all visas in the case at the time of the visa interview.** You must list your spouse here even if you plan to be divorced before you apply for a visa.

16. **CHILDREN INFORMATION** – Name, Date of Birth, Gender, City/Town of Birth, Country of Birth, and Photograph: Include all children declared in question #14 above.

SELECTION OF APPLICANTS

The computer will randomly select individuals from among all qualified entries. All Diversity Visa (DV-2012) entrants will be required to go to the E-DV website Entry Status Check to find out whether their entry has been selected in the DV lottery or to find out they have not been selected. Selectees will be notified of their selection through the Entry Status Check available starting May 1, 2011 at the E-DV website www.dvlottery.state.gov. Selectees will be directed to a confirmation page that will provide further instructions, including information on fees connected with immigration to the United States. **Entry Status Check will be the ONLY means by which selectees will be notified of their selection for DV-2012. The Kentucky Consular Center will not be mailing out notification letters. Those selected in the random drawing are NOT notified of their selection by e-mail. Those individuals NOT selected will be notified of their non-selection through the web-based Entry Status Check.** U.S. embassies and consulates will not provide a list of selectees. Selectees' spouses and unmarried children under age 21 may also apply for visas to accompany or follow-to-join the principal applicant. DV-2012 visas will be issued between October 1, 2011, and September 30, 2012.

Copyright © 2011 - GreenCard123.Com by UNorth® - All Rights Reserved

Processing of entries and issuance of DVs to selectees meeting eligibility requirements and their eligible family members MUST occur by midnight on September 30, 2012. Under no circumstances can DVs be issued or adjustments approved after this date, nor can family members obtain DVs to follow-to-join the principal applicant in the United States after this date.

In order to receive a DV to immigrate to the United States, those chosen in the random drawing must meet ALL eligibility requirements under U.S. law. These requirements may significantly increase the level of scrutiny required and time necessary for processing for natives of some countries listed in this notice including, but not limited to, countries identified as state sponsors of terrorism.

Important Notice

Electronic lottery entry in the annual DV program is free (there is no fee). The U.S. Government employs no outside consultants or private services to operate the DV program. Any intermediaries or others who offer assistance to prepare DV entries do so without the authority or consent of the U.S. Government. Use of any outside intermediary or assistance to prepare a DV entry is entirely at the entrant's discretion.

A qualified electronic entry submitted directly by an applicant has an equal chance of being randomly selected by the computer at the KCC, as does a qualified electronic entry received from an outside intermediary on behalf of the applicant. However, receipt of more than one entry per person will disqualify the person from registration, regardless of the source of the entry.

FREQUENTLY ASKED QUESTIONS

1. **WHAT DO THE TERMS "ELIGIBILITY", "NATIVE" AND "CHARGEABILITY" MEAN? ARE THERE ANY SITUATIONS IN WHICH PERSONS WHO WERE NOT BORN IN A QUALIFYING COUNTRY MAY APPLY?**

Your country of eligibility will normally be the same as your country of birth. Your country of eligibility is not related to where you live. "Native" ordinarily means someone born in a particular country, regardless of the individual's current country of residence or nationality. For immigration purposes, "native" can also mean someone who is entitled to be "charged" to a country other than the one in which he/she was born under the provisions of Section 202(b) of the Immigration and Nationality Act.

For example, if you were born in a country that is not eligible for this year's DV program, you may claim **chargeability** to the country where your derivative spouse was born, but you will not be issued a DV-1 unless your spouse is also eligible for and issued a DV-2, and both of you must enter the United States together with the DVs. In a similar manner, a minor dependent child can be "charged" to a parent's country of birth.

Finally, if you were born in a country not eligible to participate in this year's DV program, you can be "charged" to the country of birth of either of your parents as long as neither parent was a resident of the ineligible country at the time of the your birth. In general, people are not considered residents of a country in which they were not born or legally naturalized if they are only visiting the country, studying in the country temporarily, or stationed temporarily in the country for business or professional reasons on behalf of a company or government from a country other than the country in which the applicant was born. If you claim alternate chargeability, you must indicate such information on the E-DV electronic online Entry Form, in question #6. Please be aware that listing an incorrect country of **eligibility** or **chargeability** (i.e., one to which you cannot establish a valid claim) may disqualify your entry.

2. **ARE THERE ANY CHANGES OR NEW REQUIREMENTS IN THE APPLICATION PROCEDURES FOR THIS DV REGISTRATION?**

Yes. The registration period for DV-2012 will be 30 days in duration. Regarding scanning a photograph, the print must now be scanned at a resolution of at least 300 dots per inch (dpi), rather than the previous 150 dots per inch (dpi). All other requirements for scanning a submitted photograph are the same.

Additionally, the Entry Status Check available on the E-DV website www.dvlottery.state.gov will be the sole means by which DV-2012 entrants are notified of their selection, or that the entrant was not selected. The KCC will not mail selectees official notification letters, but will instead include on the selectee confirmation

6

Copyright © 2011 – GreenCard123.Com by UNorth® – All Rights Reserved

page, notification instructions on how to follow up on their selection and pursue a DV visa application. Entry Status Check will also be the means by which selectees are informed of their DV visa interview appointment date. The KCC will not sending selectees mailed letters informing them of their interview appointment.

Entry Status Check will be available for DV-2012 beginning May 1, 2011. If you applied for the DV-2011 program, you may check the status of your entry until the end of June 2011. All other requirements for DV-2012 remain the same.

3. **ARE SIGNATURES AND PHOTOGRAPHS REQUIRED FOR EACH FAMILY MEMBER, OR ONLY FOR THE PRINCIPAL ENTRANT?**

Signatures are not required on the E-DV Entry Form. Recent and individual photographs of you, your spouse, and all children under 21 years of age are required. Family or group photographs are not accepted. Refer to information on the photograph requirements located in this bulletin.

4. **WHY DO NATIVES OF CERTAIN COUNTRIES *NOT* QUALIFY FOR THE DV PROGRAM?**

DVs are intended to provide an immigration opportunity for persons from countries other than the countries that send large numbers of immigrants to the United States. The law states that no DVs shall be provided for natives of "high-admission" countries. The law defines this to mean countries from which a total of 50,000 persons in the Family-Sponsored and Employment-Based visa categories immigrated to the United States during the previous five years. Each year, U.S. Citizenship and Immigration Services (USCIS) adds the family and employment immigrant admission figures for the previous five years to identify the countries whose natives will be ineligible for the annual diversity lottery. Because there is a separate determination made before each annual E-DV entry period, the list of countries whose natives are not eligible may change from one year to the next.

5. **WHAT IS THE NUMERICAL LIMIT FOR DV-2012?**

By law, the U.S. DV program makes available a maximum of 55,000 permanent residence visas each year to eligible persons. However, the Nicaraguan Adjustment and Central American Relief Act (NACARA) passed by Congress in November 1997 stipulates that beginning as early as DV-1999, and for as long as necessary, up to 5,000 of the 55,000 annually-allocated DVs will be made available for use under the NACARA program. The actual reduction of the limit by up to 5,000 DVs began with DV-2000 and is likely to remain in effect through the DV-2012 program.

6. **WHAT ARE THE REGIONAL DV LIMITS FOR DV-2012?**

USCIS determines the regional DV limits for each year according to a formula specified in Section 203(c) of the INA. Once USCIS has completed these calculations, the regional visa limits will be announced.

7. **WHEN WILL ENTRIES FOR THE DV-2012 PROGRAM BE ACCEPTED?**

The DV-2012 entry period will run through the registration period listed above. Each year, millions of people apply for the program during the registration period. The massive volume of entries creates an enormous amount of work in selecting and processing successful individuals. Holding the entry period during October and November ensures that selectees are notified in a timely manner and gives both the visa applicants and our embassies and consulates time to prepare and complete cases for visa issuance. You are strongly encouraged to enter early in the registration period. Excessive demand at end of the registration period may slow the system down. No entries whatsoever will be accepted after noon EST Wednesday November 3, 2010.

8. **MAY PERSONS WHO ARE IN THE UNITED STATES APPLY FOR THE PROGRAM?**

Yes, an applicant may be in the United States or in another country, and the entry may be submitted from the United States or from abroad.

9. **IS EACH APPLICANT LIMITED TO ONLY ONE ENTRY DURING THE ANNUAL E-DV REGISTRATION PERIOD?**

Copyright © 2011 - GreenCard123.Com by UNorth® - All Rights Reserved

Yes, the law allows only one entry by or for each person during each registration period. **Individuals for whom more than one entry is submitted will be disqualified.** The Department of State will employ sophisticated technology and other means to identify individuals who submit multiple entries during the registration period. People submitting more than one entry will be disqualified, and an electronic record will be permanently maintained by the Department of State. Individuals may apply for the program each year during the regular registration period.

10. MAY A HUSBAND AND A WIFE EACH SUBMIT A SEPARATE ENTRY?

Yes, a husband and a wife may each submit one entry if each meets the eligibility requirements. If either is selected, the other is entitled to derivative status.

11. WHAT FAMILY MEMBERS MUST I INCLUDE ON MY E-DV ENTRY?

On your entry you must list your spouse (husband or wife) and all unmarried children under 21 years of age. You must list your spouse even if you are currently separated from him/her, unless you are legally separated (i.e., there is a written agreement recognized by a court or a court order). If you are legally separated or divorced, you do not need to list your former spouse. **You must list ALL your children who are unmarried and under 21 years of age at the time of your initial E-DV entry,** whether they are your natural children, your spouse's children, or children you have formally adopted in accordance with the laws of your country, unless such child is already a U.S. citizen or Lawful Permanent Resident. List all children under 21 years of age at the time of your electronic entry, **even if they no longer reside with you or you do not intend for them to immigrate under the DV program.** Children who are already U.S. citizens or Lawful Permanent Residents will not require or be issued a DV visa. However, you should include them on your registration.

The fact that you have listed family members on your entry does not mean that they must travel with you. They may choose to remain behind. However, if you include an eligible dependent on your visa application forms that you failed to include on your original entry, your case will be disqualified. This only applies to those who were family members at the time the original application was submitted, not those acquired at a later date. Your spouse may still submit a separate entry, even though he or she is listed on your entry, as long as both entries include details on all dependents in your family. See question #10 above.

12. MUST I SUBMIT MY OWN ENTRY, OR MAY SOMEONE ACT ON MY BEHALF?

You may prepare and submit your own entry, or have someone submit the entry for you. Regardless of whether an entry is submitted by the individual directly, or assistance is provided by an attorney, friend, relative, etc., only one entry may be submitted in the name of each person, and the entrant remains responsible for ensuring that information in the entry is correct and complete. All entrants, including those not selected, will be able to check the status of their entry through the Entry Status Check available from May 1, 2011 on the E-DV website www.dvlottery.state.gov. Entrants should keep their own confirmation page information so that they may independently check the status of their entry.

13. WHAT ARE THE REQUIREMENTS FOR EDUCATION OR WORK EXPERIENCE?

The law and regulations require that every entrant must have at least a high school education or its equivalent or have, within the past five years, two years of work experience in an occupation requiring at least two years' training or experience. A "high school education or equivalent" is defined as successful completion of a twelve-year course of elementary and secondary education in the United States or successful completion in another country of a formal course of elementary and secondary education comparable to a high school education in the United States. Only formal courses of study meet this requirement; correspondence programs or equivalency certificates (such as the G.E.D.) are not acceptable. Documentary proof of education or work experience must be presented to the consular officer at the time of the visa interview.

14. WHAT OCCUPATIONS QUALIFY FOR THE DV PROGRAM??

To determine eligibility based on work experience, definitions from the Department of Labor's (DOL) O*Net OnLine database will be used. The O*Net Online Database groups job experience into five "job zones."

8

Copyright © 2011 – GreenCard123.Com by UNorth® – All Rights Reserved

While many occupations are listed on the DOL Website, only certain specified occupations qualify for the DV Program. To qualify for a DV on the basis of your work experience, you must have, within the past five years, two years of experience in an occupation that is designated as **Job Zone 4 or 5, classified in a Specific Vocational Preparation (SVP) range of 7.0 or higher.**

15. HOW DO I FIND THE QUALIFYING OCCUPATIONS ON THE DEPARTMENT OF LABOR WEB SITE?

Qualifying DV Occupations are shown on the DOL O*Net Online Database. Follow these steps to find out if your occupation qualifies: Select "Find Occupations" and then select a specific "Job Family." For example, select Architecture and Engineering and click "GO." Then click on the link for the specific Occupation. Following the same example, click Aerospace Engineers. After selecting a specific Occupation link, select the tab "Job Zone" to find out the designated Job Zone number and Specific Vocational Preparation (SVP) rating range. For additional information see the Diversity Visa – List of Occupations webpage

16. HOW WILL SUCCESSFUL ENTRANTS BE SELECTED?

At the KCC, all entries received from each region will be individually numbered. After the end of the registration period, a computer will randomly select entries from among all the entries received for each geographic region. Within each region, the first entry randomly selected will be the first case registered; the second entry selected the second registration, etc. All entries received during the registration period will have an equal chance of being selected within each region. When an entry has been selected, the entrant will be notified of their selection through the Entry Status Check available from May 1, 2011 on the E-DV website www.dvlottery.state.gov. The KCC will continue to process the case until those selected to be visa applicants are instructed to appear for visa interviews at a U.S. consular office or until those qualifying to change status in the United States apply at a domestic USCIS office.

Important Note: Notifications to those selected in the random lottery are <u>not</u> sent by e-mail. Official notifications of selection will be made through - Entry Status Check, available from May 1, 2011 on the E-DV website www.dvlottery.state.gov. The KCC will no longer send selectee notifications or letters by regular postal mail. Should you receive an e-mail notification or a mailed letter about your E-DV selection, be aware that the notification is not legitimate. It is only after you are selected, and respond to the notification instructions made available to you via Entry Status Check, and processing begins on your case, that you may receive follow-up e-mail communication from the KCC informing you to review Entry Status Check for new information about your application. The KCC will <u>not</u> ask you to send money to them by mail or by services such as Western Union.

17. MAY SELECTEES ADJUST THEIR STATUS WITH USCIS?

Yes, provided they are otherwise eligible to adjust status under the terms of Section 245 of the INA, selected individuals who are physically present in the United States may apply to USCIS for adjustment of status to permanent resident. **Applicants must ensure that USCIS can complete action on their cases, including processing of any overseas derivatives, before September 30, 2012, since on that date registrations for the DV-2012 program expire. No visa numbers for the DV-2012 program will be available after midnight EST on September 30, 2012, under any circumstances.**

18. WILL ENTRANTS WHO ARE NOT SELECTED BE INFORMED?

All entrants, including those NOT selected, may check the status of their entry through the Entry Status Check on the E-DV website www.dvlottery.state.gov and find out if their entry was or was not selected. Entrants should keep their own confirmation page information from the time of their entry until the completion of their visa application, if selected. Status information for DV-2012 will be available online from May 1, 2011, until June 30, 2012. (Status information for the previous DV lottery, DV-2011, is available online from July 1, 2010, until June 30, 2011.)

19. HOW MANY INDIVIDUALS WILL BE SELECTED?

There are 50,000 DV visas available for DV-2012, but because it is likely that some of the first 50,000 persons who are selected will not qualify for visas or pursue their cases to visa issuance, more than 50,000 entries will be selected by the KCC to ensure that all of the available DV visas are issued. However, this also means that

9

Copyright © 2011 - GreenCard123.Com by UNorth® - All Rights Reserved

there will not be a sufficient number of visas for all those who are initially selected. All applicants who are selected will be informed promptly of their place on the list through the E-DV website's Entry Status Check. Interviews for the DV-2012 program will begin in October 2011. Selectees who provide information requested in the notification instructions will be informed of their visa interview appointment through the E-DV website's Entry Status Check four to six weeks before the scheduled interviews with U.S. consular officers at overseas posts. Each month, visas will be issued to those applicants who are ready for issuance during that month, visa-number availability permitting. Once all of the 50,000 DV visas have been issued, the program will end. In principle, visa numbers could be finished before September 2011. Selected applicants who wish to receive visas must be prepared to act promptly on their cases. **Random selection by the KCC computer as a selectee does not automatically guarantee that you will receive a visa. Only the first 50,000 selected applicants to qualify will be issued visas and you must qualify for the visa as well.**

20. IS THERE A MINIMUM AGE FOR APPLICANTS TO APPLY FOR THE E-DV PROGRAM?

There is no minimum age to apply for the program, but the requirement of a high school education or work experience for each principal applicant at the time of application will effectively disqualify most persons who are under age 18.

21. ARE THERE ANY FEES FOR THE E-DV PROGRAM?

There is no fee for submitting an electronic lottery entry. DV applicants must pay all required visa fees at the time of visa application directly to the consular cashier at the embassy or consulate. Details of required DV and immigration visa application fees will be included with the instructions sent by the KCC to applicants who are selected.

22. DO DV APPLICANTS RECEIVE WAIVERS OF ANY GROUNDS OF VISA INELIGIBILITY OR RECEIVE SPECIAL PROCESSING FOR A WAIVER APPLICATION?

Applicants are subject to all grounds of ineligibility for immigrant visas specified in the Immigration and Nationality Act (INA). There are no special provisions for the waiver of any ground of visa ineligibility aside from those ordinarily provided in the INA, nor is there special processing for waiver requests. Some general waiver provisions for people with close relatives who are U.S. Citizens or Lawful Permanent Resident aliens may be available to DV applicants as well, but the time constraints in the DV program will make it difficult for applicants to benefit from such provisions.

23. MAY PERSONS WHO ARE ALREADY REGISTERED FOR AN IMMIGRANT VISA IN ANOTHER CATEGORY APPLY FOR THE DV PROGRAM?

Yes, such persons may apply for the DV program.

24. HOW LONG DO APPLICANTS WHO ARE SELECTED REMAIN ENTITLED TO APPLY FOR VISAS IN THE DV CATEGORY?

Persons selected in the DV-2012 lottery are entitled to apply for visa issuance only during fiscal year 2012, from October 1, 2011, through September 30, 2012. **Applicants must obtain their visa or adjust status by the end of the fiscal year.** There is no carry-over of DV benefits into the next year for persons who are selected but who do not obtain visas by September 30, 2012 (the end of the fiscal year.). Also, spouses and children who derive status from a DV-2012 registration can only obtain visas in the DV category between October 1, 2011 and September 30, 2012. Applicants who apply overseas will receive an appointment notification from the KCC through Entry Status Check on the E-DV website four to six weeks before the scheduled appointment.

25. IF AN E-DV SELECTEE DIES, WHAT HAPPENS TO THE DV CASE?

The death of an individual selected in the lottery results in automatic revocation of the DV case. Any eligible spouse and/or children are no longer entitled to the DV visa for that entry.

26. WHEN WILL E-DV BE AVAILABLE ONLINE?

10

Copyright © 2011 – GreenCard123.Com by UNorth® – All Rights Reserved

Online entry will be available during the registration period beginning at noon EDT (GMT-4) on Tuesday, October 5, 2010, and ending at noon EST (GMT-5) on Wednesday, November 3, 2010.

27. **WILL I BE ABLE TO DOWNLOAD AND SAVE THE E-DV ENTRY FORM TO A MICROSOFT WORD PROGRAM (OR OTHER SUITABLE PROGRAM) AND THEN FILL IT OUT?**

No, you will not be able to save the form into another program for completion and submission later. The E-DV Entry Form is a Web form only. This makes it more "universal" than a proprietary word processor format. Additionally, it does require that the information be filled in and submitted while online.

28. **IF I DON'T HAVE ACCESS TO A SCANNER, CAN I SEND PHOTOGRAPHS TO MY RELATIVE IN THE UNITED STATES TO SCAN THE PHOTOGRAPHS, SAVE THE PHOTOGRAPHS TO A DISKETTE, AND THEN MAIL THE DISKETTE BACK TO ME TO APPLY?**

Yes, this can be done, as long as the photograph meets the photograph requirements in the instructions and the photograph is electronically submitted with, and at the same time as, the E-DV online entry. The applicants must already have the scanned photograph file when they submit the entry online. The photograph cannot be submitted separately from the online application. Only one online entry can be submitted for each person. Multiple submissions will disqualify the entry for that person for DV-2012. The entire entry (photograph and application together) can be submitted electronically from the United States or from overseas.

29. **CAN I SAVE THE FORM ONLINE SO THAT I CAN FILL OUT PART AND THEN COME BACK LATER AND COMPLETE THE REMAINDER?**

No, this cannot be done. The E-DV Entry Form is designed to be completed and submitted at one time. However, because the form is in two parts, and because of possible network interruptions and delays, the E-DV system is designed to permit up to sixty (60) minutes between the form's download and when the entry is received at the E-DV website. If more than sixty minutes elapse and the entry has not been electronically received, the information already received is discarded. This is done so that there is no possibility that a full entry could accidentally be interpreted as a duplicate of a previous partial entry. The DV-2012 instructions explain clearly and completely what information is required to fill in the form. Thus, you can be fully prepared, making sure you have all of the information needed before you start to complete the form online.

30. **IF THE SUBMITTED DIGITAL IMAGES DO NOT CONFORM TO THE SPECIFICATIONS, THE PROCEDURES STATE THAT THE SYSTEM WILL AUTOMATICALLY REJECT THE E-DV ENTRY FORM AND NOTIFY THE SENDER. DOES THIS MEAN I WILL BE ABLE RE-SUBMIT MY ENTRY?**

Yes, the entry can be resubmitted. Since the entry was automatically rejected, it was not actually considered as a submission to the E-DV website. It does not count as a submitted E-DV entry, and no confirmation notice of receipt is sent. If there are problems with the digital photograph sent, because it does not conform to the requirements, it is automatically rejected by the E-DV website. However, the amount of time it takes the rejection message to reach the sender is unpredictable, given the nature of the Internet. If the problem can be fixed by the applicant, and the Form Part One or Two is re-sent within sixty (60) minutes, there is no problem. Otherwise, the applicant will have to restart the submission process. An applicant can try to submit an application as many times as is necessary until a complete application is received and the confirmation notice sent.

31. **WILL THE ELECTRONIC CONFIRMATION NOTICE THAT THE COMPLETED E-DV ENTRY FORM HAS BEEN RECEIVED THROUGH THE ONLINE SYSTEM BE SENT IMMEDIATELY AFTER SUBMISSION?**

The response from the E-DV website which contains confirmation of the receipt of an acceptable E-DV Entry Form is sent by the E-DV website immediately. However, the amount of time it takes the response to reach the sender is unpredictable, given the nature of the Internet. If many minutes have elapsed since pressing the "Submit" button, there is no harm in pressing the "Submit" button a second time. The E-DV system will not be confused by a situation where the "Submit" button is hit a second time, because no confirmation response has been received. An applicant can try to submit an application as many times as is necessary until a complete application is received and the confirmation notice sent. However, once you receive a confirmation notice, do not resubmit your information.

11

Copyright © 2011 - GreenCard123.Com by UNorth® - All Rights Reserved

32. HOW WILL I KNOW IF THE NOTIFICATION OF SELECTION THAT I HAVE RECEIVED IS AUTHENTIC? HOW CAN I CONFIRM THAT I HAVE IN FACT BEEN CHOSEN IN THE RANDOM DV LOTTERY?

Keep your confirmation page. You will need your confirmation number to access information through the Entry Status Check available on the E-DV website www.dvlottery.state.gov. Entry Status Check will be the sole means by which DV-2012 entrants are notified of their selection, provided instructions on how to proceed with their application, and notified of their immigrant visa interview appointment date and time.

Status information will be available from May 1, 2011. If you lose your confirmation information, you will not be able to check your DV entry status by yourself, and we will not resend the confirmation page information to you. Only the randomly selected individuals will be given additional instructions on how to pursue their DV visa application. Persons not selected may verify the non-selection of their entry using their confirmation information through the official DV website, but they will not receive any additional instructions. We will NOT forward the confirmation page information to you. U.S. Embassies and Consulates will NOT provide a list of those selected to continue the visa process.

Randomly selected entrants will receive notification instructions for the DV visa application process on the selectee confirmation page available through Entry Status Check on the E-DV website www.dvlottery.state.gov. The instructions say the selected applicants will pay all diversity and immigrant visa fees in person only at the U.S. Embassy or Consulate at the time of the visa application. The consular cashier or consular officer immediately gives the visa applicant a U.S. Government receipt for payment. Selected applicants applying for an immigrant visa at a U.S. Embassy or Consulate should never send money for DV fees through the mail, Western Union, or any other delivery service. Selected applicants who are already present in the United States and who file for adjustment of status will receive separate instructions on how to mail DV fees to a US bank.

The E-DV lottery entries are submitted on the Internet, on the official U.S. Government E-DV website at www.dvlottery.state.gov. The KCC will not send notification letters to the selected applicants. The KCC, consular offices, or the U.S. Government have never sent e-mails to notify individuals they have been selected, and there are no plans to use e-mail for this purpose for the DV-2012 program. Selectees will only receive e-mail communications from the KCC alerting them that a visa appointment has been scheduled after they have responded to the notification instructions on Entry Status Check. Such e-mails will direct selectees to check their interview appointment details on Entry Status Check and will not contain information on the actual appointment date and time.

The Department of State's Bureau of Consular Affairs advises the public that only Internet sites including the ".gov" domain suffix are official government websites. Many other non-governmental websites (e.g., using the suffixes ".com" or ".org" or ".net") provide immigration and visa related information and services. Regardless of the content of non-governmental websites, the Department of State does not endorse, recommend, or sponsor any information or material shown at these other websites.

Some websites may try to mislead customers and members of the public into thinking they are official websites and may contact you by e-mail to lure you to their offers. These websites may attempt to require you to pay for services such as forms and information about immigration procedures, which are otherwise free on the Department of State Visa Services website or through U.S. embassy consular sections' websites. Additionally, these other websites may require you to pay for services you will not receive (such as fees for DV immigration applications and visas) in an effort to steal your money. If you send in money to one of these scams, you will never see it again. Also, you should be wary of sending any personal information to these websites that might be used for identity fraud/theft.

33. HOW DO I REPORT INTERNET FRAUD OR UNSOLICITED EMAIL?

If you wish to file a complaint about Internet fraud, please see the econsumer.gov website, hosted by the Federal Trade Commission, in cooperation with consumer-protection agencies from 17 nations (http://www.econsumer.gov/english/). You may also report fraud to the Federal Bureau of Investigation (FBI) Internet Crime Complaint Center. To file a complaint about unsolicited email, visit the Department of Justice Contact Us page.

Copyright © 2011 – GreenCard123.Com by UNorth® - All Rights Reserved

34. **IF I AM SUCCESSFUL IN OBTAINING A VISA THROUGH THE DV PROGRAM, WILL THE U.S. GOVERNMENT ASSIST WITH MY AIRFARE TO THE UNITED STATES, PROVIDE ASSISTANCE TO LOCATE HOUSING AND EMPLOYMENT, PROVIDE HEALTHCARE, OR PROVIDE ANY SUBSIDIES UNTIL I AM FULLY SETTLED?**

No, applicants who obtain a DV are not provided any type of assistance such as airfare, housing assistance, or subsidies. If you are selected to apply for a DV, you will be required to provide evidence that you will not become a public charge in the United States before being issued a visa. This evidence may be in the form of a combination of your personal assets, an Affidavit of Support (Form I-134) from a relative or friend residing in the United States, and/or an offer of employment from an employer in the United States.

13

Copyright © 2011 – GreenCard123.Com by UNorth® – All Rights Reserved

LIST OF COUNTRIES BY REGION WHOSE NATIVES ARE ELIGIBLE FOR DV-2012

The list below shows the countries whose natives are eligible for DV-2012, grouped by geographic region. Dependent areas overseas are included within the region of the governing country. The countries whose natives are not eligible for the DV-2012 program were identified by USCIS, according to the formula in Section 203(c) of the INA. The countries whose natives are not eligible for the DV program (because they are the principal source countries of Family-Sponsored and Employment-Based immigration or "high-admission" countries) are noted after the respective regional lists.

AFRICA

Algeria	Madagascar
Angola	Malawi
Benin	Mali
Botswana	Mauritania
Burkina Faso	Mauritius
Burundi	Morocco
Cameroon	Mozambique
Cape Verde	Namibia
Central African Republic	Niger
Chad	Nigeria
Comoros	Rwanda
Congo	Sao Tome and Principe
Congo, Democratic Republic of the	Senegal
Cote D'Ivoire (Ivory Coast)	Seychelles
Djibouti	Sierra Leone
Egypt	Somalia
Equatorial Guinea	South Africa
Eritrea	Sudan
Ethiopia	Swaziland
Gabon	Tanzania
Gambia, The	Togo
Ghana	Tunisia
Guinea	Uganda
Guinea-Bissau	Zambia
Kenya	Zimbabwe
Lesotho	
Liberia	
Libya	

Persons born in the Gaza Strip are chargeable to Egypt.

14

Copyright © 2011 – GreenCard123.Com by UNorth® – All Rights Reserved

LIST OF COUNTRIES BY REGION WHOSE NATIVES ARE ELIGIBLE FOR DV-2012

ASIA

Afghanistan	Lebanon
Bahrain	Malaysia
Bangladesh	Maldives
Bhutan	Mongolia
Brunei	Nepal
Burma	North Korea
Cambodia	Oman
East Timor	Qatar
Hong Kong Special Administrative Region	Saudi Arabia
Indonesia	Singapore
Iran	Sri Lanka
Iraq	Syria
Israel	Taiwan
Japan	Thailand
Jordan	United Arab Emirates
Kuwait	Yemen
Laos	

Natives of the following Asian countries are **not** eligible for this year's diversity program:
China (mainland-born), India, Pakistan, South Korea, Philippines, and Vietnam. Hong Kong S.A.R and Taiwan **do qualify** and are listed above. Macau S.A.R. also qualifies and is listed below (Europe).

Persons born in the areas administered prior to June 1967 by Israel, Jordan, and Syria are chargeable, respectively, to Israel, Jordan, and Syria.

15

Copyright © 2011 - GreenCard123.Com by UNorth® - All Rights Reserved

LIST OF COUNTRIES BY REGION WHOSE NATIVES ARE ELIGIBLE FOR DV-2012

EUROPE

Albania
Andorra
Armenia
Austria
Azerbaijan
Belarus
Belgium
Bosnia and Herzegovina
Bulgaria
Croatia
Cyprus
Czech Republic
Denmark (including components and dependent areas overseas)
Estonia
Finland
France (including components and areas overseas)
Georgia
Germany
Greece
Hungary
Iceland
Ireland
Italy
Kazakhstan
Kosovo
Kyrgyzstan
Latvia
Liechtenstein

Lithuania
Luxembourg
Macau Special Administrative Region
Macedonia
Malta
Moldova
Monaco
Montenegro
Netherlands (including components and dependent areas overseas)
Northern Ireland
Norway
Portugal (including components and dependent areas overseas)
Romania
Russia
San Marino
Serbia
Slovakia
Slovenia
Spain
Sweden
Switzerland
Tajikistan
Turkey
Turkmenistan
Ukraine
Uzbekistan
Vatican City

Natives of the following European countries are **not** eligible for this year's diversity program: Great Britain (United Kingdom) and Poland. Great Britain (United Kingdom) includes the following dependent areas: Anguilla, Bermuda, British Virgin Islands, Cayman Islands, Falkland Islands, Gibraltar, Montserrat, Pitcairn, St. Helena, and Turks and Caicos Islands. Note that for purposes of the diversity program only, Northern Ireland is treated separately; Northern Ireland **does qualify** and is listed among the qualifying areas.

16

Copyright © 2011 – GreenCard123.Com by UNorth® – All Rights Reserved

LIST OF COUNTRIES BY REGION WHOSE NATIVES ARE ELIGIBLE FOR DV-2012

NORTH AMERICA

The Bahamas

In North America, natives of Canada and Mexico are **not** eligible for this year's diversity program.

OCEANIA

Australia (including components and dependent areas overseas)
Fiji
Kiribati
Marshall Islands
Micronesia, Federated States of
Nauru
New Zealand (including components and dependent areas overseas)
Palau
Papua New Guinea
Solomon Islands
Tonga
Tuvalu
Vanuatu
Samoa

SOUTH AMERICA, CENTRAL AMERICA, AND THE CARIBBEAN

Antigua and Barbuda
Argentina
Barbados
Belize
Bolivia
Chile
Costa Rica
Cuba
Dominica
Grenada
Guyana
Honduras
Nicaragua
Panama
Paraguay
Saint Kitts and Nevis
Saint Lucia
Saint Vincent and the Grenadines
Suriname
Trinidad and Tobago
Uruguay
Venezuela

Countries in this region whose natives are **not** eligible for this year's diversity program:
Brazil, Colombia, Dominican Republic, Ecuador, El Salvador, Guatemala, Haiti, Jamaica, Mexico, and Peru.

Copyright © 2011 – GreenCard123.Com by UNorth® – All Rights Reserved

APPENDIX

II. HOW TO USE USCIS WEBSITE

The following is snapshot of various important tasks that can be accomplished on the USCIS.gov website. Keep in mind that the USCIS website changes over time so the links and some instructions may relocate to different section of the page or be redesigned.

Filling in forms requires a PDF reader application such as Adobe PDF or other compatible applications.

Copyright © 2011 - GreenCard123.Com by UNorth® - All Rights Reserved

HOW TO CHECK YOUR APPLICATION STATUS ON USCIS WEBSITE

A. Go to www.uscis.gov

B. On the left side click on <u>Check my Case Status</u>, or directly go to https://egov.uscis.gov

C. Enter your case number in the field

D. Click on "check status"

II-1 Checking Status of Your Application on USCIS Website

Copyright © 2011 – GreenCard123.Com by UNorth® – All Rights Reserved

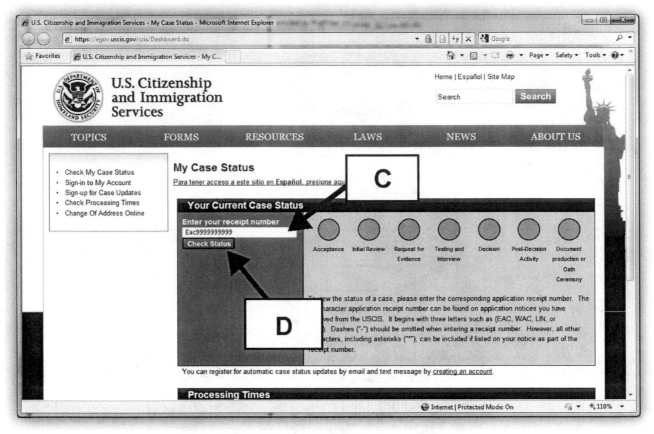

II-2 Checking Status of Your Application on USCIS Website

Copyright © 2011 – GreenCard123.Com by UNorth® – All Rights Reserved

HOW TO CHECK PROCESSING TIMES FOR YOUR VISA TYPE

A. On the homepage, check Processing Times or go to http://dashboard.uscis.gov/

B. Click on "Check Processing Time" on the left and choose visa at the bottom. **OR**

C. Click "Check Processing Time" on "My Case Status" Page

D. Choose the Field Office for your Application, if your application is being handled by Field Office, OR

E. Choose the Service Center handing your application, if your application is being handled by Service Center, **OR**

F. Click on NBC Processing Dates, if your application is currently in National Benefits Center.

G. Review the Processing Time for your Application.

Note: Depending on where the application is sent to, the Field Office or Service Center can be chosen.

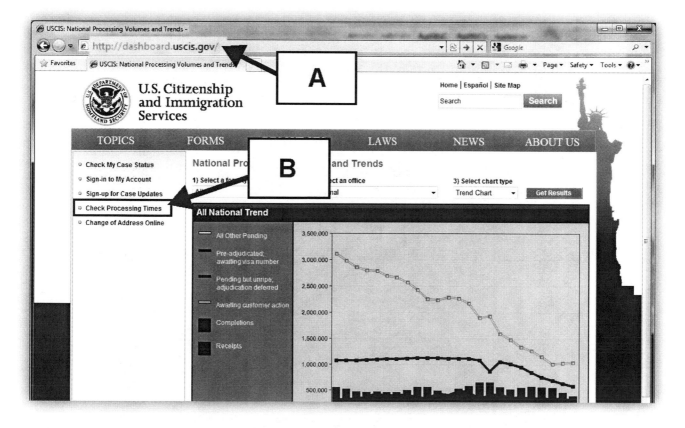

II-3CHECK PROCESSING TIMES FOR YOUR VISA TYPE

Copyright © 2011 – GreenCard123.Com by UNorth® – All Rights Reserved

II-4 CHECK PROCESSING TIMES FOR YOUR VISA TYPE

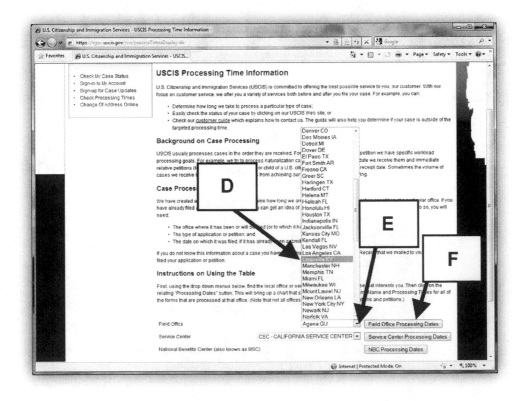

II-5CHECK PROCESSING TIMES FOR YOUR VISA TYPE

Copyright © 2011 – GreenCard123.Com by UNorth® – All Rights Reserved

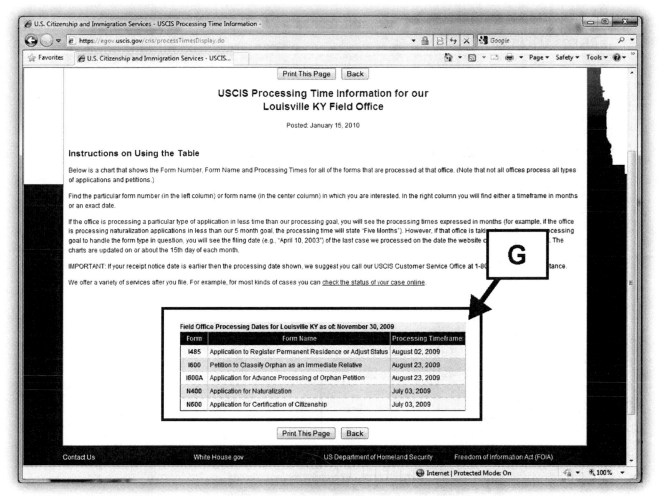

II-6CHECK PROCESSING TIMES FOR YOUR VISA TYPE

Copyright © 2011 – GreenCard123.Com by UNorth® – All Rights Reserved

HOW TO CHECK USCIS APPLICATION FEES

A. Go to www.uscis.gov

B. On the left side click on <u>Check Filing Fees</u>

C. Match your Form Type

D. See the Filing Fee

Note: If forms are being filed together, you may need to include both form's Filing Fees. Check USCIS.gov for additional information

II-7 CHECK USCIS APPLICATION FEES

Copyright © 2011 – GreenCard123.Com by UNorth® – All Rights Reserved

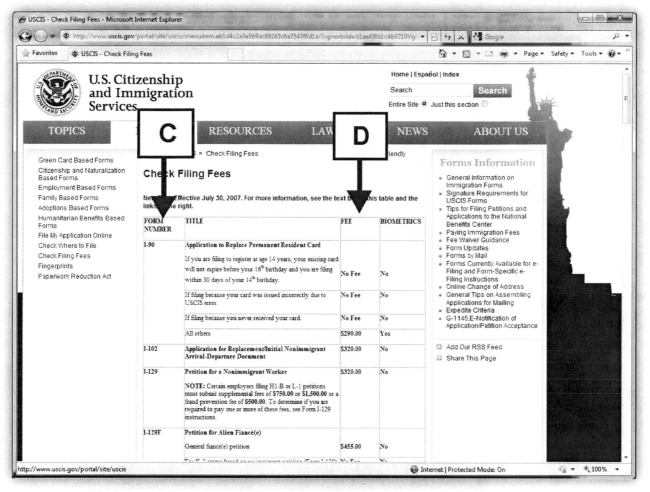

II-8CHECK USCIS APPLICATION FEES

Copyright © 2011 – GreenCard123.Com by UNorth® – All Rights Reserved

HOW TO CHANGE YOUR ADDRESS ON USCIS WEBSITE

A. Go to www.uscis.gov

B. On the left side click on <u>Change of Address Online</u>

C. Review the information on the page and click on "Change your Address Online"

D. Review and if approved, click on "I accept these terms and conditions" and on the following page change your address

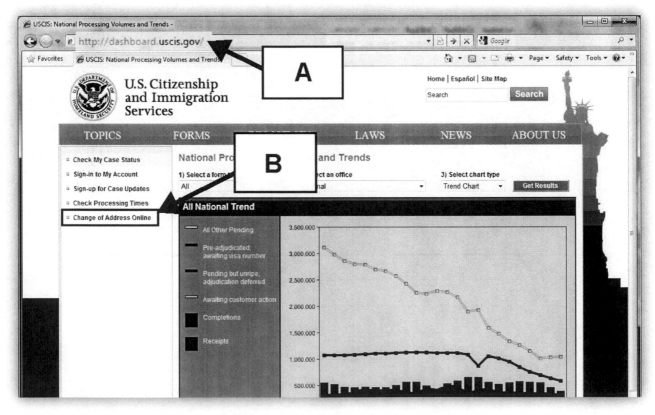

II-9 CHANGE YOUR ADDRESS ON USCIS WEBSITE

Copyright © 2011 - GreenCard123.Com by UNorth® - All Rights Reserved

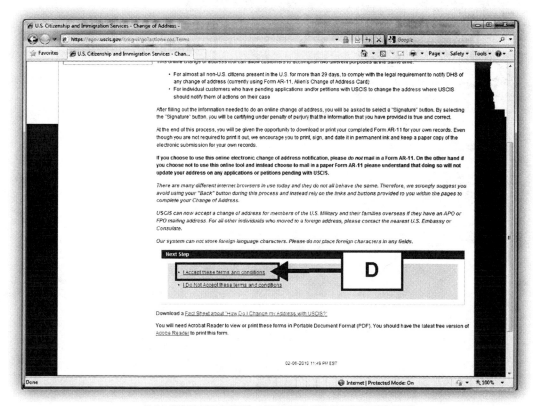

II-10 CHANGE YOUR ADDRESS ON USCIS WEBSITE

II-11 CHANGE YOUR ADDRESS ON USCIS WEBSITE

Copyright © 2011 – GreenCard123.Com by UNorth® – All Rights Reserved

HOW TO MAKE AN APPOINTMENT WITH INFOPASS

A. Go to http://infopass.uscis.giv or visit www.uscis.gov click on InfoPass Appointment

B. On the left side click on your preferred language

C. Click on "Make your appointment with Infopass"

D. Enter your Zip Code , OR select your Country from the list.

E. Click on Continue to schedule a time with Infopass

Note: Infopass may not be available in all countries

II-12MAKE AN APPOINTMENT WITH INFOPASS

Copyright © 2011 – GreenCard123.Com by UNorth® – All Rights Reserved

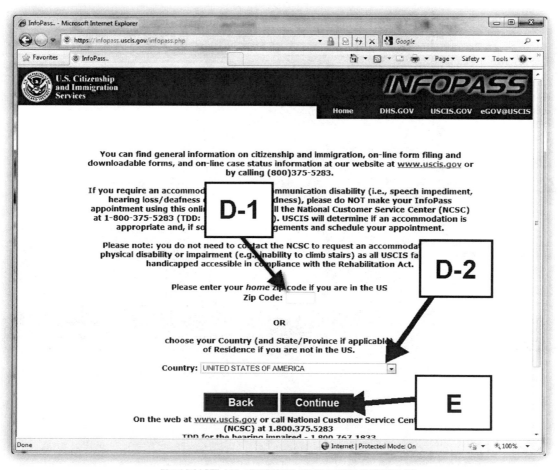

II-13 MAKE AN APPOINTMENT WITH INFOPASS

II-14 MAKE AN APPOINTMENT WITH INFOPASS

Copyright © 2011 – GreenCard123.Com by UNorth® – All Rights Reserved

HOW TO RETRIEVE THE LATEST EDITION OF VISA BULLETIN

A. Go to Department of State Website at
http://travel.state.gov
B. Click on "Visa" tab on top of the page
C. Click on "Visa Bulletin" on the left navigation bar
D. Click on the Latest issue on Visa Bulletin or archived
versions if needed.

II-15 MAKE AN APPOINTMENT WITH INFOPASS

Copyright © 2011 - GreenCard123.Com by UNorth® - All Rights Reserved

II-16 MAKE AN APPOINTMENT WITH INFOPASS

- II-17 MAKE AN APPOINTMENT WITH INFOPASS

Copyright © 2011 - GreenCard123.Com by UNorth® - All Rights Reserved

THIS PAGE WAS INTENTIONALLY LEFT BLANK

Copyright © 2011 - GreenCard123.Com by UNorth® - All Rights Reserved

APPENDIX

III. HOW TO READ VISA BULLETIN

However, when a date is shown, it means that the visa is on a waiting-list and the visa is available at the date shown (that applicant had originally applied for the visa)

WHAT IS VISA BULLETIN

Visa Bulletin is a publication of the United States Department of State. The primary purpose of this bulletin is to provide updated waiting list (also known as priority date) for the immigrants that are subject to the quota system.

United States immigrants are categorized to two groups: First, are those that are subject to annual numerical limitations (such as worker visa, and sponsored relatives of Permanent Residents) and second, those who do not have a numerical limit or a waiting list (such as visa for husband or wife of US Citizen).

There are pre-set number of annual visas available for United States immigration under those visas that fall on the waiting list.. In other words, there are only limited visas that can be issued every year. For instance, there are about 23,000 visas available for married sons and daughters of US Citizens; if the number of applicants in a year exceeds the available visa numbers, those applicants are placed in a queue and are given a priority date, which basically estimates when an applicant would get a visa based on the number of previous applicants in the queue. Think of it as a ticket system that gives you a number and you need to wait until your number is called (and if there is no one in line prior to you, you don't need a number).

The Visa Bulletin is issued every second or third week of each month and for those visas that require quota it would either show as 'CURRENT' or as a date (such as JAN10). The word CURRENT refers to those visas that are immediately available (no waiting in line).

HOW TO READ VISA BULLETIN

The Visa Bulletin follows a standard format to sort the priority dates of the applicants and is broken down into the following visa categories:

1) Family based immigrants
2) Employment based immigrants
3) Diversity based immigrants

To read the bulletin, first identify which category your visa falls under. The Codes in the table are as follows:

C means the visa limit is not reached and it is currently available to all the applicants (At the time of the publication)

DATE (such as 10JAN08) it means that if your priority date is earlier than the date shown, a visa is now available for you, otherwise you need to wait until it becomes available for you.

Copyright © 2011 - GreenCard123.Com by UNorth® - All Rights Reserved

The Unfortunate Fact of Visa Bulletin

Unfortunately, the dates in the Visa Bulletin do not follow an order. For some reasons, the priority date in the Bulletin can go forward and sometimes backwards. For example, if you applied in March 05 and the date for your visa category shows as Feb 05, it may stay at this date for quite some time or it may jump forward or even backward. It all depends on the number of applicants for the months ahead that determines who gets visa when.

DIVERSITY VISA APPLICANTS

For the purpose of the Diversity Visa, you only need to look at the category **B. DIVERSITY IMMIGRANT (DV)** section of the Visa Bulletin, and also instead of a DATE, you'll see a rank number instead that is shown on your winning letter. See the figure below for additional information

See the Figure at the end of this section for a sample Visa Bulletin issue.

Region	All DV Chargeability Areas Except Those Listed Separately	
AFRICA	CURRENT	Except: Ethiopia: 26,350
ASIA	CURRENT	
EUROPE	CURRENT	
NORTH AMERICA (BAHAMAS)	CURRENT	
OCEANIA	CURRENT	
SOUTH AMERICA, and the CARIBBEAN	CURRENT	

Table - Snapshot from September 2010 Visa Bulletin

For instance, in the table above, the status of Visa shows CURRENT, it means that the limit for all the regions (Africa, Asia, Europe, North America, Oceania, and South America/Caribbean) is not yet reached and the USCIS can keep up with the requests of visas made. In other words, if you apply for the visa, at any rank number, a visa would be immediately available for you. This is good news, meaning that your application will not have to wait and it will be processed immediately.

The Table below provides an example of a month that USCIS was not able to keep up with the visa request:

Region	All DV Chargeability Areas Except Those Listed Separately	
AFRICA	39,600	Except: Egypt 20,650 Ethiopia 19,500 Nigeria 12,750
ASIA	30,350	
EUROPE	28,000	
NORTH AMERICA (BAHAMAS)	15	
OCEANIA	930	
SOUTH AMERICA, and the CARIBBEAN	1,100	

Table - Snapshot from Jun 2009 Visa Bulletin

Recall that there are only 50,000 Diversity Visas available so once that number is reached practically no visa is available at all, but within that number, as long as USCIS can keep up with the visa requests, the status shows 'CURRENT', otherwise it would show the rank # that can apply. Your rank number# must be below the number shown on the table above in order to apply for the visa.

Priority Date

Copyright © 2011 - GreenCard123.Com by UNorth® - All Rights Reserved

The Priority date is a United States immigration concept. A common path to the green card in the United States is to obtain it through a family based or employment based petition, a very complex process that can take many years to complete.

As explained above the United States Department of State publishes a monthly visa bulletin which lists cutoff priority dates for different immigration categories and birth countries. Only those intending immigrants with priority dates before the cutoff date are permitted to file their Adjustment of Status (AOS) applications and obtain their green card. The cutoff dates generally move forward over time as old cases are disposed of. However, in certain cases, such as if a large number of old cases work their way through the system at about the same time, the cutoff dates can actually retrogress (or roll back). If an individual already has a pending AOS application on file when retrogression occurs that places the cutoff earlier than the applicant's priority date, USCIS sets the application aside and will not adjudicate it until

the priority date is current again. As an example, after months of stagnation, in June 2007 the priority date cutoffs for employment-based second and third preference (EB2 and EB3) applicants (the bulk of employment-based green card applicants) advanced dramatically for all countries of birth.

Since the Priority Date does not apply to Diversity Visa lottery, our focus is simply to compare the Rank number that is currently being processed to the rank number that is indicated on the winner's letter. The individual then can apply for the Visa as soon as the rank number that he/she is holding is below the cut-off number published by the Visa Bulletin.

A sample issue of Visa Bulletin publication is provided later in the chapter. You may also visit http://travel.state.gov to retrieve the latest version of the bulletin.

Copyright © 2011 - GreenCard123.Com by UNorth® - All Rights Reserved

Visa Bulletin for October 2010

Number 25
Volume IX
Washington, D.C.

A. STATUTORY NUMBERS

1. This bulletin summarizes the availability of immigrant numbers during **October**. Consular officers are required to report to the Department of State documentarily qualified applicants for numerically limited visas; the Bureau of Citizenship and Immigration Services in the Department of Homeland Security reports applicants for adjustment of status. Allocations were made, to the extent possible under the numerical limitations, for the demand received by September **9th** in the chronological order of the reported priority dates. If the demand could not be satisfied within the statutory or regulatory limits, the category or foreign state in which demand was excessive was deemed oversubscribed. The cut-off date for an oversubscribed category is the priority date of the first applicant who could not be reached within the numerical limits. Only applicants who have a priority date **earlier than** the cut-off date may be allotted a number. Immediately that it becomes necessary during the monthly allocation process to retrogress a cut-off date, supplemental requests for numbers will be honored only if the priority date falls within the new cut-off date which has been announced in this bulletin.

2. Section 201 of the Immigration and Nationality Act (INA) sets an annual minimum family-sponsored preference limit of 226,000. The worldwide level for annual employment-based preference immigrants is at least 140,000. Section 202 prescribes that the per-country limit for preference immigrants is set at 7% of the total annual family-sponsored and employment-based preference limits, i.e., 25,620. The dependent area limit is set at 2%, or 7,320.

3. Section 203 of the INA prescribes preference classes for allotment of immigrant visas as follows:

FAMILY-SPONSORED PREFERENCES

First: Unmarried Sons and Daughters of Citizens: 23,400 plus any numbers not required for fourth preference.

Second: Spouses and Children, and Unmarried Sons and Daughters of Permanent Residents: 114,200, plus the number (if any) by which the worldwide family preference level exceeds 226,000, and any unused first preference numbers:

A. Spouses and Children: 77% of the overall second preference limitation, of which 75% are exempt from the per-country limit;

B. Unmarried Sons and Daughters (21 years of age or older): 23% of the overall second preference limitation.

Third: Married Sons and Daughters of Citizens: 23,400, plus any numbers not required by first and second preferences.

Fourth: Brothers and Sisters of Adult Citizens: 65,000, plus any numbers not required by first three preferences.

EMPLOYMENT-BASED PREFERENCES

First: Priority Workers: 28.6% of the worldwide employment-based preference level, plus any numbers not required for fourth and fifth preferences.

Second: Members of the Professions Holding Advanced Degrees or Persons of Exceptional Ability: 28.6% of the worldwide employment-based preference level, plus any numbers not required by first preference.

Third: Skilled Workers, Professionals, and Other Workers: 28.6% of the worldwide level, plus any numbers not required by first and second preferences, not more than 10,000 of which to "Other Workers".

Fourth: Certain Special Immigrants: 7.1% of the worldwide level.

Fifth: Employment Creation: 7.1% of the worldwide level, not less than 3,000 of which reserved for investors in a targeted rural or high-unemployment area, and 3,000 set aside for investors in regional centers by Sec. 610 of P.L. 102-395.

4. INA Section 203(e) provides that family-sponsored and employment-based preference visas be issued to eligible immigrants in the order in which a petition in behalf of each has been filed. Section 203(d) provides that spouses and children of preference immigrants are entitled to the same status, and the same order of consideration, if accompanying or following to join the principal. The visa prorating provisions of Section 202(e) apply to allocations for a foreign state or dependent area when visa demand exceeds the per-country limit. These provisions apply at present to the following oversubscribed chargeability areas: CHINA-mainland born, INDIA, MEXICO, and PHILIPPINES.

5. On the chart below, the listing of a date for any class indicates that the class is oversubscribed (see paragraph 1); "C" means current, i.e., numbers are available for all qualified applicants; and "U" means unavailable, i.e., no numbers are available. (NOTE: Numbers are available only for applicants whose priority date is **earlier** than the cut-off date listed below.)

Family	All Chargeability Areas Except Those Listed	CHINA-mainland born	INDIA	MEXICO	PHILIPPINES
1st	15FEB06	15FEB06	15FEB06	15DEC92	01MAR97
2A	01APR10	01APR10	01APR10	01JAN10	01APR10
2B	01APR05	01APR05	01APR05	22JUN92	01SEP02
3rd	01MAY02	01MAY02	01MAY02	22OCT92	01MAR95
4th	01DEC01	01DEC01	01DEC01	08DEC95	01APR91

*NOTE: For October, 2A numbers **EXEMPT from per-country limit** are available to applicants from all countries with priority dates **earlier** than 01JAN10. 2A numbers **SUBJECT to per-country limit** are available to applicants chargeable to all countries **EXCEPT the MEXICO** with priority dates beginning 01JAN10 and earlier than 01APR10. (All 2A numbers provided for the MEXICO are exempt from the per-country limit; there are no 2A numbers for MEXICO subject to per-country limit.)

Employment-Based	All Chargeability Areas Except Those Listed	CHINA-mainland born	INDIA	MEXICO	PHILIPPINES
1st	C	C	C	C	C
2nd	C	22MAY06	08MAY06	C	C
3rd	08JAN05	08NOV03	15JAN02	22APR01	08JAN05
Other Workers	22MAR03	22MAR03	15JAN02	22APR01	22MAR03
4th	C	C	C	C	C
Certain Religious Workers	C	C	C	C	C
5th	C	C	C	C	C
Targeted Employment Areas/ Regional Centers	C	C	C	C	C

Copyright © 2011 - GreenCard123.Com by UNorth® - All Rights Reserved

5th Pilot Programs	C	C	C	C	C

The Department of State has available a recorded message with visa availability information which can be heard at: (area code 202) 663-1541. This recording will be updated in the middle of each month with information on cut-off dates for the following month.

Employment Third Preference Other Workers Category: Section 203(e) of the NACARA, as amended by Section 1(e) of Pub. L. 105-139, provides that once the Employment Third Preference Other Worker (EW) cut-off date has reached the priority date of the latest EW petition approved prior to November 19, 1997, the 10,000 EW numbers available for a fiscal year are to be reduced by up to 5,000 annually beginning in the following fiscal year. This reduction is to be made for as long as necessary to offset adjustments under the NACARA program. Since the EW cut-off date reached November 19, 1997 during Fiscal Year 2001, the reduction in the EW annual limit to 5,000 began in Fiscal Year 2002.

B. DIVERSITY IMMIGRANT (DV) CATEGORY

Section 203(c) of the Immigration and Nationality Act provides a maximum of up to 55,000 immigrant visas each fiscal year to permit immigration opportunities for persons from countries other than the principal sources of current immigration to the United States. The Nicaraguan and Central American Relief Act (NACARA) passed by Congress in November 1997 stipulates that beginning with DV-99, and for as long as necessary, up to 5,000 of the 55,000 annually-allocated diversity visas will be made available for use under the NACARA program. **This reduction has resulted in the DV-2011 annual limit being reduced to 50,000.** DV visas are divided among six geographic regions. No one country can receive more than seven percent of the available diversity visas in any one year.

For **October**, immigrant numbers in the DV category are available to qualified DV-2011 applicants chargeable to all regions/eligible countries as follows. When an allocation cut-off number is shown, visas are available only for applicants with DV regional lottery rank numbers **BELOW** the specified allocation cut-off number:

Region	All DV Chargeability Areas Except Those Listed Separately	
AFRICA	9,000	Except: Egypt 5,550 Ethiopia 7,450 Nigeria 7,450
ASIA	9,000	
EUROPE	9,600	
NORTH AMERICA (BAHAMAS)	1	
OCEANIA	350	
SOUTH AMERICA, and the CARIBBEAN	450	

Entitlement to immigrant status in the DV category lasts only through the end of the fiscal (visa) year for which the applicant is selected in the lottery. The year of entitlement for all applicants registered for the DV-2011 program ends as of September 30, 2011. DV visas may not be issued to DV-2011 applicants after that date. Similarly, spouses and children accompanying or following to join DV-2011 principals are only entitled to derivative DV status until September 30, 2011. DV visa availability through the very end of FY-2011 cannot be taken for granted. Numbers could be exhausted prior to September 30.

C. ADVANCE NOTIFICATION OF THE DIVERSITY (DV) IMMIGRANT CATEGORY RANK CUT-OFFS WHICH WILL APPLY IN OCTOBER

For **November**, immigrant numbers in the DV category are available to qualified DV-2011 applicants chargeable to all regions/eligible countries as follows. When an allocation cut-off number is shown, visas are available only for applicants with DV regional lottery rank numbers **BELOW** the

Copyright © 2011 - GreenCard123.Com by UNorth® - All Rights Reserved

specified allocation cut-off number:

Region	All DV Chargeability Areas Except Those Listed Separately	
AFRICA	12,000	Except: Egypt 9,300 Ethiopia 11,000 Nigeria 10,000
ASIA	10,750	
EUROPE	12,500	
NORTH AMERICA (BAHAMAS)	2	
OCEANIA	650	
SOUTH AMERICA, and the CARIBBEAN	675	

D. OBTAINING THE MONTHLY VISA BULLETIN

The Department of State's Bureau of Consular Affairs offers the monthly "Visa Bulletin" on the INTERNET'S WORLDWIDE WEB. The INTERNET Web address to access the Bulletin is:

http://travel.state.gov

From the home page, select the VISA section which contains the Visa Bulletin.

To be **placed on** the Department of State's E-mail subscription list for the "Visa Bulletin", please send an E-mail to the following E-mail address:

listserv@calist.state.gov

and in the message body type:
Subscribe Visa-Bulletin *First name/Last name*
(example: Subscribe Visa-Bulletin Sally Doe)

To be **removed from** the Department of State's E-mail subscription list for the "Visa Bulletin", **send an e-mail message to the following E-mail address:**

listserv@calist.state.gov

and in the message body type: **Signoff Visa-Bulletin**

The Department of State also has available a recorded message with visa cut-off dates which can be heard at: (area code 202) 663-1541. The recording is normally updated by the middle of each month with information on cut-off dates for the following month.

Readers may submit questions regarding Visa Bulletin related items by E-mail at the following address:

VISABULLETIN@STATE.GOV

(This address cannot be used to subscribe to the Visa Bulletin.)

Department of State Publication 9514
CA/VO: September 9, 2010

Copyright © 2011 - GreenCard123.Com by UNorth® - All Rights Reserved

APPENDIX

IV. ONE JOB LIST

Code	Occupation
13-2011.01	Accountants
15-2011.00	Actuaries
23-1021.00	Administrative Law Judges, Adjudicators, and Hearing Officers
11-3011.00	Administrative Services Managers
25-3011.00	Adult Literacy, Remedial Education, and GED Teachers and Instructors
11-2011.00	Advertising and Promotions Managers
17-3021.00	Aerospace Engineering and Operations Technicians
17-2011.00	Aerospace Engineers
13-1011.00	Agents and Business Managers of Artists, Performers, and Athletes
17-2021.00	Agricultural Engineers
25-1041.00	Agricultural Sciences Teachers, Postsecondary
53-2011.00	Airline Pilots, Copilots, and Flight Engineers
29-1061.00	Anesthesiologists
19-1011.00	Animal Scientists
19-3091.01	Anthropologists
25-1061.00	Anthropology and Archeology Teachers, Postsecondary
13-2021.02	Appraisers, Real Estate
11-9011.03	Aquacultural Managers
23-1022.00	Arbitrators, Mediators, and Conciliators
19-3091.02	Archeologists
17-1011.00	Architects, Except Landscape and Naval
25-1031.00	Architecture Teachers, Postsecondary
25-4011.00	Archivists
25-1062.00	Area, Ethnic, and Cultural Studies Teachers, Postsecondary
27-1011.00	Art Directors
25-1121.00	Art, Drama, and Music Teachers, Postsecondary
19-2011.00	Astronomers
29-9091.00	Athletic Trainers
19-2021.00	Atmospheric and Space Scientists
25-1051.00	Atmospheric, Earth, Marine, and Space Sciences Teachers, Postsecondary
25-9011.00	Audio-Visual Collections Specialists
29-1121.00	Audiologists
13-2011.02	Auditors
19-1021.00	Biochemists and Biophysicists
25-1042.00	Biological Science Teachers, Postsecondary
19-4021.00	Biological Technicians
19-1020.01	Biologists
17-2031.00	Biomedical Engineers
27-3021.00	Broadcast News Analysts
13-2031.00	Budget Analysts
25-1011.00	Business Teachers, Postsecondary
17-2041.00	Chemical Engineers
25-1052.00	Chemistry Teachers, Postsecondary
19-2031.00	Chemists
11-1011.00	Chief Executives
21-1021.00	Child, Family, and School Social Workers
29-1011.00	Chiropractors
27-2032.00	Choreographers
19-4061.01	City and Regional Planning Aides
17-2051.00	Civil Engineers
21-2011.00	Clergy
19-3031.02	Clinical Psychologists
27-2022.00	Coaches and Scouts
27-1021.00	Commercial and Industrial Designers
25-1122.00	Communications Teachers, Postsecondary
11-3041.00	Compensation and Benefits Managers
13-1072.00	Compensation, Benefits, and Job Analysis Specialists
15-1011.00	Computer and Information Scientists, Research
11-3021.00	Computer and Information Systems Managers
17-2061.00	Computer Hardware Engineers
15-1021.00	Computer Programmers
25-1021.00	Computer Science Teachers, Postsecondary
15-1071.01	Computer Security Specialists
15-1031.00	Computer Software Engineers, Applications
15-1032.00	Computer Software Engineers, Systems Software
15-1051.00	Computer Systems Analysts
15-1099.02	Computer Systems Engineers/Architects
11-9021.00	Construction Managers
27-3043.04	Copy Writers
13-1041.06	Coroners
13-1051.00	Cost Estimators

Copyright © 2011 - GreenCard123.Com by UNorth® - All Rights Reserved

19-3031.03	Counseling Psychologists	29-1062.00	Family and General Practitioners
13-2041.00	Credit Analysts	25-9021.00	Farm and Home Management Advisors
33-3021.03	Criminal Investigators and Special Agents	13-2051.00	Financial Analysts
25-1111.00	Criminal Justice and Law Enforcement Teachers, Postsecondary	13-2061.00	Financial Examiners
11-9011.02	Crop and Livestock Managers	11-3031.02	Financial Managers, Branch or Department
25-4012.00	Curators	17-2111.02	Fire-Prevention and Protection Engineers
15-1061.00	Database Administrators	45-1011.06	First-Line Supervisors/Managers of Aquacultural Workers
29-1021.00	Dentists, General	41-1012.00	First-Line Supervisors/Managers of Non-Retail Sales Workers
29-1031.00	Dietitians and Nutritionists	33-3031.00	Fish and Game Wardens
27-2012.02	Directors- Stage, Motion Pictures, Television, and Radio	19-1012.00	Food Scientists and Technologists
21-2021.00	Directors, Religious Activities and Education	25-1124.00	Foreign Language and Literature Teachers, Postsecondary
25-1063.00	Economics Teachers, Postsecondary	19-4092.00	Forensic Science Technicians
19-3011.00	Economists	19-1032.00	Foresters
27-3041.00	Editors	25-1043.00	Forestry and Conservation Science Teachers, Postsecondary
11-9032.00	Education Administrators, Elementary and Secondary School	53-6051.08	Freight and Cargo Inspectors
11-9033.00	Education Administrators, Postsecondary	19-3092.00	Geographers
11-9031.00	Education Administrators, Preschool and Child Care Center/Program	25-1064.00	Geography Teachers, Postsecondary
25-1081.00	Education Teachers, Postsecondary	19-4041.01	Geophysical Data Technicians
21-1012.00	Educational, Vocational, and School Counselors	19-2042.00	Geoscientists, Except Hydrologists and Geographers
17-2071.00	Electrical Engineers	25-1191.00	Graduate Teaching Assistants
17-2072.00	Electronics Engineers, Except Computer	27-1024.00	Graphic Designers
25-2021.00	Elementary School Teachers, Except Special Education	21-1091.00	Health Educators
13-1061.00	Emergency Management Specialists	25-1071.00	Health Specialties Teachers, Postsecondary
11-9041.00	Engineering Managers	19-3093.00	Historians
25-1032.00	Engineering Teachers, Postsecondary	25-1125.00	History Teachers, Postsecondary
25-1123.00	English Language and Literature Teachers, Postsecondary	25-1192.00	Home Economics Teachers, Postsecondary
13-1041.01	Environmental Compliance Inspectors	11-3040.00	Human Resources Managers
17-2081.00	Environmental Engineers	19-2043.00	Hydrologists
19-4091.00	Environmental Science and Protection Technicians, Including Health	33-3021.05	Immigration and Customs Inspectors
25-1053.00	Environmental Science Teachers, Postsecondary	17-2112.00	Industrial Engineers
19-2041.00	Environmental Scientists and Specialists, Including Health	17-2111.01	Industrial Safety and Health Engineers
19-1041.00	Epidemiologists	19-3032.00	Industrial-Organizational Psychologists
13-1041.03	Equal Opportunity Representatives and Officers	25-9031.00	Instructional Coordinators
		29-1063.00	Internists, General
		27-3091.00	Interpreters and Translators
		23-1023.00	Judges, Magistrate Judges, and Magistrates

Copyright © 2011 - GreenCard123.Com by UNorth® - All Rights Reserved

25-2012.00	Kindergarten Teachers, Except Special Education
17-1012.00	Landscape Architects
23-2092.00	Law Clerks
25-1112.00	Law Teachers, Postsecondary
23-1011.00	Lawyers
11-1031.00	Legislators
25-4021.00	Librarians
25-1082.00	Library Science Teachers, Postsecondary
13-2071.00	Loan Counselors
13-1081.00	Logisticians
13-1111.00	Management Analysts
17-2121.02	Marine Architects
17-2121.01	Marine Engineers
19-3021.00	Market Research Analysts
11-2021.00	Marketing Managers
21-1013.00	Marriage and Family Therapists
17-2131.00	Materials Engineers
19-2032.00	Materials Scientists
25-1022.00	Mathematical Science Teachers, Postsecondary
15-2091.00	Mathematical Technicians
15-2021.00	Mathematicians
17-2141.00	Mechanical Engineers
29-2011.00	Medical and Clinical Laboratory Technologists
11-9111.00	Medical and Health Services Managers
21-1022.00	Medical and Public Health Social Workers
19-1042.00	Medical Scientists, Except Epidemiologists
13-1121.00	Meeting and Convention Planners
21-1023.00	Mental Health and Substance Abuse Social Workers
21-1014.00	Mental Health Counselors
19-1022.00	Microbiologists
25-2022.00	Middle School Teachers, Except Special and Vocational Education
17-2151.00	Mining and Geological Engineers, Including Mining Safety Engineers
49-3042.00	Mobile Heavy Equipment Mechanics, Except Engines
27-1014.00	Multi-Media Artists and Animators
27-2041.01	Music Directors
11-9121.00	Natural Sciences Managers
15-1071.00	Network and Computer Systems

	Administrators
17-2161.00	Nuclear Engineers
25-1072.00	Nursing Instructors and Teachers, Postsecondary
29-1064.00	Obstetricians and Gynecologists
29-9011.00	Occupational Health and Safety Specialists
29-1122.00	Occupational Therapists
15-2031.00	Operations Research Analysts
29-1041.00	Optometrists
29-1022.00	Oral and Maxillofacial Surgeons
29-1023.00	Orthodontists
29-2091.00	Orthotists and Prosthetists
19-1031.03	Park Naturalists
29-1065.00	Pediatricians, General
13-2052.00	Personal Financial Advisors
13-1071.02	Personnel Recruiters
17-2171.00	Petroleum Engineers
29-1051.00	Pharmacists
25-1126.00	Philosophy and Religion Teachers, Postsecondary
29-1123.00	Physical Therapists
29-1071.00	Physician Assistants
19-2012.00	Physicists
25-1054.00	Physics Teachers, Postsecondary
29-1081.00	Podiatrists
27-3043.05	Poets, Lyricists and Creative Writers
25-1065.00	Political Science Teachers, Postsecondary
19-3094.00	Political Scientists
21-1092.00	Probation Officers and Correctional Treatment Specialists
27-2012.01	Producers
17-2111.03	Product Safety Engineers
27-2012.03	Program Directors
43-9081.00	Proofreaders and Copy Markers
29-1024.00	Prosthodontists
29-1066.00	Psychiatrists
25-1066.00	Psychology Teachers, Postsecondary
11-2031.00	Public Relations Managers
27-3031.00	Public Relations Specialists
11-3061.00	Purchasing Managers
19-1031.02	Range Managers
25-1193.00	Recreation and Fitness Studies Teachers, Postsecondary

Copyright © 2011 – GreenCard123.Com by UNorth® – All Rights Reserved

39-9032.00	Recreation Workers
29-1125.00	Recreational Therapists
21-1015.00	Rehabilitation Counselors
27-3022.00	Reporters and Correspondents
41-3031.02	Sales Agents, Financial Services
41-3031.01	Sales Agents, Securities and Commodities
41-9031.00	Sales Engineers
11-2022.00	Sales Managers
41-4011.00	Sales Representatives, Wholesale and Manufacturing, Technical and Scientific Products
19-3031.01	School Psychologists
25-2031.00	Secondary School Teachers, Except Special and Vocational Education
27-1027.00	Set and Exhibit Designers
11-9151.00	Social and Community Service Managers
19-4061.00	Social Science Research Assistants
25-1113.00	Social Work Teachers, Postsecondary
19-3041.00	Sociologists
25-1067.00	Sociology Teachers, Postsecondary
15-1099.01	Software Quality Assurance Engineers and Testers
19-1013.00	Soil and Plant Scientists
19-1031.01	Soil and Water Conservationists
25-2042.00	Special Education Teachers, Middle School
25-2041.00	Special Education Teachers, Preschool, Kindergarten, and Elementary School
25-2043.00	Special Education Teachers, Secondary School
29-1127.00	Speech-Language Pathologists
15-2041.00	Statisticians
11-3071.02	Storage and Distribution Managers
21-1011.00	Substance Abuse and Behavioral Disorder Counselors
29-1067.00	Surgeons
19-3022.00	Survey Researchers
17-1022.00	Surveyors
27-2012.04	Talent Directors
27-3042.00	Technical Writers
11-3042.00	Training and Development Managers
13-1073.00	Training and Development Specialists
11-3031.01	Treasurers and Controllers
19-3051.00	Urban and Regional Planners
29-1131.00	Veterinarians
25-2023.00	Vocational Education Teachers, Middle School
25-1194.00	Vocational Education Teachers, Postsecondary
25-2032.00	Vocational Education Teachers, Secondary School
19-1023.00	Zoologists and Wildlife Biologists

Copyright © 2011 – GreenCard123.Com by UNorth® – All Rights Reserved

APPENDIX

V. FREQUENTLY ASKED QUESTIONS

Q: What if my status changes

A:If your status changes in the form of AOS (Adjustment of Status) you will be disqualified from the Lottery Visa. In other words, if after applying for US Lottery, you become eligible for another type of visa (e.g. marry a US Citizen), your eligibility under Lottery Visa is invalid since you'll receive AOS under different Category.

Q: How is the Diversity Visa Year Number coded?

A: DV-2010 means that should you in the drawing, you'll be receiving your actual visa in 2010. DV-2011 means that you'll will receive a visa in 2011 should your application be drawn as winner and (and assuming that you have all the documentation necessary to be qualified and are not inadmissible, etc)

Q: How many people participate in the Lottery Application every year?

A: This number changes every year since there is no actual cap-limit on the number of applicants for the diversity visa lottery (while there is a 50,000 limit on the actual visa number issued for the winners of diversity visa app.,

In 2008, 8.9 million people applied for the lottery application

Q: Is there any data available regarding where people physically apply for visa from? And whether is assisted or not?

A: According to House Judiciary committee, in 2004 approximately 50% of the applicants were from the United States and 70% of applicants used a facilitator to assist with the registration (Those agents that charge fee to simply apply on your behalf over the internet, and of course not you !) .
Source:
http://judiciary.house.gov/Legacy/patterson042904.htm

Q: Why is the lottery program Free?

A: This is not correct. Diversity Lottery visa is not free at all. It is only free to apply for your initial application. There has been debates in the past to charge small fee to cover administration cost and at the same time, this may alone reduce number of fraud cases (e.g. by monitoring duplicate method of payment or the fact that the payment source would reveal partial identity, etc). However, as of 2010 there is no fee to apply for the Visa Lottery application.

This does not mean that USCIS is acting like Charity. The fee is actually covered by all the winners of lottery. All the winners need to pay fee (Currently $375) per application per person to apply for green card

Q: What if my spouse is from a different country

A: As explained in chapter 2, if you and your spouse is born in an eligible country, each one of you can participate in Lottery program and submit two separate form to USCIS (in which one your spouse would be the primary, claiming you as spouse, and in the other you would be the primary, listing your spouse. You both will choose the country of birth as your "chargeability country"

However, if you or your spouse are not born in an eligible country, but one of you is born in an eligible country, you may still file via the same process but your "Chargeability country" would be the country that makes you eligible (either yours or your spouse's)

Q: What is NACARA?

A: As of 1997, United States enacted Nicaraguan and Central American Relieve Act (NACARA). As part of this act, an additional 5,000 visa are

Copyright © 2011 - GreenCard123.Com by UNorth® - All Rights Reserved

allocated solely to Nicaraguan and Central American. Department of States defines NACARA as follows:

"The Nicaraguan and Central American Relief Act (NACARA) passed by Congress in November 1997 stipulated that up to 5,000 of the 55,000 annually-allocated diversity visas be made available for use under the NACARA program. The reduction of the limit of available visas to 50,000 began with DV-2000. "

Source <http://travel.state.gov/visa/immigrants/types/types_4574.html>

Q: Is there a time difference if I file my case inside the United States and through adjustment of Status compared to if I file my case outside and through Embassy/consular?
A: Hard to say. Some embassies have a faster turnaround time and some don't (mostly dependent on how busy the embassy is)When you file your application with USCIS there has been times that unexpected things may happen and your application gets delayed for no reason (e.g. backlogged). Unfortunately, once your application gets stuck there is almost no way to get it out of there. However, at the same time, USCIS personnel (especially during the interview) are known to be much nicer since you are already inside the United States and the fraudulent rate drops dramatically. Embassy interviews are known to be more difficult.

Q: How long do I have to enter United States once my Visa is approved?
A: You need to enter United States within six months of receiving your Visa. That is, unless beyond extreme emergency.

Q: My child turned 21 after we submit the application for Lottery visa, and I'm notified as a winner Can he/she apply for green card ?
A: Technically, your child is 21 and ineligible to apply for green card since he/she is considered independent. However, law does provide some protection that allows you to subtract the days between the date you received your winning notification letter, and the date you were first eligible to apply for Diversity Visa from the age of your child. Sounds confusing? See the example below

Example: John and Mary have a daughter named Rose. The Diversity visa lottery program opened on October 01, 2010. They apply for Diversity Visa Application on November 20, 2010. Rose's birthday is December 10, 1989 (meaning that she will turn 21 in March 20, 2010). Later John is notified as winner of lottery on May 30, 2011 and they apply for green card with interview date of August 10, 2011.

Technically, by August 10, 2011 when they are all at the interview, Rose is already 21 (143 days to be exact). However, the law allows the duration between October 01, 2010 (the application availability date) and winner notification letter date (May 30, 2011) be deducted from her age, or 241 days. That would put her about 3 months prior to becoming ineligible and thus the application is approved for John, Mary, and Rose.

If the above numbers don't work for you unfortunately, your child is considered independent and is not eligible to receive green card . The parents however are still eligible to receive green card

Q: What is the minimum age to apply for Lottery application independently?
A: As of 2010 there is no specific age requirement to apply for Diversity Visa. That said, keep in mind that there are Education or Job experience that normally prevents anyone under age of 18 to apply to the program. Exceptions apply. For example, if you completed your high school earl or you have eligible job-experience prior turning to 18.

Q: An agent offers me to increase my chances in winning if I chose their company. Is that correct?
A: Keep in mind that there is no need for an agent to apply for your Lottery application. Lottery program has been design with as ease-as-

Copyright © 2011 - GreenCard123.Com by UNorth® - All Rights Reserved

possible steps to make it "do-it-yourself". Your can save some money by doing so as well.

Either way, it is highly recommended to perform a thorough research, before selecting an agent.

Q: Would I be able to apply if I'm on a non-immigrant visa currently in the US?

A: Yes, if you are on a non-immigrant visa (e.g. H1 visa) you can still apply for Diversity Visa, assuming that you qualify for the other requirements and are from eligible country. That's assuming that your current visa has not expired and you are currently legally in the United States. If you are currently illegal in the US or in removal proceeding, seek an experienced attorney immediately.

Q: If I don't win the lottery in the current visa year, would I need to re-apply or my application would be included?

A: Yes, you'll need to re-apply to the Lottery program every year in order to be considered for the drawing.

Q: I'm born in one of the countries that is identified as state sponsors of terrorism. Would I need any special paperwork?

A: For applying to Lottery program, no other paperwork is required.

After you win the lottery, if you are born in one of the countries that are identified as state sponsors of terrorism (as of 2010, Cuba, Libya, Syria, and Iran) USCIS generally requires through background check but no special form is designated for those countries for the lottery program.

Q: If I don't win, would I get any notification?

A: Kentucky Service Center will only notify the applicants that have been selected in the drawing. You'll not receive any notification if you are not the winner.

Q: My child is turning to 21 years after I submitted my application. Do I need to worry?

A: If you're notified as a Lottery winner and you or your child are/is turning 21, you should notify embassy immediately. They can expedite processing of your application, assuming that your priority date is "current"

In addition, under certain circumstances, special exception applies to this rule: If you win the lottery you'll be able to deduct number of days from the date you filed your application until the date of interview, if your child was not 21years of age.

Q: Some agencies claim that they can increase my chances in the lottery and for that they request large sum of money. Is that for real?

A: As the term "lottery" refers, It is generally impossible to select the winners of lottery. Kentucky service center of USCIS is specially staffed to randomly select the candidates. Any agency, individual, attorney, or entity that is claiming they can increase your chances in winning lottery by other means than those mentioned in the book is purely false advertisement.

Some of these agencies may be sending your application more than once, thinking that would increase your chance. Beware that such action would disqualify you from the entire lottery year.

Q: I was born in one of the ineligible countries but my wife was not so I claimed my wife's country to apply for Diversity Visa. We were among the winners but my wife does not want to come to US. Can I apply alone?

A: No, if you claimed your wife's country of birth as your chargeability country, you and your wife

Copyright © 2011 - GreenCard123.Com by UNorth® - All Rights Reserved

must apply simultaneously and enter United States together.

Q: If the selectee dies, what happens?
A: If the selectee (primary applicant) dies, the visa eligibility is also terminated.

Q: Isn't the Lottery visa an unfair visa because it is discriminating other nationalities
A: The opponents of the Visa Lottery argue that visa is targeting certain population and races in the world which basically contradicts the basic believe of American people against discrimination by favoring certain races more than others. At the same time, the reason diversity visa was placed at the first place was the fact that certain ethnic groups (majority) were applying so many visas that minorities did not have chance to get in line.

The other argument about the Lottery visa is the fact that there is no specific educational or "outstanding" status is needed to improve the country. In other words, any one from any background, as long as he/she has high-school diploma can potentially be given green card to United States. Of course, filtering people on basis of education itself is discriminatory which

Q: I was born in one of the ineligible countries but my spouse is born in eligible country. Can I apply?
A: As explained earlier in the book, you are allowed to claim your spouse's birth place if that makes you eligible

Q: My Country Name is not in use, what should I choose?
A: Use the Current name of the country. For example if you were born in Yugoslavia, but that country no longer exists, you should select "Slovenia" as your Country.

Q: When I'm selected as green card Lottery Winner, do I automatically get green card ?
A: No. Remember that although the maximum visas available is 50,000 , the number of winners selected is 100,000. In other words, 100,000 people will be notified that they have been selected as a winner. The prediction is that by the time everyone applies and considering the people who may be disqualified or change their mind to apply, the actual number of visa applicants will reduce to close to 50,000. Once you are selected, you'll be assigned a "Rank Number". You'll need to wait until your rank number is "current," meaning that you can apply for the visa. Assuming that there are still visas left (out of 50,000) and you are a qualified candidate, you'll be issued a visa. That being the case, it is highly recommended that if you're selected as a winner, you must act quickly or may loose your chance.

Q: What if my photo is with Cover?
A: Normally, the face should not be covered with any obstacle, such as hat, religious hijab, etc, unless the cover is worn on daily basis for purpose of Religious. Please contact USCIS/State.GOV for details of you're planning to supply pictures with cover. Photos with cover still must adhere to other photo requirements to be fully met (e.g. background, contract, ...)

Q: What if I have a Criminal History?
A: If you are in any way inadmissible (including having a criminal record, etc) you may be eligible to file a Waiver. Consult with your attorney for more detail.

Q: My country allows for multiple wife/husband. How can I proceed?

Copyright © 2011 - GreenCard123.Com by UNorth® - All Rights Reserved

A: Having more than one wife/husband is called Polygamy. US Law does not allow Polygamy. In your immigration form, you'll see a question on whether or not you practice polygamy and checking the box would make you ineligible to apply for visa.

A spouse is a legally wedded husband or wife. Cohabiting partners do not qualify as spouses for immigration purposes. Common-law spouses may qualify as spouses for immigration purposes depending on the laws of the country where the common-law marriage occurs. In cases of polygamy only the first spouse qualifies as a spouse for immigration.

US law does not allow polygamy. If you were married before, you and your spouse must show that you ended (terminated) all previous marriages before your current marriage. The death and divorce documents that show termination of marriages must be legal and verifiable in the country that issued them. Divorces must be final. In cases of legal marriage to two or more spouses at the same time, or marriages overlapping for a period of time, you may file only for the first spouse.

Q: What are some of the Fraud Cases that I should be aware of?
A: Should you win your visa, and you're offered any type of compensation for the visa that you won, you should know for sure that this is a scheme by some foreign companies to act as middle man to buy winning applications from people who cannot afford to pay for the visa process and sell to the rich community by switching the application.
(Source http://judiciary.house.gov/Legacy/patterson042904.htm)

Although recently KCC has implemented electronic application program to check for all photographs in the system and application information to decide whether or not the entry is legitimate and/or duplicate and if so would reject the application.

Q: I don't have high-school diploma but have a GED Certificate or correspondence program. Is that acceptable?
A: No, USCIS is clear to specifically ask for Formal education of First and Second level elementary school (Equal to 12 year education in US). Documentary proof of this education completion must be provided to consulate at the time of the interview.

Q: What happens if Wife and Husband Participate and both supply separate applications and they both win?
A: Although very unlikely, if both applicants win, you should choose the applicant with the lower Ranking number, thus shortening your wait time until visa becomes current, and apply via the lower ranking visa.

Copyright © 2011 - GreenCard123.Com by UNorth® - All Rights Reserved

THIS PAGE WAS INTENTIONALLY LEFT BLANK

Copyright © 2011 – GreenCard123.Com by UNorth® – All Rights Reserved

APPENDIX

VI. GETTING TECHNICAL

LEGAL HISTORY:

In December 2005, the United States House of Representatives voted 273-148 to add an amendment to the border enforcement bill H.R. 4437 abolishing the DV. Opponents of the lottery said it was susceptible to fraud and was a way for terrorists to enter the country. The Senate never passed the bill.

In March 2007, Congressman Bob Goodlatte (R-VA) introduced H.R. 1430, which would eliminate the diversity visa program.

In June 2007, the U.S. House passed H.R. 2764 to eliminate funding for the program, and the Senate did likewise in September.[10] However, the final version of this bill with amendments, signed into law on December 26, 2007, did not include the removal of funds for the program. H.R. 2764

Several attempts have been made over the last several years to eliminate the lottery. Although H.R. 2764 was an appropriation bill and could only cut funds for the lottery during one fiscal year, this was the first time that both the House and the Senate passed a bill to halt the diversity visa program.

Rep. Bob Goodlatte (R-VA) reintroduced his Security and Fairness Enhancement for America Act (formerly H.R. 1430, now H.R. 2305) on May 7, 2009. The bill amends the Immigration and Nationality Act to eliminate the diversity immigrant program completely.

Rep. Sheila Jackson-Lee (D-TX) introduced the Save America Comprehensive Immigration Act of 2009 (H.R. 264) on January 7, 2009. The bill would increase the number of diversity visas from 55,000 to 110,000 per year.[11]

In this section, a copy of Immigration and Nationality Act 203 (C) regarding allocation of Visas to Diversity Application is provided.

Further Readings:

SECURITY AND FAIRNESS ENHANCEMENT FORAMERICA ACT OF 2003 - A BILL TO ELIMINATE DIVERSITY VISA PROGRAM http://frwebgate.access.gpo.gov/cgi-bin/getdoc.cgi?dbname=108_cong_reports&docid=f:hr747.108.pdf

Diversity Visa Immigration Code – INA ACT 201

INA: ACT 201 - WORLDWIDE LEVEL OF IMMIGRATION 1/

§ 201. [8 U.S.C.A. § 1151]

(a) In general – Exclusive of aliens described in subsection (b), aliens born in a foreign state or dependent area who may be issued immigrant visas or who may otherwise acquire the status of an alien lawfully admitted to the United States for permanent residence are limited to –

(1) family-sponsored immigrants described in section 203(a) (or who are admitted under section 211(a) on the basis of a prior issuance of a visa to their accompanying parent under section 203(a)) in a number not to exceed in any fiscal year the number specified in subsection (c) for that year, and not to exceed in any of the first 3 quarters of any fiscal year 27 percent of the worldwide level under such subsection for all of such fiscal year;

(2) employment-based immigrants described in section 203(b) (or who are admitted under section 211(a) on the basis of a prior issuance of a visa to their accompanying parent under section 203(b)),

Copyright © 2011 - GreenCard123.Com by UNorth® - All Rights Reserved

in a number not to exceed in any fiscal year the number specified in subsection (d) for that year, and not to exceed in any of the first 3 quarters of any fiscal year 27 percent of the worldwide level under such subsection for all of such fiscal year; and

(3) for fiscal years beginning with fiscal year 1995, diversity immigrants described in section 203(c) (or who are admitted under section 211(a) on the basis of a prior issuance of a visa to their accompanying parent under section 203(c)) in a number not to exceed in any fiscal year the number specified in subsection (e) for that year, and not to exceed in any of the first 3 quarters of any fiscal year 27 percent of the worldwide level under such subsection for all of such fiscal year.

(b) Aliens Not Subject to Direct Numerical Limitations – Aliens described in this subsection, who are not subject to the worldwide levels or numerical limitations of subsection (a), are as follows:

(1)(A) Special immigrants described in subparagraph (A) or (B) of section 101(a)(27).

(B) Aliens who are admitted under section 207 or whose status is adjusted under section 209.

(C) Aliens whose status is adjusted to permanent residence under section 210 or 245A.

(D) Aliens whose removal is canceled under section 240A(a).

(E) Aliens provided permanent resident status under section 249.

(2)(A)(i) Immediate relatives – For purposes of this subsection, the term "immediate relatives" means the children, spouses, and parents of a citizen of the United States, except that, in the case of parents, such citizens shall be at least 21 years of age. In the case of an alien who was the spouse of a citizen of the United States for at least 2 years at the time of the citizen's death and was not legally separated from the citizen at the time of the citizen's death, the alien (and each child of the alien) shall be considered, for purposes of this subsection, to remain an immediate relative after the date of the citizen's death but only if the spouse files a petition under section 204(a)(1)(A)(ii) within 2 years after such date and only until the date the spouse remarries. **3/** For purposes of this clause, an alien who has filed a petition under clause (iii) or (iv) of section 204(a)(1)(A) of this Act remains an immediate relative in the event that the United States citizen spouse or parent loses United States citizenship on account of the abuse.

(ii) Aliens admitted under section 211(a) on the basis of a prior issuance of a visa to their accompanying parent who is such an immediate relative.

(B) Aliens born to an alien lawfully admitted for permanent residence during a temporary visit abroad.

(c) Worldwide Level of Family-Sponsored Immigrants

(1)(A) The worldwide level of family-sponsored immigrants under this subsection for a fiscal year is, subject to subparagraph (B), equal to –

> **(i)** 480,000, minus

> **(ii)** the sum of the number computed under paragraph (2) and the number computed under paragraph (4), plus

> **(iii)** the number (if any) computed under paragraph (3).

(B)(i) For each of fiscal years 1992, 1993, and 1994, 465,000 shall be substituted for 480,000 in subparagraph (A)(i).

Copyright © 2011 - GreenCard123.Com by UNorth® - All Rights Reserved

(ii) In no case shall the number computed under subparagraph (A) be less than 226,000.

(2) The number computed under this paragraph for a fiscal year is the sum of the number of aliens described in subparagraphs (A) and (B) of subsection (b)(2) who were issued immigrant visas or who otherwise acquired the status of aliens lawfully admitted to the United States for permanent residence in the previous fiscal year.

(3)(A) The number computed under this paragraph for fiscal year 1992 is zero.

(B) The number computed under this paragraph for fiscal year 1993 is the difference (if any) between the worldwide level established under paragraph (1) for the previous fiscal year and the number of visas issued under section 203(a) during that fiscal year.

(C) The number computed under this paragraph for a subsequent fiscal year is the difference (if any) between the maximum number of visas which may be issued under section 203(b) (relating to employment-based immigrants) during the previous fiscal year and the number of visas issued under that section during that year.

(4) The number computed under this paragraph for a fiscal year (beginning with fiscal year 1999) is the number of aliens who were paroled into the United States under section 212(d)(5) in the second preceding fiscal year-

> **(A)** who did not depart from the United States (without advance parole) within 365 days; and

> **(B)** who (i) did not acquire the status of aliens lawfully admitted to the United States for permanent residence in the two preceding fiscal years, or (ii) acquired such status in such years under a

provision of law (other than section 201(b)) which exempts such adjustment from the numerical limitation on the worldwide level of immigration under this section.

(5) If any alien described in paragraph (4) (other than an alien described in paragraph (4)(B)(ii)) is subsequently admitted as an alien lawfully admitted for permanent residence, such alien shall not again be considered for purposes of paragraph (1). **2/**

(d) Worldwide level of employment-based immigrants

(1) The worldwide level of employment-based immigrants under this subsection for a fiscal year is equal to –

> **(A)** 140,000 plus

> **(B)** the number computed under paragraph (2).

(2)(A) The number computer under this paragraph for fiscal year 1992 is zero.

(B) The number computed under this paragraph for fiscal year 1993 is the difference (if any) between the worldwide level established under paragraph (1) for the previous fiscal year and the number of visas issued under section 203(b) during that fiscal year.

(C) The number computed under this paragraph for a subsequent fiscal year is the difference (if any) between the maximum number of visas which may be issued under section 203(a) (relating to family-sponsored immigrants) during the previous fiscal year and the number of visas issued under that section during that year.

(e) Worldwide level of diversity immigrants –

Copyright © 2011 - GreenCard123.Com by UNorth® - All Rights Reserved

The worldwide level of diversity immigrants is equal to 55,000 for each fiscal year.

(f) Rules for determining whether certain aliens are immediate relatives 4/

(1) Age on petition filing date – Except as provided in paragraphs (2) and (3), for purposes of subsection (b)(2)(A)(i), a determination of whether an alien satisfies the age requirement in the matter preceding subparagraph (A) of section 101(b)(1) shall be made using the age of the alien on the date on which the petition is filed with the Attorney General under section 204 to classify the alien as an immediate relative under subsection (b)(2)(A)(i).

(2) Age on parent's naturalization date – In the case of a petition under section 204 initially filed for an alien child's classification as a family-sponsored immigrant under section 203(a)(2)(A), based on the child's parent being lawfully admitted for permanent residence, if the petition is later converted, due to the naturalization of the parent, to a petition to classify the alien as an immediate relative under subsection (b)(2)(A)(i), the determination described in paragraph (1) shall be made using the age of the alien on the date of the parent's naturalization.

(3) Age on marriage termination date – In the case of a petition under section 204 initially filed for an alien's classification as a family-sponsored immigrant under section 203(a)(3), based on the alien's being a married son or daughter of a citizen, if the petition is later converted, due to the legal termination of the alien's marriage, to a petition to classify the alien as an immediate relative under subsection (b)(2)(A)(i) or as an unmarried son or daughter of a citizen under section 203(a)(1), the determination described in paragraph (1) shall be made using the age of the alien on the date of the termination of the marriage.

(4) Application to self-petitions 5/ – Paragraphs (1) through (3) shall apply to self-petitioners and derivatives of self-petitioners.

FOOTNOTES FOR SECTION 201

INA ACT 201 FN 1

FN1   This section was amended in its entirety by § 101(a) of IMMACT and further amended by § 302(a)(1) of MTINA.

INA ACT 201 FN 2

FN 2   Paragraphs (4) and (5) added by § 603 of IIRIRA.

INA ACT 201 FN 3

FN 3   Language inserted at the end by section 1507(a)(3) of Public Law 106-386, dated October 28, 2000.

INA ACT 201 FN 4

FN 4   Paragraph (f) added by section 2 of the Child Status Protection Act, Public Law 107-208, dated August 6, 2002. Effective Date: The amendments made by this Act shall take effect on the date of the enactment of this Act (August 6, 2002) and shall apply to any alien who is a derivative beneficiary or any other beneficiary of –

(1) a petition for classification under section 204 of the Immigration and Nationality Act (8 U.S.C. 1154) approved before such date but only if a final determination has not been made on the beneficiary's application for an immigrant visa or adjustment of status to lawful permanent residence pursuant to such approved petition;

(2) a petition for classification under section 204 of the Immigration and Nationality Act (8 U.S.C. 1154) pending on or after such date; or

Copyright © 2011 - GreenCard123.Com by UNorth® - All Rights Reserved

(3) an application pending before the Department of Justice or the Department of State on or after such

INA ACT 201 FN 5

FN 5   Section 805(b)(1) of Public Law 109-162 dated January 5, 2006, is amended by adding paragraph (4) to section 201(f) of the Immigration and Nationality Act.

Diversity Visa Immigration Code – INA ACT 203

INA: ACT 203 - ALLOCATION OF IMMIGRANT VISAS
Sec. 203. [8 U.S.C. 1153]

US DEPARTMENT OF STATE
IMMIGRATION AND NATIONALITY ACT
TITLE II - IMMIGRATION CHAPTER 1 - SELECTION SYSTEM

(c) Diversity Immigrants

(1) In general – Except as provided in paragraph (2), aliens subject to the worldwide level specified in section 201(e) for diversity immigrants shall be allotted visas each fiscal year as follows:

(A) Determination of preference immigration – The Attorney General shall determine for the most recent previous 5-fiscal-year period for which data are available, the total number of aliens who are natives of each foreign state and who (i) were admitted or otherwise provided lawful permanent resident status (other than under this subsection) and (ii) were subject to the numerical limitations of section 201(a) (other than paragraph (3) thereof) or who were

admitted or otherwise provided lawful permanent resident status as an immediate relative or other alien described in section 201(b)(2).

(B) Identification of high-admission and low-admission regions and high-admission and low-admission states – The Attorney General –

(i) shall identify –

(I) each region (each in this paragraph referred to as a "high-admission region") for which the total of the numbers determined under subparagraph (A) for states in the region is greater than 1/6 of the total of all such numbers, and

(II) each other region (each in this paragraph referred to as a "low-admission region"); and

(ii) shall identify –

(I) each foreign state for which the number determined under subparagraph (A) is greater than 50,000 (each such state in this paragraph referred to as a "high-admission state"), and

(II) each other foreign state (each such state in this paragraph referred to as a "low-admission state").

(C) Determination of percentage of worldwide immigration attributable to high-admission regions – The Attorney General shall determine the percentage of the total of the numbers determined under subparagraph (A) that are numbers for foreign states in high-admission regions.

Copyright © 2011 - GreenCard123.Com by UNorth® - All Rights Reserved

(D) Determination of regional populations excluding high-admission states and ratios of populations of regions within low-admission regions and high-admission regions – The Attorney General shall determine –

(i) based on available estimates for each region, the total population of each region not including the population of any high-admission state;

(ii) for each low-admission region, the ratio of the population of the region determined under clause (i) to the total of the populations determined under such clause for all the low-admission regions; and

(iii) for each high-admission region, the ratio of the population of the region determined under clause (i) to the total of the populations determined under such clause for all the high-admission regions.

(E) Distribution of visas

(i) No visas for natives of high-admission states – The percentage of visas made available under this paragraph to natives of a high-admission state is 0.

(ii) For low-admission states in low-admission regions – Subject to clauses (iv) and (v), the percentage of visas made available under this paragraph to natives (other than natives of a high-admission state) in a low-admission region is the product of –

(I) the percentage determined under subparagraph (C), and

(II) the population ratio for that region determined under subparagraph (D)(ii).

(iii) For low-admission states in high-admission regions – Subject to clauses (iv) and (v), the percentage of visas made available under this paragraph to natives (other than natives of a high-admission state) in a high-admission region is the product of –

(I) 100 percent minus the percentage determined under subparagraph (C), and

(II) the population ratio for that region determined under subparagraph (D)(iii).

(iv) Redistribution of unused visa numbers – If the Secretary of State estimates that the number of immigrant visas to be issued to natives in any region for a fiscal year under this paragraph is less than the number of immigrant visas made available to such natives under this paragraph for the fiscal year, subject to clause (v), the excess visa numbers shall be made available to natives (other than natives of a high-admission state) of the other regions in proportion to the percentages otherwise specified in clauses (ii) and (iii).

(v) Limitation on visas for natives of a single foreign state – The percentage of visas made available under this paragraph to natives of any single foreign state for any fiscal year shall not exceed 7 percent .

(F) Region defined – Only for purposes of administering the diversity program under this subsection, Northern Ireland shall be treated as a separate foreign state, each colony

Copyright © 2011 - GreenCard123.Com by UNorth® - All Rights Reserved

or other component or dependent area of a foreign state overseas from the foreign state shall be treated as part of the foreign state, and the areas described in each of the following clauses shall be considered to be a separate region:

(i) Africa.
(ii) Asia.
(iii) Europe.
(iv) North America (other than Mexico).
(v) Oceania.
(vi) South America, Mexico, Central America, and the Caribbean.

(2) Requirement of education or work experience – An alien is not eligible for a visa under this subsection unless the alien –

(A) has at least a high school education or its equivalent, or

(B) has, within 5 years of the date of application for a visa under this subsection, at least 2 years of work experience in an occupation which requires at least 2 years of training or experience.

(3) Maintenance of information – The Secretary of State shall maintain information on the age, occupation, education level, and other relevant characteristics of immigrants issued visas under this subsection.

(d) Treatment of Family Members – A spouse or child as defined in subparagraph (A), (B), (C), (D), or (E) of section 101(b)(1) shall, if not otherwise entitled to an immigrant status and the immediate issuance of a visa under subsection (a), (b), or (c), be entitled to the same status, and the same order of consideration provided in the respective subsection, if accompanying or following to join, the spouse or parent.

(e) Order of Consideration

(1) Immigrant visas made available under subsection (a) or (b) shall be issued to eligible immigrants in the order in which a petition in behalf of each such immigrant is filed with the Attorney General (or in the case of special immigrants under section 101(a)(27)(D), with the Secretary of State) as provided in section 204(a).

(2) Immigrant visa numbers made available under subsection (c) (relating to diversity immigrants) shall be issued to eligible qualified immigrants strictly in a random order established by the Secretary of State for the fiscal year involved.

(3) Waiting lists of applicants for visas under this section shall be maintained in accordance with regulations prescribed by the Secretary of State.

(f) Authorization for issuance – In the case of any alien claiming in his application for an immigrant visa to be described in section 201(b)(2) or in subsection (a), (b), or (c) of this section, the consular officer shall not grant such status until he has been authorized to do so as provided by section 204.

(g) Lists – For purposes of carrying out the Secretary's responsibilities in the orderly administration of this section, the Secretary of State may make reasonable estimates of the anticipated numbers of visas to be issued during any quarter of any fiscal year within each of the categories under subsections (a), (b), and (c) and to rely upon such estimates in authorizing the issuance of visas. The Secretary of State shall terminate the registration of any alien who fails to apply for an immigrant visa within one year following notification to the alien of the availability of such visa, but the Secretary shall reinstate the registration of any such alien who establishes within 2 years following the date of notification of the availability of such visa that such failure to apply was due to circumstances beyond the alien's control.

(h) Rules for determining whether certain aliens are children

(1) In general – For purposes of subsections (a)(2)(A)

Copyright © 2011 - GreenCard123.Com by UNorth® - All Rights Reserved

and (d), a determination of whether an alien satisfies the age requirement in the matter preceding subparagraph (A) of section 101(b)(1) shall be made using –

(A) the age of the alien on the date on which an immigrant visa number becomes available for such alien (or, in the case of subsection (d), the date on which an immigrant visa number became available for the alien's parent), but only if the alien has sought to acquire the status of an alien lawfully admitted for permanent residence within one year of such availability; reduced by

(B) the number of days in the period during which the applicable petition described in paragraph (2) was pending.

(2) Petitions described – The petition described in this paragraph is –

(A) with respect to a relationship described in subsection (a)(2)(A), a petition filed under section 204 for classification of an alien child under subsection (a)(2)(A); or

(B) with respect to an alien child who is a derivative beneficiary under subsection (d), a petition filed under section 204 for classification of the alien's parent under subsection (a), (b), or (c).

(3) Retention of priority date – If the age of an alien is determined under paragraph (1) to be 21 years of age or older for the purposes of subsections (a)(2)(A) and (d), the alien's petition shall automatically be converted to the appropriate category and the alien shall retain the original priority date issued upon receipt of the original petition.

(4) Application to self-petitions – Paragraphs (1) through (3) shall apply to self-petitioners and derivatives of self-petitioners.

Copyright © 2011 – GreenCard123.Com by UNorth® – All Rights Reserved

APPENDIX

VII. FRAUD AND SCAM IN IMMIGRATION PROCESS

Copyright © 2011 - GreenCard123.Com by UNorth® - All Rights Reserved

A. DON'T BE A VICTIM OF IMMIGRATION FRAUD
(Source: USCIS.gov)

Notarios, Notary Publics and Immigration Consultants

Notarios, notary publics and immigration consultants may NOT represent you before USCIS. While in many other countries the word "Notario"" means that the individual is an attorney, this is not true in the United States and they may not provide the same services that an attorney or accredited representative does.

A notario may NOT:

- Give you legal advice on what immigration benefit you may apply for or what to say in an immigration interview
- Hold him or herself out as qualified in legal matters or in immigration and naturalization procedure

If you are seeking help with immigration questions, you should be very careful before paying money to a non-attorney. Please use the following guidelines when selecting an individual to represent you:

How to Protect Yourself from Becoming a Victim:

- DO NOT sign blank applications, petitions or other papers.
- DO NOT sign documents that you do not understand.
- DO NOT sign documents that contain false statements or inaccurate information.
- DO NOT let anyone keep your original documents.
- DO NOT make payments to a representative without getting a receipt.
- DO NOT pay more than a nominal fee to non-attorneys or make payments on the internet.
- DO obtain copies of all documents prepared or submitted for you.
- DO verify an attorney's or accredited representative's eligibility to represent you.
- DO report any representative's unlawful activity to USCIS, State Bar Associations and/or State Offices of Attorneys General.

For more information on how to report unlawful activity, please visit the National Association of Attorney Generals website and the American Bar Association. These websites contain contact information for your state Attorney General or State Board.

Attorneys and Accredited Representatives

You may choose to have someone, such as an attorney or accredited representative of a recognized organization, represent you when filing an application or petition with USCIS. Only attorneys and accredited representatives may communicate on your behalf regarding your application with USCIS. For more information on finding an attorney or accredited representative to help you file an application or petition, please see the "Finding Legal Advice" link on the left side of this page. (http://www.uscis.gov/files/nativedocuments/USCIS%20fraud%20brochure.pdf)

B. FTC CONSUMER ALERT REGARDING DIVERSITY VISA LOTTERY
Diversity Visa Lottery Fraud and Rip-Offs:

Copyright © 2011 - GreenCard123.Com by UNorth® - All Rights Reserved

FTC Consumer Alert

Federal Trade Commission ■ Bureau of Consumer Protection ■ Division of Consumer & Business Education

Diversity Visa Lottery:
Read the Rules, Avoid the Rip-Offs

If you or someone you know is trying to get a green card — the right to live in the United States permanently — be on the lookout for unscrupulous businesses and attorneys. They'll claim that, for a fee, they can make it easier to enter the U. S. State Department's annual Diversity Visa (DV) lottery (also known as the "green card lottery") or increase your chances of winning the DV lottery.

Each year, the State Department conducts a lottery through its DV program to distribute applications for 50,000 immigrant visas. Winners of the lottery have a chance to apply for an immigrant visa, which can be used to enter the U. S. Winners are selected randomly, and there is no fee to enter the lottery.

Entries to the DV lottery must be submitted online at www.dvlottery.state.gov. (This site is only accessible during the application period.) Paper entries or mail-in requests will not be accepted. Lottery entrants must include a passport-style digital photograph and separate digital photographs of any spouse and children under 21 years of age. Group photographs are not allowed. Check with the State Department for technical requirements of the digital photograph.

Entries are accepted for a limited time. **For the DV-2009 Lottery (to be conducted in 2007), the application period is from October 3, 2007, through December 2, 2007.** DV-2009 visas will be issued between October 1, 2008 and September 30, 2009. Check with the State Department for entry dates for future DV lotteries.

Entrants may submit only one entry during any particular DV lottery; those who submit more than one entry will be disqualified. Spouses may submit separate entries, however, if each meets the eligibility requirements. If only one spouse is selected, the other may enter the country on the Diversity Visa of the winning spouse.

The DV lottery has two eligibility requirements:

1. **The entrant must be from an eligible country.** You must have been born in an eligible country, or have parents who were born in eligible countries and who were not residents of your country of birth, when you were born. For example, your parents might have lived temporarily in the ineligible country because of their jobs.

   Every year, the State Department announces the countries whose natives are ineligible for application. **For the DV-2009 lottery, natives of the following countries are not eligible to apply:** Brazil, Canada, China (mainland born), Colombia, Dominican Republic, Ecuador, El Salvador, Guatemala, Haiti, India, Jamaica, Mexico, Pakistan, Peru, Philippines, Poland, Russia, South Korea, United Kingdom (except Northern Ireland) and its dependent territories,

Copyright © 2011 - GreenCard123.Com by UNorth® - All Rights Reserved

and Vietnam. Persons born in Hong Kong, Macau, and Taiwan are eligible. Applicants should check with the State Department to determine the ineligible countries for future DV lotteries.

2. **Entrants must meet an education or training requirement.** You will have met the *education requirement* if you have a high school education or have successfully completed a 12-year course of elementary and secondary education. You will have met the *training requirement* if you have at least two years of work experience within the past five years in an occupation requiring at least two years of training or experience to perform. The U.S. Department of Labor's O*Net OnLine database will be used to determine qualifying work experience.

Green Card Lottery Scams

According the Federal Trade Commission (FTC), the nation's consumer protection agency, some businesses and attorneys misrepresent their services by saying that:

- they are affiliated with the U.S. government;
- they have special expertise or a special entry form that is required to enter the lottery;
- their company has never had a lottery entry rejected;
- their company can increase an entrant's chances of "winning" the lottery;
- people from ineligible countries still are "qualified" to enter the lottery.

In addition, some companies jeopardize an entrant's opportunity to participate in the lottery by filing several entries. These companies also may charge lottery-winning applicants substantial fees to complete the application process.

Protecting Yourself from Fraud

The FTC says the best way to protect against green card lottery scams is to understand how the State Department's lottery works.

- **There's no charge to enter the green card lottery.** You can enter on your own at the State Department's website — www.dvlottery.state.gov. You'll need to answer a few questions and provide passport-style digital photographs. You'll get an acknowledgment from the State Department once you've submitted your entry.

  Hiring a company or attorney to enter the lottery for you is your decision, but the person you pay will have to follow the same procedure. And your chance of being selected is the same whether you submit the entry or you pay someone to do it for you.

- **Submit only one entry.** If you submit more than one, you will be disqualified.

- **Selection of entries is random.** Spouses who are eligible for the DV lottery can apply separately; the "losing" spouse can enter the country on the Diversity Visa of the "winning" spouse. This is the only legitimate way to significantly increase your chance of entering the U.S. through the DV lottery.

- **Be alert to websites promising government travel or residency documents online or by mail.** Except for entering the DV lottery, most applications for visas, passports, green cards,

Copyright © 2011 – GreenCard123.Com by UNorth® – All Rights Reserved

and other travel and residency documents must be completed in person before an officer of the U.S. government.

- **Be thoughtful about who you send your personal documents to.** Unless you have an established relationship with a business, do not mail birth certificates, passports, drivers' licenses, marriage certificates, Social Security cards, or other documents with your personal identifying information to businesses promising to complete your application for travel or residency documents. These businesses may be engaged in identity theft.

- **Be skeptical of websites posing as U.S. government sites.** They may have domain names similar to government agencies, official-looking emblems (eagles, flags, or other American images like the Statue of Liberty or the U.S. Capitol), the official seals or logos of — and links to — other government sites, and list Washington, D.C., mailing addresses. **If the domain name doesn't end in ".gov," it's not a government site.** Bogus sites may charge for government forms. Don't pay; government forms and instructions for completing them are available from the issuing U.S. government agency for free.

For More Information

For details about the State Department's Diversity Visa lottery, visit www.dvlottery.state.gov. You also may call the State Department's Visa Services' Public Inquiries Branch at 202-663-1225. This number has recorded information with an option to speak with a visa specialist during normal business hours. Those overseas should contact the nearest U.S. embassy or consulate.

The FTC works for the consumer to prevent fraudulent, deceptive, and unfair business practices in the marketplace and to provide information to help consumers spot, stop, and avoid them. To file a complaint or to get free information on consumer issues, visit ftc.gov or call toll-free, 1-877-FTC-HELP (1-877-382-4357); TTY: 1-866-653-4261. The FTC enters Internet, telemarketing, identity theft, and other fraud-related complaints into Consumer Sentinel, a secure online database available to hundreds of civil and criminal law enforcement agencies in the U.S. and abroad.

FEDERAL TRADE COMMISSION	ftc.gov
1-877-FTC-HELP	FOR THE CONSUMER

October 2007

Copyright © 2011 - GreenCard123.Com by UNorth® - All Rights Reserved

APPENDIX

VIII. LIST OF U.S. EMBASSIES
AND ADDRESSES

List of United States embassies are provided in the following pages. The list is divided to regions below:

A) AFRICA
B) THE AMERICAS
C) EASE ASIA AND PACIFIC
D) EUROPE AND EURASIA
E) MIDDLE EAST AND NORTH AFRICA
F) CENTRAL AND SOUTH ASIA

For latest list and contact information visit http://www.usembassy.gov

A. AFRICA

Africa Regional Services
14, boulevard Haussmann
75009 - Paris FRANCE
Tel : (33) 1.43.12.70.22
Fax : (33) 1.43.12.71.88
http://ars-paris.state.gov/

Angola: Luanda
Rua Houari Boumedienne, #32
Luanda, Angola
Tel: (244) 222-641-000, (244) 222-445-727, (244) 222-445-481
Fax: (244) 222-641-232
E-mails for:
Economic/Commercial Section:
econusembassyluanda@yahoo.com
Small Grants Coordinator:
LuandaSmallGrants@yahoo.com.br
http://angola.usembassy.gov/

Benin: Cotonou
American Embassy
01BP 2012
Cotonou Benin
Tel. (229) 21 30 06 50
Fax: (229)21 30 03 84
http://cotonou.usembassy.gov/

Botswana: Gaborone
U.S. Embassy Gaborone, Botswana
Embassy Drive, Government Enclave, Gaborone, Botswana
P.O. Box 90 Gaborone, Botswana
(+267) 395-3982 (Monday-Friday, 7:30AM - 5:00PM)
(+267) 395-7111 (After Hours)
(+267) 318-0232
ConsularGaborone@state.gov
http://botswana.usembassy.gov/

Ouagadougou, Burkina Faso
Avenue Sembene Ousmane
Ouaga 2000, Secteur 15
Tel: (226) 50-49-53-00
Fax: (226) 50-49-56-28
e-mail: amembouaga@state.gov
http://ouagadougou.usembassy.gov/

Burundi: Bujumbura
American Embassy Bujumbura
B.P. 1720
Avenue Des Etats-Unis
Bujumbura, Burundi
Tel: +257 22-207-000
Tel (after hours): +257 22-214-853
Fax: +257 22-222-926
http://burundi.usembassy.gov/

Cameroon: Yaounde
The United States Embassy in Cameroon
Avenue Rosa Parks
P.O. Box 817
Yaounde
Cameroon
Phone: (237) 2220-1500
Fax: (237) 2220-1500x4531
http://yaounde.usembassy.gov/

Cameroon: VPP Septentrion
Septentrion camerounais (Mission diplomatique virtuelle)
B.P. 817
Yaoundé, Cameroun
Tel. : (237) 22-20-15-00
Fax : (237) 22-20-14 02
Email: vppseptentrion@state.gov
http://septentrion.usvpp.gov/

Copyright © 2011 - GreenCard123.Com by UNorth® - All Rights Reserved

Cape Verde: Praia
Rua Abilio Macedo 6, Praia, Cape Verde
Telephone: (238)-260-89-00
Fax: (238)-261-13-55
Consular Section
U.S. Embassy Praia
Rua Abilio Macedo 6, Praia
Fax: (238)-261-2551
Email: praiaconsular@state.gov
http://praia.usembassy.gov/

Central African Republic: Bangui
The United States Embassy in the Central African Republic
Avenue David Dacko
P.O. Box 924
Bangui
CENTRAL AFRICAN REPUBLIC
Phone: (236) 2161-0200
Fax: (236) 2161-4494
http://bangui.usembassy.gov

Chad: N'Djamena
The U.S. Embassy is located in N'Djamena on Avenue Felix
Eboue;
mailing address is B.P. 413;
Telephone: (235) 2251-62-11, 2251-70-09, 2251-77-59,
2251-90-52, 2251-92-18, and 2251-92-33;
Fax: (235) 2251-56-54
http://ndjamena.usembassy.gov/

Democratic Republic of the Congo: Kinshasa
Congolese Mailing Address:
American Embassy, Kinshasa
310, Avenue des Aviateurs
Kinshasa, Gombe
République Démocratique du Congo
http://kinshasa.usembassy.gov/

American Embassy, Kinshasa
B.P. 697, Kinshasa 1
République Démocratique du Congo

Republic of the Congo: Brazzaville
Boulevard De La Revolution
BDEAC Building, 4th Floor
Brazzaville, Republic of Congo
Country Code: 242
Telephone: 81 1481

To call from the United States: 011 242 81 1481
E-mail Address: greggcf@state.gov
http://brazzaville.usembassy.gov/

Côte d'Ivoire: Abidjan
Email Addresses:
Consular - consularabidja@state.gov
Press Section - tekofx@state.gov
Mailing Address:
01 B.P. 1712 Abidjan 01
Côte d'Ivoire
Telephone Numbers:
Switchboard: (225) 22 49 40 00
Fax: (225) 22 49 43 23
http://abidjan.usembassy.gov/

Republic of Djibouti: Djibouti
American Embassy, Djibouti
Plateau du Serpent
Blvd du Marechal Joffre
B.P. 185
Djibouti
Phone: 253 35 39 95
Fax: 253 35 39 40
http://djibouti.usembassy.gov/

Republic of Djibouti: Djibouti
American Embassy, Djibouti
Plateau du Serpent
Blvd du Marechal Joffre
B.P. 185
Djibouti
Phone: 253 35 39 95
Fax: 253 35 39 40
http://djibouti.usembassy.gov/

Equatorial Guinea: Malabo
K-3, Carretera de Aeropuerto,
Al lado de Restaurante El Paraíso,
Malabo,
Guinea Ecuatorial
Phone Number (+240) 098-895
Fax (+240) 098-894
http://malabo.usembassy.gov/

Eritrea: Asmara

Copyright © 2011 - GreenCard123.Com by UNorth® - All Rights Reserved

179 Ala Street
P.O. Box 211
Asmara, Eritrea
Tel. (291)(1) 12-00-04
Fax: (291)(1) 12-75-84
usembassyasmara@state.gov
http://eritrea.usembassy.gov/

Ethiopia: Addis Ababa
Address: Entoto Street
P.O. Box 1014
Addis Ababa
Phone: 517-40-00 (Embassy Switchboard)
124-24-00 (Embassy After Hours)
517-40-07 (Public Affairs Section)
124-24-24 (Consular Services)
466-95-66 (CDC Switchboard)
551-00-88 (USAID Switchboard)
320-0316 (Peace Corps)
Fax: 517-40-01 (Embassy)
124-24-54 (Public Affairs Section)
124-24-35 (Consular Section)
466-95-67 (CDC)
124-24-45 (DAO)
551-00-43 (USAID)
320-0315 (Peace Corps)
E-mail: pasaddis@state.gov
http://ethiopia.usembassy.gov/

Gabon: Libreville
Blvd. du Bord de Mer
B.P. 4000
Libreville, Gabon
Phone: (241) 76-20-03 or 76-20-04
After Hours: (241) 07-38-01-71
Fax: (241) 74-55-07
usembassylibreville@state.gov.
http://libreville.usembassy.gov/

Ghana: Accra
No. 24, Fourth Circular Rd., Cantonments, Accra
P.O. Box GP 2288
Accra, Ghana
Telephone: (233) 21-741-150
Fax: (233) 21-741-692/741-763
Email: pressaccra@state.gov
http://ghana.usembassy.gov/

Guinea: Conakry
American Embassy Conakry
P.O. Box 603
Transversale No. 2
Centre Administratif de Koloma
Commune de Ratoma
Conakry, Republic of Guinea
Telephone: +224-65-10-40-00
Fax:+224-65-10-42-97
ConsularConakr@state.gov
http://conakry.usembassy.gov/

Kenya: Nairobi
Embassy of the United States
United Nations Avenue Nairobi
P. O. Box 606 Village Market
00621 Nairobi, Kenya
Embassy Switchboard: 363-6000
Fax: 363-3410
U.S. Mailing Address
American Embassy Nairobi
U.S. Department of State
Washington, DC 20521-8900
http://nairobi.usembassy.gov/

Lesotho: Maseru
American Embassy Maseru
P.O. Box 333
Maseru 100
Lesotho
Physical Address: 254 Kingsway Road Maseru Lesotho
Tel: +266 22 312 666
Fax: +266 22 310 116
E-mail: infomaseru@state.gov
URL: http://maseru.usembassy.gov/

Liberia: Monrovia
111 UN Drive
Mamba Point
P. O. Box 98
Monrovia, Liberia
Switchboard:
+231-77-054-826 (cell)
+231-77-210-948 (cell)
+231-77-010-370 (fax)
ConsularMonrovia@state.gov
http://monrovia.usembassy.gov/

Copyright © 2011 - GreenCard123.Com by UNorth® - All Rights Reserved

Madagascar: Antananarivo
14 - 16 rue Rainitovo
Antsahavola - Antananarivo
Madagascar
Tel: 261 20 22 212 57
Fax: 261 20 22 345 39
http://www.antananarivo.usembassy.gov/

Malawi: Lilongwe
Embassy of the United States of America
P.O Box 30016
16 Jomo Kenyatta Road, Lilongwe 3, Malawi
Telephone: (265) 1 773 166
Fax: (265) 1 770 471
consularlilong@state.gov
http://lilongwe.usembassy.gov/

Mali: Bamako
ACI 2000
Rue 243, Porte 297
Bamako, Mali
Tel: +223 20 70 23 00
Fax: +223 20 70 24 79
http://mali.usembassy.gov/

Mauritania: Nouakchott
Phone: 222-525-2660 or 2663
Fax: 222-525-1592
Street Address: 288, rue 42-100, (rue Abdallaye)
Mailing Address: BP 222, Nouakchott, Mauritania
Email Address: tayebho@state.gov
http://mauritania.usembassy.gov/

Mauritius: Port Louis
4th Floor, Rogers House
John Kennedy Avenue
P.O. Box 544
Port Louis
Republic of Mauritius
Tel: (230) 202-4400
Fax: (230) 208-9534
Email: usembass@intnet.mu
http://mauritius.usembassy.gov/

Mauritius: VPP Seychelles

U.S. Consular Agency
Victoria, Seychelles
Tel: (248) 22 22 56
Fax: (248) 22 51 59
Email: usoffice@seychelles.net
http://seychelles.usvpp.gov/

Mozambique: Maputo
Maputo, Mozambique
Av. Kenneth Kaunda, 193
Caixa Postal, 783
Tel: (258) 21-49 27 97
Fax:(258) 21-49 01 14
E-mail: maputoirc@state.gov
http://maputo.usembassy.gov/

Namibia: Windhoek
Mailing Address: Private Bag 12029
Windhoek, Namibia
Street Address: 14 Lossen Street
Windhoek, Namibia
Local Phone: 061-295-8500
Local Fax: 061-295-8603
International Phone: +264-61-295-8500
http://windhoek.usembassy.gov/

Niger: Niamey
Public Affairs Section (PAS) Niamey
BP 11201
Niamey, Niger
Public Affairs Section (PAS) Niamey
BP 11201
Niamey, Niger
From U.S.:
Public Affairs Section (PAS)
2420 Niamey PL
DULLES, VA 20189-2420
Telephone: (227) 20-73-31-69 or (227) 20-72-39-41
Fax: (227) 20-73-55-60
Email: NiameyPASN@state.gov
http://niamey.usembassy.gov/

Nigeria: Abuja
Embassy of the United States of America
Plot 1075 Diplomatic Drive
Central District Area, Abuja, Nigeria
Telephone: (234)-9-461-4000

Copyright © 2011 - GreenCard123.Com by UNorth® - All Rights Reserved

Fax: (234)-9-461-4036
pepfaruniv@state.gov
http://nigeria.usembassy.gov/

Rwanda: Kigali
#2657 Avenue de la Gendarmerie (Kacyiru)
Tel: (250) 596 400 Extension: 2553
Fax: (250) 596 771 / 596 591
P.O. Box 28 Kigali
RWANDA
ConsularKigali@state.gov
http://rwanda.usembassy.gov/

Senegal: Dakar | Français
American Embassy Dakar
BP 49
Avenue Jean XXIII, angle Rue Kleber
Dakar, Senegal
Telephone: (221) 33-829-2100
After hours: (221) 33-823-6520
Fax: (221) 33-822-2991
ConsularDakar@state.gov
http://dakar.usembassy.gov/

Sierra Leone: Freetown
Embassy of the United States of America
Southridge - Hill Station
Freetown, Sierra Leone
Telephone: +232 22 515 000 or +232 76 515 000
Fax: +232 22 515 355
http://freetown.usembassy.gov/

Somalia: VPP Somalia
U.S Embassy, Public Affairs Section
American Reference Center
United Nations Avenue, Gigiri
P.O Box 606, Village Market
00621 Nairobi, Kenya
PHONE: 254-2-363-6196/197/205
FAX: 254-2-363-6353
E-MAIL: ircnairobi@state.gov
SomaliaPublicDiploma@state.gov
http://somalia.usvpp.gov/

South Africa: Pretoria

PO Box 9536, Pretoria 0001
877 Pretorius St, Arcadia, Pretoria
Tel: (27-12) 431-4000
Fax: (27-12) 342-2299
consularjohannesburg@state.gov.
http://southafrica.usembassy.gov/

Sudan: Khartoum
U.S. Embassy Khartoum
P.O. Box 699
Kilo 10, Soba
Khartoum, Sudan
Tel: +249-1-870-2-2000
http://sudan.usembassy.gov/

Swaziland: Mbabane
Embassy of the United States, Mbabane Swaziland
7th Floor, Central Bank Building
Mahlokohla Street
P.O. Box 199
Mbabane, Swaziland
Tel: (268) 404-6441
Fax: (268) 404-5959
http://swaziland.usembassy.gov/

Tanzania: Dar es Salaam
American Embassy
686 Old Bagamoyo Road,
Msasani
P.O. Box 9123,
Dar es Salaam
Tel: 255-22-266-8001
Fax: 255-22-266-8238 or 8373
http://tanzania.usembassy.gov/

Tanzania: VPP Zanzibar
Address: 8 Mazizini Road
Adjacent to Omani Consulate Residence
P.O. Box 4
Zanzibar
Tel/Fax: (255-24) 223 1976
http://zanzibar-tanzania.usvpp.gov/

The Gambia: Banjul
American Embassy Banjul

Copyright © 2011 - GreenCard123.Com by UNorth® - All Rights Reserved

Kairaba Avenue, Fajara
P.M.B. 19
Banjul
The Gambia
Tel: (220) 439-2856
Fax: (220) 439-2475
http://banjul.usembassy.gov

Togo: Lome
Department of State /2300 Lome Place
Washington, D.C., 20521-2300
Phone: (+228) 261 5470
Fax: (+228) 261 5501
lomewebmaster@state.gov
http://togo.usembassy.gov/

Uganda: Kampala
Embassy of the United States of America
U. S. Embassy Kampala
Plot 1577 Ggaba Road,
P.O. Box 7007,
Kampala
Uganda.
Tel: 0414 25 97 91 /2/3/5
Fax: 0414 259 794
For all Visa inquiries: KampalaVisa@state.gov
http://kampala.usembassy.gov/

VPP Northern Uganda
U.S. Embassy
Plot: 1577 Ggaba Road,U.S. Embassy,Plot: 1577 Ggaba Road,
Tel: 256-414-259791
Fax: 256-414-259794
Email: KampalaWebContact @state.gov
Web Site: http://kampala.usembassy.gov

Zambia: Lusaka
Embassy of the United States of America
Corner of the United Nations and Independence Road
P.O.Box 31617
Lusaka, ZAMBIA
Telephone: +(260)-211-250955, Fax: +(260)-211-252225
ACSLuasaka@state.gov
http://zambia.usembassy.gov/

Zimbabwe: Harare
Consular Section of the United States Embassy Harare, Zimbabwe
172 Herbert Chitepo Avenue Harare, Zimbabwe
Tel: 263-4-250593/4
Fax: 263- 4-796488
Email: consularharare@state.gov (Only for US Citizens)
http://harare.usembassy.gov/

U.S. Mission to the African Union
U.S. Mission to the African Union:
phone: 251-11-517-4055
fax: 251-11-124-7037
U.S. Address: 2035 USAU Place
Washington, D.C. 20521-2035
Email: USAU@state.gov
http://www.usau.usmission.gov/

B. THE AMERICAS

Argentina: Buenos Aires
Mailing address:
Av. Colombia 4300
(C1425GMN) Buenos Aires - Argentina
Telephone: (54-11) 5777-4533
Fax: (54-11) 5777-4240
http://argentina.usembassy.gov/

Bahamas: Nassau
Mailing Address:
The U.S. Embassy
P.O. Box N-8197
Nassau, Bahamas
Telephone: (242) 322-1181
E-mail: embnas@state.gov
http://nassau.usembassy.gov/

Barbados: Bridgetown
American Embassy
Wildey Business Park
Wildey
St. Michael BB 14006
Barbados, W.I.
 (246) 227-4000

Copyright © 2011 - GreenCard123.Com by UNorth® - All Rights Reserved

(246) 227-4399
http://barbados.usembassy.gov/

Belize: Belmopan
Floral Park Road
Belmopan, Cayo
Belize
International: Dial 011 +
Phone: (501) 822-4011
Fax: (501) 822-4012
Email: embbelize@state.gov
http://belize.usembassy.gov/

Bermuda: Hamilton

Street Address:	Mailing Address:
Crown Hill	P.O. Box HM 325
16 Middle Road	Hamilton HM BX
Devonshire DV 03	Bermuda
Bermuda	

(441) 295-1342
http://hamilton.usconsulate.gov/

Bolivia: La Paz
Avenida Arce 2780
Casilla 425
La Paz, Bolivia
Tel: (591) 2-216-8000
Fax: (591) 2-216-8111
Email: lpzwebmail@state.gov
http://bolivia.usembassy.gov/

Bolivia: VPP Cochabamba
Embasssy of the United States
Avenida Arce 2780
Casilla 425
La Paz, Bolivia
Telephone: (591) 2-216-8000
FAX: (591) 2-216-8111
Email: cochabambavpp@state.gov
http://cochabamba.usvpp.gov/

Bolivia: VPP Santa Cruz
Avenida Arce 2780
Casilla 425
La Paz, Bolivia
Telephone: (591) 2-216-8000
FAX: (591) 2-216-8111
Email: santacruzvpp@state.gov
http://santacruz.usvpp.gov/

Bolivia: VPP Sucre
Embasssy of the United States
Avenida Arce 2780
Casilla 425
La Paz, Bolivia
Telephone: (591) 2-216-8000
FAX: (591) 2-216-8111
Email: sucrevpp@state.gov
http://sucre.usvpp.gov/

Brazil: Brasilia
Phone: (61) 3312-7000 during Consulate's working hours
(8am to 5pm)
Phone: (61) 3312-7400 after hours
Fax: (61) 3312-7651
E-mail: BrasiliaACS@state.gov
http://brazil.usembassy.gov/

Canada: Ottawa
The Embassy of the United States of America
PO Box 866
Station B
Ottawa, Ontario K1P 5T1 Canada
http://canada.usembassy.gov/

Canada: Calgary
Consulate General Calgary
Address:
615 Macleod Trail S.E.,
10th Floor
Calgary, Alberta, T2G 4T8 Canada
http://calgary.usconsulate.gov/

Canada: Halifax
Physical Address
Purdy's Wharf Tower II
1969 Upper Water Street, Suite 904
Halifax, NS B3J 3R7
Mailing Address
1973 Upper Water Street
Halifax, NS B3J 0A9
Phone
1-902-429-2480
Email address for questions on visas and services for American citizens only
consularh@state.gov
http://halifax.usconsulate.gov

Copyright © 2011 - GreenCard123.Com by UNorth® - All Rights Reserved

Canada: Montreal
The United States Consulate General's mailing address is:
P.O. Box 65
Station Desjardins
http://montreal.usconsulate.gov/

Canada: Quebec
Consulate General of the United States of America
2, rue de la Terrasse-Dufferin, Quebec, Qc G1R 4T9 Canada
Telephone: 418.692.2095   Fax: 418.692.4640
http://quebec.usconsulate.gov/

Canada: Toronto
United States Consulate General
360 University Avenue
Toronto, Ontario M5G 1S4
http://toronto.usconsulate.gov/

Canada: Vancouver
Consulate General of the United States of America
1095 W. Pender St., Vancouver, B.C. V6E 2M6 Canada
Tel: 604.685.4311   Fax: 604.685.5285
http://vancouver.usconsulate.gov/

Canada: Winnipeg
Consulate of the United States of America
201 Portage Avenue, Suite 860, Winnipeg, Manitoba R3B 3K6 Canada
Tel: 204.940.1800   Fax: 204.940.1809
http://winnipeg.usconsulate.gov/

Canada: VPP Northwest Territories
United States Consulate General
615 Macleod Trail S.E., Room 1000
Calgary, Alberta T2G 4T8
Tel: (403) 266-8962
Fax: (403) 264-6630
Email: nwtvpp@state.gov
http://www.canadanorth.usvpp.gov/nwt/index.asp

Canada: VPP Nunavut
United States Consulate General
2, rue de la Terrasse Dufferin
Quebec, Quebec G1R 4T9
Tel: (418) 692-2095
Email: NunavutVPP@state.gov
http://www.canadanorth.usvpp.gov/nunavut/index.asp

Canada: VPP Southwest Ontario
United States Consulate General
360 University Avenue
Toronto, Ontario M5G 1S4
http://www.swontario.usvpp.gov/

Canada: VPP Yukon
U.S. Consulate-General
1095 W. Pender St.
Vancouver, B.C. V6E 2M6
Tel: 604.685.4311
Fax: 604.685.5285
Email: yukonvc@state.gov
http://www.canadanorth.usvpp.gov/yukon/index.asp

Chile: Santiago
Embassy of the United States in Chile
Address: Av. Andrés Bello 2800, Las Condes
Santiago, Chile
Switchboard: (56-2) 330-3000
Fax: (56-2) 330-3710, 330-3160
http://chile.usembassy.gov/

Colombia: Bogota
Mailing address: Carrera 45 No. 24B-27 Bogotá, D.C. Colombia
Embassy phone: (571) 315-0811 Embassy fax: (571) 315-2197
Consular Section phone: (571) 315-1566
USAID phone: (571) 423-6880
Immigrant Visa Unit fax: (571) 315-4155
Non-Immigrant Visa Unit fax: (571) 315-2127
Public Affairs Section fax: (571) 315-2208
http://bogota.usembassy.gov/

Costa Rica: San Jose
Location: At the intersection of Avenida Central and Calle 120 in the Pavas Section of San José, Costa Rica.
Street Address: Calle 120 Avenida 0, Pavas, San José, Costa Rica
Local Mailing Address: 920-1200 San José, Costa Rica
U.S. Mailing Address: US Embassy San Jose, APO AA 34020
Telephone: [506] 2519-2000 From the U.S.: 011-506-2519-2000
http://sanjose.usembassy.gov/

Cuba: U.S. Interests Section
Calzada between L & M Streets,
Vedado, Havana

Copyright © 2011 - GreenCard123.Com by UNorth® - All Rights Reserved

Phone: (53) (7) 833-3551 through 59
Hours: 8:00 a.m. to 4:30 p.m (We are closed on U.S. and Cuban Holidays)
Emergencies/After Hours:
Phone: (53) (7) 833-2302
http://havana.usint.gov/

Dominican Republic: Santo Domingo
The Embassy of the United States in the Dominican Republic
Cesar Nicolas Penson esq. Leopoldo Navarro,
Telephone: 809 221-2171, Fax 809 686-7437
http://santodomingo.usembassy.gov/

Ecuador: Quito
Ave. Avigiras E12-170 y Ave. Eloy Alfaro (next to SOLCA)
Quito, Ecuador
http://ecuador.usembassy.gov/

Ecuador: Guayaquil
U.S. Consulate General
9 de Octubre y Garcia Moreno
Guayaquil, Ecuador
acsguayaquil@state.gov
http://guayaquil.usconsulate.gov/

El Salvador: San Salvador
Embajada de Los Estados Unidos
Final Boulevard Santa Elena
Antiguo Cuscatlán, La Libertad
Telephone: 2501-2999
Fax: 2501-2150
http://sansalvador.usembassy.gov/

Guatemala: Guatemala City
Embajada de los Estados Unidos de América
Avenida Reforma 7-01, Zona 10
Guatemala Ciudad, Guatemala
http://guatemala.usembassy.gov/

Guatemala: VPP Xela
Embajada de los Estados Unidos de América
Avenida Reforma 7-01, Zona 10
Guatemala Ciudad, Guatemala
http://xela.usvpp.gov/

Haiti: Port-au-Prince
Tabarre 41, Boulevard 15 Octobre
Port-au-Prince, Haiti
http://haiti.usembassy.gov/

Honduras: Tegucigalpa
Embajada de los Estados Unidos de América
Avenida La Paz
Tegucigalpa M.D.C.
Honduras
Telephone Numbers: 236-9320, 238-5114
Fax Number: 236-9037
http://honduras.usembassy.gov/

Honduras: VPP San Pedro Sula
Embassy of the United States of America
Avenida La Paz
Tegucigalpa M.D.C.
Honduras
Tel: (504) 236-9320 / 238-5114
Fax: (504) 236-9037
http://sanpedrosula.usvpp.gov/

Jamaica: Kingston
American Embassy
142, Old Hope Road
Kingston 6
Jamaica, W.I.
Telephone: (876) 702-6000
http://kingston.usembassy.gov/

Mexico: Mexico City
Desde México:
Embajada de Estados Unidos
Paseo de la Reforma 305
Col. Cuauhtémoc
06500 Mexico, D.F
Desde México: (01−55) 5080−2000
Desde E.U.:
011−52−55−5080−2000
http://mexico.usembassy.gov/eng/main.html

Mexico: Ciudad Juarez
U.S. Consulate General
Paseo de la Victoria #3650
Fracc. Partido Senecú
Ciudad Juárez, Chihuahua, Mexico C.P. 32543
http://ciudadjuarez.usconsulate.gov/

Mexico: Guadalajara
U.S. Consulate Guadalajara
Progreso 175
Col. Americana
Guadalajara, Jalisco, Mexico
C.P. 44160

Copyright © 2011 - GreenCard123.Com by UNorth® - All Rights Reserved

Tel : (01-33) 3268-2100
Fax: (01-33) 3826-6549
http://guadalajara.usconsulate.gov/

Mexico: Hermosillo
Consulado Americano
Monterrey #141 entre las calles
Rosales y Galeana
Col. Esqueda, C.P. 83000
Hermosillo, Sonora, México
In México: 01-662-289-3500
From the United States: 011-52-662-289-3500
http://hermosillo.usconsulate.gov/

Mexico: Matamoros
Calle Primera #2002
Col. Jardin
Matamoros, Tamps., 87330
Telephone: 011 52 (868) 812-4402
Fax: 011 52 (868) 812-217
http://matamoros.usconsulate.gov/

Mexico: Merida
Calle 60 No. 338-K x 29 y 31
Col. Alcala Martin
Merida, Yucatan, Mexico 97050
Fax:
(011)(52)(999) 942-5759 (dialing from the U.S.)
(01)(999) 942-5759 (dialing from within Mexico)
E-Mail: meridacons@state.gov
http://merida.usconsulate.gov/

Mexico: Monterrey
Ave. Constitución 411 Pte.
Monterrey, Nuevo León. México 64000
Telephone (01 81) 8047-3100
http://monterrey.usconsulate.gov/

Mexico: Nogales
Calle San José s/n
Fraccionamiento los Alamos
C. P. 84065 Nogales, Sonora.
Telephone Number: (52) - (631) - 311 - 8150
Fax Number: (52) - (631) - 313 - 4652
http://nogales.usconsulate.gov/

Mexico: Nuevo Laredo
American Consulate Nuevo Laredo
Calle Allende 3330
Nuevo Laredo Tamaulipas, Mexico

Tel: (867) 714-0512
Fax: (867) 714-6075
http://nuevolaredo.usconsulate.gov/

Mexico: Puerto Vallarta
U.S. Consulate Guadalajara
Progreso 175
Col. Americana
Guadalajara, Jalisco, Mexico
C.P. 44160
Telephones:
From Mexico:
Tel : (01-33) 3268-2100
Fax: (01-33) 3826-6549
http://guadalajara.usconsulate.gov/puerto_vallarta.html

Mexico: Tijuana
American Consulate General
P.O. Box 439039
San Diego, CA 92143-9039
http://tijuana.usconsulate.gov/

Mexico: VPP El Bajio
Embassy of the United States of America
Paseo de la Reforma 305
Col. Cuauhtémoc
06500 Mexico, D.F
Telephone
From México: (01-55) 5080-2000
From the U.S.: 011-52-55-5080-2000
http://elbajio.usvpp.gov/

Mexico: VPP Chiapas-Tabasco
Embajada de los Estados Unidos
ACS, Virtual Presence Posts, Oficina 101
Paseo de la Reforma #305
Col. Cuauhtémoc, Delegación Cuauhtémoc
C.P. 06500, Ciudad de México, D.F.
MEXICO
Telephone:
From Mexico (01-55) 50-80-20-00, extension 4369
From the US (011-52) (55)50-80-20-00, extension 4369
http://chiapas-tabasco.usvpp.gov/

Netherlands Antilles: Curacao
United States Consulate General Curacao
P.O. Box 158, J.B. Gorsiraweg 1
Tel 599-9-461-3066, fax 599-9-461-6489
Email: infocuracao@state.gov

Copyright © 2011 - GreenCard123.Com by UNorth® - All Rights Reserved

http://curacao.usconsulate.gov/

Nicaragua: Managua
Kilometer 5 1/2 (5.5) Carretera Sur, in Managua, Nicaragua.
Embassy Telephone: +(505) 2252-7100
Consular Section phone: +(505) 2252-7888
Consular fax: +(505) 2252-7304
Consular E-mail: consularmanagua@state.gov
http://nicaragua.usembassy.gov/

Panama: Panama City
American Embassy Panama
Building 783, Demetrio Basilio Lakas Avenue
Clayton, Panama
Press Section Fax: (507) 207-7352
Cultural Section Fax: (507) 207-7350
E-mail: Panamaweb@state.gov
http://panama.usembassy.gov/

Panama: VPP Colon
Embajada de los Estados Unidos
Apartado 0816-02561
Panamá 5, República de Panamá
Tel: (507) 207-7000
Fax: (507) 207-7352
http://colon.usvpp.gov/

Paraguay: Asuncion
1776 Mariscal Lopez Avenue
Asunción, Paraguay
Tel: 595 21 213-715
Fax: 595 21 213-728
http://paraguay.usembassy.gov/

Peru: Lima
Embassy of the United States
Avenida La Encalada cdra. 17 s/n
Surco, Lima 33, Peru
Telephone: (51-1) 618-2000
Fax: (51-1) 618-2397
http://lima.usembassy.gov/

Suriname: Paramaribo
United States Embassy Suriname
129 Dr. Sophie Redmondstraat
Paramaribo, Suriname
Phone: (597) 472-900
Fax (Consular) (597) 425-788
Fax: (597) 425-690

Fax: (597) 410-972
http://suriname.usembassy.gov/

Trinidad & Tobago: Port of Spain
United States Embassy
15 Queen's Park West
Port of Spain
TRINIDAD & TOBAGO
Tel: (868) 622-6371-6
Fax: (868) 822-5905
E-mail: ircpos@state.gov
http://trinidad.usembassy.gov

Uruguay: Montevideo
EMBASSY OF THE UNITED STATES OF AMERICA
Lauro Muller 1776 - Montevideo 11200 - URUGUAY
Tel: (+598 2) 1770-2000 - Fax: (+598 2) 418-8611
http://montevideo.usembassy.gov/

Venezuela: Caracas
Calle F con Calle Suapure, Urb. Colinas de Valle Arriba, Caracas, Venezuela 1080.
Telephone: [58] (212) 975-6411
Fax: [58] (212) 907-8199
http://caracas.usembassy.gov/?b=48

U.S. Mission to the OAS
Telephone 202-647-9430
Fax: 202-647-0911
Address: U.S. Permanent Mission to the Organization of American
States (OAS)
U.S. Department of State
2201 C Street, NW
Room 5914
Washington, D.C. 20515
http://www.usoas.usmission.gov/

U.S. Mission to the U.N.-New York
Press and Public Diplomacy Section
United States Mission to the United Nations
140 East 45th Street
New York, N.Y. 10017
Accredited Journalists: 212-415-4050
Opinion & Comment line: 212-415-4062
Fax: 212-415-4053
http://www.usunnewyork.usmission.gov/

Copyright © 2011 - GreenCard123.Com by UNorth® - All Rights Reserved

EAST ASIA AND PACIFIC

Australia: Canberra
American Embassy
Moonah Place
Yarralumla, ACT 2600
Telephone: (02) 6214-5600
Web: http://canberra.usembassy.gov/

Australia: Melbourne
Address
American Embassy
Moonah Place
Yarralumla, ACT 2600
http://melbourne.usconsulate.gov/melbourne/index
.html

Australia: Perth
4th Floor
16 St. George's Terrace
Perth, WA 6000
Telephone: (08) 9202-1224, 8:30am - 4:30pm
Email: usrsaustralia@state.gov
http://perth.usconsulate.gov/

Australia: Sydney
American Embassy
Moonah Place
Yarralumla, ACT 2600
Email: usrsaustralia@state.gov
http://sydney.usconsulate.gov/sydney/index.html

Australia: VPP Adelaide
American Embassy
Moonah Place
Yarralumla, ACT 2600
Email: usrsaustralia@state.gov
http://adelaide.usvpp.gov/adelaide/
http://canberra.usembassy.gov/

Australia: VPP Brisbane
American Embassy
Moonah Place
Yarralumla, ACT 2600
http://brisbane.usvpp.gov/brisbane/

Brunei: Bandar Seri Begawan
The American Embassy is located at:
Third Floor, Teck Guan Plaza
Jalan Sultan (Corner of Jalan
McArthur)
Bandar Seri Begawan BS8811
Tel: 222-0384 (Ext.2111)
Fax: 222-5293
Email: consularbrunei@state.gov
http://brunei.usembassy.gov/

Burma: Rangoon
The Embassy110 University Ave,
Kamayut Township,
Rangoon, Burma.
Telephone: (95)-(1) 536-509, 535-756, 538-038
Fax: (95)-(1)-511-069
http://burma.usembassy.gov/

Cambodia: Phnom Penh
Embassy of the United States of America
#1, Street 96, Sangkat Wat Phnom, Khan Daun
Penh, Phnom Penh
Embassy Tel: (855-23) 728-000
Embassy Fax: (855-23) 728-600
http://cambodia.usembassy.gov/

China: Beijing
United States Embassy of Beijing, China
Jon Huntsman
No. 55 An Jia Lou Lu 100600
Tel: (86-10) 8531-3000
http://beijing.usembassy-china.org.cn/

China: Chengdu
U.S. Consulate General in Chengdu
4 Lingshiguan Road
Chengdu, Sichuan 610041
Switchboard: (86-28) 8558 3992
Public Affairs Section
Tel: (86-28) 8558 3792
Fax: (86-28) 8557 7540
http://chengdu.usembassy-china.org.cn/

Copyright © 2011 - GreenCard123.Com by UNorth® - All Rights Reserved

China: Guangzhou
No. 1 Shamian Street South, Guangzhou   (510133)
Mailing Address: No. 1 Shamian Street South,
Guangzhou 510133
Phone: 020-8121-8000
Fax: 020-8121-9001
http://guangzhou.usembassy-china.org.cn/

China: Shanghai
U.S. Consulate General in Shanghai
Main U.S. Consulate General Building
1469 Huai Hai Zhong Road
(Near Wulumuqi Nan Lu)
200031 Shanghai
http://shanghai.usembassy-china.org.cn/

China: Shenyang
United States Consulate General Shenyang, China
52, 14th Wei Road, Heping District, 110003 China
Tel [86] (24) 2322-1198
Fax [86] (24) 2322-2374
http://shenyang.usembassy-china.org.cn/

China: Wuhan
New World International Trade Tower I
No. 568, Jianshe Avenue
Hankou, Wuhan 430022
Tel：027-8555-7791
Fax：027-8555-7761
CG assistant: Wen Cuihong
传真: (86-10)8531-4222
E-mail: wencx@state.gov
http://wuhan.usembassy-china.org.cn/

China: VPP Fuzhou
No. 1 Shamian Street South, Guangzhou
 510133
http://fuzhou.usvpp.gov/

China: VPP Kunming
VPPKunming@state.gov.
http://kunming.usvpp.gov/

China: VPP Lhasa
usiscd@mail.sc.cninfo.net.
http://lhasa.usvpp.gov/

China: VPP Nanjing
美国驻上海总领事馆主楼
地址: 中国, 上海市, 淮海中路1469号.
(近乌鲁木齐南路)
邮编: 200031
新闻文化处
(处理有关总领事馆同新闻媒介的关系并负责美国
政府在中国华东地区的所有官方教育和文化交流
项目)
地址: 中国,上海,南京西路1376号,
上海商城东峰532室(位于上海展览中心对面)
邮编: 200040
电话: (86-21) 6279-7662
传真: (86-21) 6279-7603
http://nanjing.usembassy-china.org.cn/

China: VPP Nanning
No. 1 Shamian Street South, Guangzhou 510133
Phone: 020-8121-8000
After-hours Emergency Number: 020-8121-6077
Fax: 020-8121-9001
http://nanning.usvpp.gov/

China: VPP Xiamen
No. 1 Shamian Street South, Guangzhou 510133
Phone: 020-8121-8000
After-hours Emergency Number: 020-8121-6077
Fax: 020-8121-9001
http://xiamen.usvpp.gov/

China: VPP Zhengzhou
美国驻华大使馆
美国驻华大使:雷德
北京市秀水北街3号,
邮编：100600, 电话：(86-10) 6532-3831
美国驻华大使馆地图
新闻文化处
新闻文化官：元敦奎
传真：（86-10）6532-2039
网络管理员：负责使馆网络的技术问题
电子邮件：BeijingWebmaster@state.gov
http://zhengzhou.usembassy-china.org.cn/

Copyright © 2011 - GreenCard123.Com by UNorth® - All Rights Reserved

Fiji: Suva
Embassy of the United States of America,
31 Loftus Street, Suva, Fiji
P.O. Box 218,
Suva, Fiji.
Telephone: (679) 3314-466
Facsimile: (679) 3308-685
http://suva.usembassy.gov/

Fiji: VPP Tonga
Commercial Section,
Embassy of the United States of America,
31 Loftus Street, Suva, Fiji
P.O. Box 218,
Suva, Fiji.
Other Contact Info
Telephone: (679) 3314-466
Facsimile: (679) 3308-685
Email: usembsuva@connect.com.fj
http://tonga.usvpp.gov/

Hong Kong and Macau
Address: 26 Garden Road, Hong Kong
Tel: (852) 2523-9011
(Please note that visa inquiries will not be answered
on this line)
Fax: (852) 2845-1598
http://hongkong.usconsulate.gov/

Indonesia: Jakarta
Jl. Medan Merdeka Selatan No. 3 - 5
Jakarta 10110, Indonesia
Telephone: (62)(21) 3435-9000
Fax: (62)(21) 385-7189
http://jakarta.usembassy.gov

Indonesia: Surabaya
Jl. Dr. Sutomo No. 33
Surabaya, Indonesia 60264
Tel: (62) 31-295-6400
Email: consurabaya@state.gov
http://surabaya.usconsulate.gov/

Japan: Tokyo
1-10-5 Akasaka
Minato-ku, Tokyo 107-8420 JAPAN
03-3224-5000
03-3505-1862

http://tokyo.usembassy.gov/

Japan: Fukuoka
5-26 Ohori 2-chome, Chuo-ku, Fukuoka 810-0052
Tel. (092) 751-9331
Fax: (092) 725-3772
Email: Unavailable
http://japan.usembassy.gov/fukuoka/f-main.html

Japan: Nagoya
Nagoya International Center Bldg. 6F
1-47-1 Nagono, Nakamura-ku, Nagoya
450-0001
Tel: 052-581-4501
Fax: 06-6315-5914
Email: AOK@state.gov
http://nagoya.usconsulate.gov

Japan: Osaka/Kobe
2-11-5, Nishitenma,
Kita-ku, Osaka 530-8543
06-6315-5900
http://osaka.usconsulate.gov/

Japan: Sapporo
Kita 1-jo Nishi 28-chome,
Chuo-ku, Sapporo 064-0821, Japan
Phone: 011-641-1115
http://sapporo.usconsulate.gov/

Japan: Naha, Okinawa
The Consulate General
Route 241 just west of the intersection of Route 330
and Route 241
next to the Barkley's Court.
http://naha.usconsulate.gov/

Korea: Seoul
International Mailing Address:
Embassy of the United States Seoul
32 Sejongno, Jongno-gu
Seoul 110-710
Republic of Korea
FAX: 82-2-397-4080 DSN FAX: 721-4080
E-mail: SeoulInfo@state.gov
http://seoul.usembassy.gov/

Korea: Busan

Copyright © 2011 - GreenCard123.Com by UNorth® - All Rights Reserved

Address: Room #612, Lotte Gold Rose Building, #150-3,
Yangjung-dong, Busan jin-gu, Busan, Korea
Tel: 051-863-0731/0732,   Fax: 051-863-0734
http://busan.usconsulate.gov/

Laos: Vientiane
U.S. Embassy, Vientiane, Laos
Public Diplomacy Section
Tel: (856-21) 267089
Fax: (856-21) 267160
Email: webmastervientiane@state.gov
http://laos.usembassy.gov

Malaysia: Kuala Lumpur
International Mailing Address:
Embassy of the United States Kuala Lumpur
376 Jalan Tun Razak
50400 Kuala Lumpur
Malaysia
http://malaysia.usembassy.gov/

Republic of the Marshall Islands: Majuro
(692) 247-4012
Email the Embassy at: majuropd@state.gov
http://majuro.usembassy.gov/

Federated States of Micronesia: Kolonia
P.O. Box 1286
Kolonia, Pohnpei
FSM 96941
Phone: (691) 320-2187
Fax: (691) 320-2186
USEmbassy@mail.fm
http://kolonia.usembassy.gov/

Mongolia: Ulaanbaatar
P.O. Box 1021
Ulaanbaatar-13
Mongolia
Phone: 976-11-329095
Fax: 976-11-320776
http://mongolia.usembassy.gov/

New Zealand: Wellington
Embassy of the United States of America
P.O. Box 1190,
Wellington,
New Zealand

(04) 462 6000
+64 4 462 6000
http://newzealand.usembassy.gov/

Papua New Guinea: Port Moresby
Embassy of the United States of America
P.O. Box 1492
Port Moresby, Papua New Guinea
http://portmoresby.usembassy.gov/

Republic of Palau: Koror
usembassykoror@palaunet.com
(680) 587-2920.
http://palau.usembassy.gov/

Philippines: Manila
U.S. Embassy
1201 Roxas Boulevard
Manila, Philippines 1000
http://manila.usembassy.gov/

Philippines: VPP Mindinao
USVirtConDavao@State.gov
http://mindanao.usvpp.gov/

Samoa: Apia
5th Floor,
Accident Corporation Building,
Matafele
Apia
Ph: +685 21436 / 21631 / 21452 or 22696
Fax: +685 22030
Email: AmEmbApia@state.gov
http://samoa.usembassy.gov/

Singapore
American Embassy
27 Napier Road
Singapore 258508
Main Tel. No: (65) 6476-9100
Main Fax No: (65) 6476-9340
http://singapore.usembassy.gov/

Thailand: Bangkok
American Citizen Services, U.S. Consulate General
Chiang Mai
387 Witchayanond Road, Chiang Mai 50300,
Thailand
Tel: +66-53-107-777
Fax: +66-53-252-633

Copyright © 2011 - GreenCard123.Com by UNorth® - All Rights Reserved

E-mail: acschn@state.gov
http://bangkok.usembassy.gov/

Thailand: Chiang Mai
Consulate General of the United States of America
387 Wichaynond Road
Chiang Mai 50300 THAILAND
Tel.: 053-107-700 (from inside Thailand); +66-53-
107-700 (from outside Thailand)
Fax: 053-252-633 (from inside Thailand); +66-53-
252-633 (from outside Thailand)
http://chiangmai.usconsulate.gov/

Timor-Leste: Dili
Avenida de Portugal, Praia dos Coqueiros,
Dili, Timor-Leste,
tel: (670) 332-4684,
fax: (670) 331-3206.
ConsDili@state.gov
http://timor-leste.usembassy.gov/

Vietnam: Hanoi
The American Center
1st Floor, Rose Garden Tower
170 Ngoc Khanh Street, Hanoi, Vietnam
Tel: 844-3850-5000
Email: hanoiac@state.gov
http://vietnam.usembassy.gov/

Vietnam: Ho Chi Minh City
U.S. Consulate General in Ho Chi Minh City
4 Le Duan Blvd., District 1
Ho Chi Minh City Vietnam
Tel: + 84-8-3520-4200
Fax: +84-8-3520-4244
http://hochiminh.usconsulate.gov/

C. EUROPE AND EURASIA

Albania: Tirana
http://tirana.usembassy.gov/

EMBASSY OF THE UNITED STATES OF AMERICA
Address: Rruga e Elbasanit No. 103, Tirana, ALBANIA
Phone: +(355) 4 2247 285
Fax: +(355) 4 2232 222

Armenia: Yerevan

Embassy of the United States of America
1 American Avenue
Yerevan 0082, Republic of Armenia
Telephone: (+37410) 464-700
Fax:(+37410) 464-742
E-mail: usinfo@usa.am
http://armenia.usembassy.gov/

Austria: Vienna
Embassy of the United States
Boltzmanngasse 16
1090 Vienna
Tel.: (+43-1) 31339-0
Fax: (+43-1) 310 06 82
E-mail: embassy@usembassy.at
http://austria.usembassy.gov/

Azerbaijan: Baku
83 Azadlig Prospecti
AZ1007 Baku, Azerbaijan
Switchboard: (+994 12) 4980-335
Switchboard: (+994 12) 4980-336
Switchboard: (+994 12) 4980-337
Fax: (+994 12) 4656-671
Consular Section Fax: (+994 12) 4983755
http://azerbaijan.usembassy.gov/

Belarus: Minsk
United States Embassy
46 Starovilenskaya St.
Minsk 220002, Belarus
Telephone: +375 17 210-12-83 / 217-7347 / 217-
7348
Fax: +375 17 234-78-53
http://minsk.usembassy.gov/

Belgium: Brussels
Embassy of the United States of America
Regentlaan 27 Boulevard du Régent, B-1000
Brussels
Phone: (32-2) 811-4000
Fax: (32-2) 811-4500
http://belgium.usembassy.gov/

Bosnia & Herzegovina: Sarajevo
UNITED STATES EMBASSY SARAJEVO
Alipašina 43, 71000 SARAJEVO
tel: +387 33 445-700
fax: +387 33 659-722
e-mail: bhopa@state.gov

Copyright © 2011 - GreenCard123.Com by UNorth® - All Rights Reserved

For urgent inquiries, please call the U.S. Embassy at
387-33-445-700
http://sarajevo.usembassy.gov/

Bulgaria: Sofia
The U.S. Embassy in Sofia is located at
16, Kozyak Street
Sofia 1407, Bulgaria
Telephone: +359 2 937 5100
*   +359 2 939 5500*
Fax number: +359 2 937 5320
http://bulgaria.usembassy.gov
http://sofia.usembassy.gov

Croatia: Zagreb
Embassy of the United States of America
2 Thomas Jefferson Street
10010 Zagreb
Croatia
Telephone: 385-1-661-2200
http://zagreb.usembassy.gov/

Cyprus: Nicosia
Metochiou & Ploutarchou Street
2407, Engomi
Nicosia, Cyprus
or
P.O. Box 24536
1385 Nicosia
Cyprus
Telephone: 357-22-393939
Fax: 357-22-780944
http://cyprus.usembassy.gov/

Czech Republic: Prague
Tržiště 15
118 01 Praha 1
Czech Republic
Phone:
(+420) 257 022 000
Fax:
(+420) 257 022 809
http://prague.usembassy.gov/

Denmark: Copenhagen
Embassy of the United States of America
Dag Hammarskjölds Allé 24
2100 København Ø.
Tlf. (+45) 33 41 71 00
Fax: (+45) 35 43 02 23
http://denmark.usembassy.gov/

Estonia: Tallinn
Embassy of the United States of America
Kentmanni 20
15099 Tallinn
Estonia
Embassy phone: (372) 668 8100
Fax: (372) 668 8134
e-mail: USASaatkond@state.gov
http://estonia.usembassy.gov/

Finland: Helsinki
Embassy of the United States of America
Itäinen Puistotie 14 B
00140 Helsinki
Finland
Telephone: +358-9-616 250
http://finland.usembassy.gov/

France: Paris
US Embassy in France
2, avenue Gabriel
75382 Paris Cedex 08
Switchboard: +33 1 43 12 22 22
Fax: +33 1 42 66 97 83
http://france.usembassy.gov/

France: Bordeaux
S Embassy in France
2, avenue Gabriel
75382 Paris Cedex 08
Switchboard: +33 1 43 12 22 22
Fax: +33 1 42 66 97 83
http://france.usembassy.gov/bordeaux.html

France: Lille
US Embassy in France
2, avenue Gabriel
75382 Paris Cedex 08
Switchboard: +33 1 43 12 22 22
Fax: +33 1 42 66 97 83
http://france.usembassy.gov/lille.html

Copyright © 2011 - GreenCard123.Com by UNorth® - All Rights Reserved

France: Lyon
US Embassy in France
2, avenue Gabriel
75382 Paris Cedex 08
Switchboard: +33 1 43 12 22 22
Fax: +33 1 42 66 97 83
http://france.usembassy.gov/lyon.html
France: Rennes

US Embassy in France
2, avenue Gabriel
75382 Paris Cedex 08
Switchboard: +33 1 43 12 22 22
Fax: +33 1 42 66 97 83
http://france.usembassy.gov/rennes.html

France: Toulouse
US Embassy in France
2, avenue Gabriel
75382 Paris Cedex 08
Switchboard: +33 1 43 12 22 22
Fax: +33 1 42 66 97 83
http://france.usembassy.gov/toulouse.html
France: Marseille

US Embassy in France
2, avenue Gabriel
75382 Paris Cedex 08
Switchboard: +33 1 43 12 22 22
Fax: +33 1 42 66 97 83
http://france.usembassy.gov/marseille.html

France: Strasbourg
US Embassy in France
2, avenue Gabriel
75382 Paris Cedex 08
Switchboard: +33 1 43 12 22 22
Fax: +33 1 42 66 97 83
http://france.usembassy.gov/strasbourg.html

Georgia: Tbilisi
1 George Balanchine Street
Tbilisi, Georgia, 0131
Telephone: (995 32) 27-70-00
Fax: (995 32) 53-23-10
http://georgia.usembassy.gov/

Germany: Berlin
http://germany.usembassy.gov/

Germany: Düsseldorf
U.S. Consulate General Duesseldorf
Willi - Becker - Allee 10
40227 Duesseldorf
Tel.: (0211) 788 - 8927
Fax: (0211) 788 - 8938
http://duesseldorf.usconsulate.gov/

Germany: Frankfurt
Gießener Str. 30
60435 Frankfurt am Main
Federal Republic of Germany
Phone: (069) 7535-0
http://frankfurt.usconsulate.gov/

Germany: Hamburg
Consulate General of the United States
Alsterufer 27/28
20354 Hamburg
Federal Republic of Germany
Tel: (040) 411 71 100
Fax: (040) 411 71 222
http://hamburg.usconsulate.gov/

Germany: Leipzig
Consulate General of the United States Leipzig
Wilhelm-Seyfferth- Straße 4
04107 Leipzig
Federal Republic of Germany
Administration: (0341) 213-84-70 or -53
Protocol: (0341) 213-84-52
Information Resource Center (IRC): (0341) 213-84-69
E-mail: leipzig@usconsulate.de
http://leipzig.usconsulate.gov/

Germany: Munich
Consulate General of the United States
Königinstraße 5
80539 Munich
ConsMunich@state.gov
http://munich.usconsulate.gov/

Greece: Athens
U.S. Embassy Athens
91 Vasilisis Sophias Avenue
10160 Athens, Greece
Phone (Main Switchboard/Info): 30-210-721-2951

Copyright © 2011 – GreenCard123.Com by UNorth® – All Rights Reserved

E-mail: AthensAmEmb@state.gov
http://athens.usembassy.gov/

Greece: Thessaloniki
United States Consulate General
43 Tsimiski, 7th Floor
546 23 Thessaloniki GREECE
+30 2310 242 905,6,7
+30 2310 242 927
+30 2310 242 910
info@usconsulate.gr
http://thessaloniki.usconsulate.gov

Hungary: Budapest
Embassy of the United States of America
Szabadság tér 12
H-1054 Budapest
Hungary
http://hungary.usembassy.gov/

Iceland: Reykjavik
American Embassy
Laufásvegur 21
101 Reykjavík
Tel: (354) 562-9100
http://iceland.usembassy.gov/

Ireland: Dublin
U.S. Embassy Dublin
42 Elgin Road
Ballsbridge
Dublin 4
Telephone:
+353 1 668-8777 During Business Hours
+353 1 668 9612, for emergencies involving
American citizens
http://dublin.usembassy.gov/

Italy: Rome
Vittorio Veneto 121 - 00187 ROMA
website: rome.usembassy.gov
Telephone (switchboard): (+39) 06.46741
http://rome.usembassy.gov

Italy: Florence
Vittorio Veneto 121 - 00187 ROMA
website: rome.usembassy.gov
Telephone (switchboard): (+39) 06.46741
http://florence.usconsulate.gov

Italy: Milan
Consulate General of the United States
Via Principe Amedeo 2/10
20121 Milano (Italia)
Tel. (+39) 02.29035.1
Fax (+39) 02.2900.1165
http://milan.usconsulate.gov/

Italy: Naples
Vittorio Veneto 121 - 00187 ROMA
website: rome.usembassy.gov
Telephone (switchboard): (+39) 06.46741
http://naples.usconsulate.gov
Italy: Vatican

American Embassy to the Holy See
Via delle Terme Deciane, 26
00153 - Rome, Italy
Email: Vatican-Info@state.gov
Website: vatican.usembassy.gov
http://vatican.usembassy.gov

Kosovo: Pristina
U.S. Embassy in Pristina
Arberia/Dragodan, Nazim Hikmet 30, Pristina,
Kosovo
Telephone: + 381 38 59 59 3000
Fax: + 381 38 549 890
E-mail: PaPristina@state.gov
For Consular related issues:
E-mail: ConsularPristina@state.gov
http://pristina.usembassy.gov/

Latvia: Riga
U.S. Embassy Riga
Raiņa Blvd. 7
Riga LV-1510
Latvia
Tel: +371 67036200
Fax: +371 67820047
http://riga.usembassy.gov/

Copyright © 2011 - GreenCard123.Com by UNorth® - All Rights Reserved

Lithuania: Vilnius
United States Embassy
Akmenų gatvė 6
Vilnius, Lithuania
LT-03106
Tel: (370-5)2665500
Fax: (370-5)2665510
http://vilnius.usembassy.gov/

Luxembourg
22 Boulevard Emmanuel Servais
L-2535 Luxembourg
Phone: +352 46 01 23
Fax: +352 46 14 01
http://luxembourg.usembassy.gov/

Macedonia: Skopje
Str. "Samoilova" Nr.21
1000 Skopje
Republic of Macedonia
Phone: +389 2 310-2000 (0 -for Switchboard Operator);
Fax: +389 2 310-2499
http://macedonia.usembassy.gov/

Malta: Valletta
Development House, 3rd Floor
St. Anne Street, Floriana, Malta VLT 01
Mailing address:
P.O. Box 535, Valletta, Malta, CMR 01
Telephone Number: (356) 2561 4000
Fax: (356) 21 243229
http://malta.usembassy.gov/

Moldova: Chisinau
103 Mateevici street
Chisinau MD-2009
Republic of Moldova
Tel: (+373 22) 408 300 (Reception)
Fax: (+373 22) 233 044
http://moldova.usembassy.gov/

Montenegro: Podgorica
John Jackson 2
81000 Podgorica
Montenegro
Embassy Switchboard: +382 20 410 500
Embassy Fax: +382 20 241 358
http://podgorica.usembassy.gov/

The Netherlands: The Hague
Embassy of the United States of America
Lange Voorhout 102
2514 EJ The Hague.
T: +31 70 310-2209
F: +31 70 361-4688
http://thehague.usembassy.gov/

The Netherlands: Amsterdam
Museumplein 19
1071 DJ AMSTERDAM
The Netherlands
Tel number 020 575 5331 or 5333
Fax number (31)(0)20-575 5389
E-mail: ImmigrantVisasAms@state.gov
http://amsterdam.usconsulate.gov/

Norway: Oslo
Visas and all matters concerning entering, working in, or residing in the U.S.: oslovisa@state.gov
Federal Benefits: fbu.oslo@ssa.gov
American Citizen Services: osloamcit@state.gov
http://norway.usembassy.gov/

Poland: Warsaw
U.S. Embassy Warsaw
Aleje Ujazdowskie 29/31
00-540 Warsaw Poland
Tel.: +48-22/504-2000
http://poland.usembassy.gov/

Poland: Krakow
Consulate of the United States
Krakow, Poland
Tel: (48 12) 424-5138
Fax: (48 12) 424-5145
http://krakow.usconsulate.gov/

Portugal: Lisbon
United States Embassy
Avenida das Forças Armadas
1600-081 Lisboa
And
Apartado 43033
1601-301 Lisboa
Phone: 351-21-727-3300
Fax: 351-21-726-9109
E-mail: lisbonweb@state.gov
http://portugal.usembassy.gov/

Copyright © 2011 - GreenCard123.Com by UNorth® - All Rights Reserved

Portugal: Ponta Delgada, Azores
Av. Príncipe do Mónaco No, 6-2 F
9500-237 Ponta Delgada, Açores
Portugal
Tel: 351 296-282-216
Fax: 351 296-287-216
ConsPontaDelgada@state.gov
http://pontadelgada.usconsulate.gov/

Romania: Bucharest
The United States Embassy
7-9, Tudor Arghezi Street,
District 2, Bucharest
020942 Romania
Telephone: (+40) 21 200-3300
Fax: (+40) 21 200-3442
http://romania.usembassy.gov/

Russia: Moscow
Bolshoy Deviatinsky Pereulok No. 8
Moscow 121099, Russian Federation - PSC-77, APO
AE 09721
Tel: +7 (495) 728-5000, fax: 728-5090
http://moscow.usembassy.gov/

Russia: St. Petersburg
Bolshoy Deviatinsky Pereulok No. 8
Moscow 121099, Russian Federation - PSC-77, APO
AE 09721
Tel: +7 (495) 728-5000, fax: 728-5090
Russia: Vladivostok
Public Affairs Section
U.S. Consulate General
32 Pushkinskaya St.
Vladivostok 690001
Russia
Tel: +7 (4232) 30 00 70, ext. 4107 or 4109
Fax: +7 (4232) 30 00 95
Email: pavlad@state.gov
http://vladivostok.usconsulate.gov/

Russia: Yekaterinburg
15 Gogol Street,
Yekaterinburg, 620151
Russia
http://yekaterinburg.usconsulate.gov/

Serbia: Belgrade
Kneza Miloša 50
11000 Belgrade

Serbia
Embassy Switchboard: +381 11 361 9344
http://serbia.usembassy.gov/

Slovakia: Bratislava
http://slovakia.usembassy.gov/

Embassy of the U.S.A.
P.O. Box 309
814 99 Bratislava
Slovak Republic
Fax: +421-2-5441 8861
Tel: +421-2-5443 3338
Slovenia: Ljubljana
Prešernova 31
1000 Ljubljana
Slovenia
Phone: +386 (1) 2005500
Fax.: +386 (1) 200-5555
E-mail: USEmbassyLjubljana@state.gov
Web Site: http://slovenia.usembassy.gov/

Spain: Madrid
Phone: 91-587-2200
Fax: 91-587-2303
http://madrid.usembassy.gov/

Spain: Barcelona
Phone: 93-280-2227
 Fax: 93-280-6175
http://barcelona.usconsulate.gov/

Sweden: Stockholm
Embassy of the United States of America
Dag Hammarskjölds Väg 31
SE-115 89 Stockholm, Sweden
Tel: (+46) 8 783 5300
http://stockholm.usembassy.gov/

Switzerland: Bern
Embassy of the United States Bern
Sulgeneckstrasse 19
CH-3007 Bern, Switzerland
Tel: 031 357 70 11
http://bern.usembassy.gov/

Turkey: Ankara
AMERICAN EMBASSY ANKARA
110 Atatürk Blvd.
Kavaklıdere, 06100 Ankara - TURKEY

Copyright © 2011 - GreenCard123.Com by UNorth® - All Rights Reserved

Phone: (90-312) 455-5555
Fax: (90-312) 467-0019
e-mail: webmaster_ankara@state.gov
http://turkey.usembassy.gov/

Turkey: Adana
Amerikan Konsoloslugu / Consulate of the United
States
Girne Bulvari No:212 Guzelevler Mah.
Yuregir, Adana - TURKEY
Local number: (322) 346-6262
http://adana.usconsulate.gov

Turkey: Istanbul
U.S. CONSULATE GENERAL ISTANBUL
İstinye Mahallesi, Kaplıcalar Mevkii
No.2
İstinye 34460 - Istanbul / Turkey
Phone: (90) 212-335 90 00
Webmaster: istanbul-webmaster@state.gov
http://istanbul.usconsulate.gov/

Turkey: VPP Izmir
Izmir Chamber of Commerce
Atatürk Caddesi, No:126, 5th floor
35210 Pasaport
Izmir, Turkey
**Berrin Erturk, Commercial Specialist
(Berrin.Erturk@mail.doc.gov)**
Tel: [90] (232) 441 24 46
Fax: [90] (232) 489 02 67
E-mail: Izmir.Office.Box@mail.doc.gov
http://izmir.usvpp.gov/

United Kingdom: London
Mailing Address
24 Grosvenor Square
London, W1A 1AE
United Kingdom
Switchboard: [44] (0)20 7499-9000
http://london.usembassy.gov/

United Kingdom: VPP Cardiff
Welsh Affairs Office:
Patricia Morales
Welsh Affairs Officer
US EMBASSY LONDON
24 Grosvenor Square
London UK W1A 1AE
Phone:

From Wales: [44] (0)29-2002-6419
From outside Wales: [44](0)20 7984 0131
fax: [44](0)20 7894-0117
http://cardiff.usvpp.gov/

The Vatican
American Embassy to the Holy See
Via delle Terme Deciane, 26
00153 - Rome, Italy
Email: Vatican-Info@state.gov
Website: vatican.usembassy.gov
http://vatican.usembassy.gov

U.S. Mission to International: Organizations in
Vienna
IZD Tower
Wagramerstrasse 17-19
1220 Vienna
Mail-Address:
Boltzmanngasse 16
Vienna, Austria
Phone: (43) (1) 31339 0
E-Mail: pavienna@state.gov
http://vienna.usmission.gov/

U.S. Mission to the EU
United States Mission to the European Union
Zinnerstraat - 13 - Rue Zinner
B-1000 Brussels, Belgium
Telephone: +32-2-508-2111
Public Affairs Office
Email: useupa@state.gov
Fax: +32-2-508-2063
http://useu.usmission.gov/

U.S. Mission to NATO
http://nato.usmission.gov/

U.S. Mission to the OECD
USOECD Mailing Address:
18, avenue Gabriel
75008 Paris, FRANCE
Telephone: +33 (0) 1 43 12 22 22
Fax: +33 (0) 1 45 24 74 80
E-mail: usoecdpao@state.gov
http://usoecd.usmission.gov/

U.S. Mission to the OSCE
U.S. Mission to the OSCE
Obersteinergasse 11/1

Copyright © 2011 - GreenCard123.Com by UNorth® - All Rights Reserved

A-1190 Vienna, Austria
Tel: (+43 1) 31339 0
Fax: (+43 1) 31339 3136
http://osce.usmission.gov/

U.S. Mission to the UN-Geneva
U.S. Mission to the UN Agencies in Rome
Piazza del Popolo 18, 4th Floor
Phone: (06) 4674-3500
Fax: (06) 4674-3535
http://usunrome.usmission.gov

U.S. Mission to the UN-Rome
U.S. Mission to the UN Agencies in Rome
Piazza del Popolo 18, 4th Floor
Phone: (06) 4674-3500
Fax: (06) 4674-3535
http://usunrome.usmission.gov

U.S. Mission to UNESCO
18, avenue Gabriel
75008 Paris, FRANCE
Telephone: +33 (0) 1 45 24 74 56
Fax: +33 (0) 1 45 24 74 58
E-mail: ParisUNESCO@state.gov
http://unesco.usmission.gov/

D. MIDDLE EAST AND NORTH AFRICA

Algeria: Algiers
American Embassy Algiers, Algeria
05 Chemin Cheikh Bachir Ibrahimi
El-Biar 16030
Alger Algerie
Tel: 0770-08-2000
Fax: 021-60-7335
Email: Algiers_webmaster@state.gov
Web Site: http://algiers.usembassy.gov

Bahrain: Manama
Embassy of the United States of America
Bldg 979, Road 3119, Block 331, Zinj
Kingdom of Bahrain
Tel: (973)1724-2700
Fax: (973)1727-0547
http://bahrain.usembassy.gov/

Egypt: Cairo
U.S. Embassy Cairo - 8 Kamal El Din Salah St.,
Garden City, Cairo, Egypt. Tel: [20] [2] 2797-3300
http://cairo.usembassy.gov/

Iraq: Baghdad
irc-baghdad@state.gov
http://iraq.usembassy.gov/

Israel: Tel Aviv
nivtelaviv@state.gov
http://telaviv.usembassy.gov/

Jerusalem
U.S. Consulate General, Jerusalem
18 Agron Road
Jerusalem 94190
Tel.: +972.2.622.7230
Fax: +972.2.625.9270
http://jerusalem.usconsulate.gov/

VPP Gaza
18 Agron Road, Jerusalem 94190
27 Nablus Road, Jerusalem 94190
PHONE: 972-2-6227230 / 972-2-6253288
FAX: 972-2-6259270
E-MAIL: uscongenjerusalem@state.gov
http://gaza.usvpp.gov/

Jordan: Amman
American Embassy
P.O. Box 354, Amman
11118 Jordan
Location:
Abdoun, Al-Umawyeen St.
Amman – Jordan
Telephone: 962-6-590-6000
Fax: 962-6-592-0163
http://jordan.usembassy.gov/

Kuwait: Kuwait City
American Embassy

Copyright © 2011 - GreenCard123.Com by UNorth® - All Rights Reserved

P. O. Box 77
Safat 13001
Kuwait
Telephone: 00-(965) 2259-1001
Fax: 00-(965) 2538-0282
E-mail: paskuwaitm@state.gov
http://kuwait.usembassy.gov/

Lebanon: Beirut
U.S. Embassy in Beirut, Lebanon
Address: Awkar facing the Municipality
P.O. Box 70-840 Antelias
Telephone: (961) 4 542600 - 543600
Fax: (961) 4 544136
http://lebanon.usembassy.gov/

Libya: Tripoli
United States Embassy
Ben Ashour Area, Jraba Street
Tripoli, Libya
TripoliPAO@state.gov
Phone: 218-91-220-3239
http://libya.usembassy.gov/

Morocco: Rabat
Embassy
PSC 74 Box 021
APO AE 09718
Telephone: (212)(537)-76-22-65
Fax: (212)(537)-76-56-61
http://rabat.usembassy.gov/

Morocco: Casablanca
8, Boulevard Moulay Youssef
Casablanca 20000
Morocco
Fax: 212-2-220-4127
http://casablanca.usconsulate.gov/

Oman: Muscat
P.O. Box 202
P.C. 115
Madinat Al Sultan Qaboos
Muscat, Oman
Telephone: (968) 24-643-400
Fax: (968) 24-699-771
http://oman.usembassy.gov/

Qatar: Doha
Embassy of the United States of America

22nd February Street
Al Luqta district
P.O. Box 2399
Doha, Qatar
Telephone: (974) 4488-4101
Fax: (974) 4488-4298
Email: PASDoha@state.gov
http://qatar.usembassy.gov/

Saudi Arabia: Riyadh
American Embassy
P.O. Box 94309
Riyadh 11693
Saudi Arabia
Telephone: 9661-4883800
Fax: 9661-4887360
http://riyadh.usembassy.gov/

Saudi Arabia: Dhahran
Main Telephone: (966-3) 330-3200
Fax: (966-3) 330-0464
P.O. Box 38955, Dhahran Airport, 31942, Saudi
Arabia
http://dhahran.usconsulate.gov/

Saudi Arabia: Jeddah
American Citizen Services,
Consular Section
U.S. Consulate General
Phone: (966-2) 667-0080
Fax: (966-2) 669-3098
P.O. Box 149, Jeddah 21411
Email: Jeddahacs@state.gov
http://jeddah.usconsulate.gov/

Syria: Damascus
Embassy of the United States of America
Abou Roumaneh, 2 Al Mansour Street
P.O. Box 29
Damascus, Syria
Regular/ Operator: 3391-4444
Emergency calls: 3391-3333
damasweb-query@state.gov
http://damascus.usembassy.gov/

Tunisia: Tunis | Français
Les Berges du Lac
1053 TUNIS
Tunisia
Main switchboard: +216 71 107 000

Copyright © 2011 - GreenCard123.Com by UNorth® - All Rights Reserved

Fax: +216 71 963 263
http://tunisia.usembassy.gov/

United Arab Emirates: Abu Dhabi
P.O. Box 4009, Abu Dhabi, UAE
Tel. +971-2 414 2200
http://abudhabi.usembassy.gov/

United Arab Emirates: Dubai
Consulate General of the United States of america
Dubai World Trade Center
PO BOX 9343
Dubai, United Arab Emirates
Tel: +971-(0)4-311-6000
http://dubai.usconsulate.gov/

Yemen: Sana'a
Address: Sa'awan Street, P.O. Box 22347
Telephone: (967) 1 755-2000 EXT. 2153 or 2266
Fax: Main (967) 1 303-182 Consular (967) 1 303-175
http://yemen.usembassy.gov/

E. CENTRAL AND SOUTH ASIA

Afghanistan: Kabul
Embassy of the United States
Kabul, Afghanistan
Tel: (00 93) (0)700-10-8001
Fax: (00 93) (0)700-108-564 or (0)202-300-546
http://kabul.usembassy.gov/

Bangladesh: Dhaka
Embassy of the United States Dhaka
Madani Avenue Baridhara
Dhaka Bangladesh 1212
Main Switchboard: (880) (2) 8855500
http://dhaka.usembassy.gov/

Bangladesh: VPP Chittagong
http://dhaka.usembassy.gov/virtual_consulate_chit tagong3.html
Embassy of the United States Dhaka
Madani Avenue Baridhara
Dhaka Bangladesh 1212
Main Switchboard: (880) (2) 8855500

Bangladesh: VPP Jessore
http://dhaka.usembassy.gov/virtual_consulate_jess ore.html
Embassy of the United States Dhaka
Madani Avenue Baridhara
Dhaka Bangladesh 1212

Bangladesh: VPP Sylhet Embassy of the United States Dhaka
Madani Avenue Baridhara
Dhaka Bangladesh 1212
http://dhaka.usembassy.gov/virtual_consulate_sylh et3.html

India: New Delhi
U.S. Embassy
Shantipath, Chanakyapuri
New Delhi - 110021
Tel: 011-2419-8000
Fax: +91-11-2419-0017
http://newdelhi.usembassy.gov/

India: Hyderabad
Paigah Palace
1-8-323, Chiran Fort Lane
Begumpet, Secunderabad 500 003
Telephone: +91 (40) 4033-8300
Non-Immigrant Visas: HydNIV@state.gov
http://hyderabad.usconsulate.gov/

India: Kolkata
Consulate General of the United States of America
5/1, Ho Chi Minh Sarani,
Kolkata - 700071,
West Bengal, India.
Telephone: 91-33-3984 2400
Facsimile: 91-33-2282 2335
http://kolkata.usconsulate.gov/

India: Chennai
U.S. Consulate General
Gemini Circle
Chennai 600 006
Phone: 044-2857-4000
Fax: 044-2811-2020
http://chennai.usconsulate.gov/

India: Mumbai
U.S. Consulate General, Mumbai
Consul General: Paul A. Folmsbee
Lincoln House
78 Bhulabhai Desai Road

Copyright © 2011 - GreenCard123.Com by UNorth® - All Rights Reserved

Mumbai 400 026
Phone: (22) 2363-3611
Fax: (22) 2363-0350
http://mumbai.usconsulate.gov/

India: VPP Bangalore
Consulate General of the United States of America
Gemini Circle
220 Anna Salai
Chennai 600 006
Telephone: 91-44-2857 4242
Facsimile: 91-44-2811 2020 or 2811-2027
http://bangalore.usvpp.gov/

Kazakhstan: Astana
Ak Bulak 4,
Str. 23-22, building #3, Astana 010010
Astana, Kazakhstan
Phone: +7 (7172) 70-21-00
Fax: +7 (7172) 34-08-90
email: info@usembassy.kz
http://kazakhstan.usembassy.gov/

Kyrgyz Republic: Bishkek
mbassy of the United States of America in the
Kyrgyz Republic
171 Prospect Mira, Bishkek 720016
Kyrgyz Republic
Telephone: +996(312) 551-241
Fax: +996(312) 551-264
Website: http://bishkek.usembassy.gov
Nepal: Kathmandu
Embassy of the United States of America
Maharajgunj, Kathmandu, Nepal
Tel.: 977-1-400-7200
Fax: 977-1-400-7280
kathmandupdlibrary@state.gov
http://nepal.usembassy.gov/

Pakistan: Islamabad
American Embassy
Diplomatic Enclave, Ramna 5
Islamabad, Pakistan
Telephone: (+92) 51-208-0000
Fax: (+92) 51-2276427
webmasterisb@state.gov
http://islamabad.usembassy.gov/

Pakistan: Karachi
Public Affairs Section

Embassy of the United States of America
Diplomatic Enclave, Ramna 5
Islamabad, Pakistan
Tel: (+92-51) 2082060
Fax: (+92-51) 2278607
E-mail: webmasterisb@state.gov
http://karachi.usconsulate.gov/

Pakistan: Lahore
Public Affairs Section
Embassy of the United States of America
Diplomatic Enclave, Ramna 5
Islamabad, Pakistan
Tel: (92-51) 2082060
Fax: (92-51) 2278607
E-mail: webmasterisb@state.gov
http://lahore.usconsulate.gov

Pakistan: Peshawar
Public Affairs Section
Embassy of the United States of America
Diplomatic Enclave, Ramna 5
Islamabad, Pakistan
Tel: (+92-51) 2082060
Fax: (+92-51) 2278607
E-mail: webmasterisb@state.gov
http://peshawar.usconsulate.gov/

Sri Lanka: Colombo
U. S. Embassy
210 Galle Road,
Colombo 03,
Sri Lanka
Phone: +94(11)249-8500
Commercial Affairs:
Phone: +94 (11) 249-8500
E-mail: commercialcolombo@state.gov
http://srilanka.usembassy.gov/

Sri Lanka: VPP Maldives
U.S. Embassy
210 Galle Road,
Colombo 03,
Sri Lanka
Phone: +94 (11) 249-8500
http://maldives.usvpp.gov/

Tajikistan: Dushanbe |
109-A Ismoili Somoni Avenue (Zarafshon district)
Dushanbe, Tajikistan 734019

Copyright © 2011 - GreenCard123.Com by UNorth® - All Rights Reserved

Phone: [992] (37) 229 20 00
Fax: [992] (37) 229 20 50, 236 04 30
Email: usembassydushanbe@state.gov
http://dushanbe.usembassy.gov/

Turkmenistan: Ashgabat
American Embassy
9 1984 Street (formerly Pushkin Street)
Ashgabat, Turkmenistan 744000
Tel: (99312) 35 00 45
Fax:(993-12) 39 26 14
E-mail: consularashgab@state.gov
http://turkmenistan.usembassy.gov/

Uzbekistan: Tashkent
3 Moyqorghon Street, 5th Block,

Yunusobod District, 100093 Tashkent.
The Embassy's switchboard number: (998) (71) 120 5450;
  Fax number: (998) (71) 120 6335
E-mail: TashkentInfo@state.gov
http://uzbekistan.usembassy.gov/

Copyright © 2011 - GreenCard123.Com by UNorth® - All Rights Reserved

APPENDIX

IX. GLOSSARY

Term	Description
A Number	Alien Number, File number, Green Card number, Alien Registration Number, Registered alien Number, case number. File Number, assigned numbers by USCIS or ICE permanent file number for the alien and will appear on work permit green card , naturalization certificate. Should be used in all correspondence with USCIS This is the alien registration number, which the Department of Homeland Security assigns to each alien. It is an "A" followed by eight numbers. For example: A12 345 678. Some recently-issued A numbers consist of an "A" followed by nine digits. For example: A 200 345 678.
Accompanying	A type of visa in which family members travel with the principal applicant, (in immigrant visa cases, within six months of issuance of an immigrant visa to the principal applicant).
Accredited Representative	A person who is approved by the Board of Immigration Appeals (the Board) to represent aliens before the Immigration Courts, the BIA and USCIS. He or she must work for a specific nonprofit, religious, charitable, social service, or similar organization. The organization must be authorized by the Board to represent aliens.
Acquired Citizenship	Citizenship conferred at birth on children born abroad to a U.S. citizen parent(s).
Adjust Status	1) To change from a nonimmigrant visa status or other status 2) To adjust the status of a permanent resident (green card holder). To apply learn more on USCIS's website as it is a Department of Homeland Security (DHS) process.
Adjustment of Status (AOS)	Process in which one becomes permanent resident
Adjustment to Immigrant Status	Procedure allowing certain aliens already in the United States to apply for immigrant status. Aliens admitted to the United States in a nonimmigrant, refugee, or parolee category may have their status changed to that of lawful permanent resident if they are eligible to receive an immigrant visa and one is immediately available. In such cases, the alien is counted as an immigrant as of the date of adjustment, even though the alien may have been in the

United States for an extended period of time. Beginning in October 1994, section 245(i) of the INA allowed illegal residents who were eligible for immigrant status to remain in the United States and adjust to permanent resident status by applying at a USCIS office and paying an additional penalty fee. Section 245(i) is no longer available unless the alien is the beneficiary of a petition under section 204 of the Act or of an application for a labor certification under section 212(a)(5)(A), filed on or before April 30, 2001. And, if filed after January 1, 1998, the alien must have been present in the United States on December 21, 2000. Prior to October 1994, most illegal residents were required to leave the United States and acquire a visa abroad from the Department of State as they are again now.

Term	Description
Administrative processing	Some visa applications require further administrative processing, which takes additional time after the visa applicant's interview by a Consular Officer. Applicants are advised of this requirement when they apply. To learn more review our Administrative Processing webpage.
Admission	Into the U.S. is authorized by a DHS, Customs and Border Protection (CBP) officer.
Adopted Child	An unmarried child under age 21
Adopted Decision	A decision of the Administrative Appeals Office (AAO) binding on all USCIS adjudication officers, but not yet published as a precedent decision.
Adoption	See "Orphan"
Advance Parole	Permission to return to the U.S. after travel abroad granted by DHS prior to leaving the U.S. The following categories of people may need advance parole
Advisory Opinion	An opinion regarding a point of law from the Office of Visa Services in the Department of State, Washington, D.C
Advisory Opinion ("J" Visa) Waiver of Foreign Residence Requirement, INA 212(e):	A J-1 visa /DS 2019 or IAP 66 form will have a statement in the bottom left hand corner of the form, as follows
Affidavit	A document in which a person states facts, swearing that the facts are true and accurate. The person (the affiant) must

Copyright © 2011 - GreenCard123.Com by UNorth® - All Rights Reserved

	include their full printed name and address, date and place of birth, relationship to the parties, if any, and complete details concerning how the affiant acquired knowledge of the events. The affiant should sign the affidavit under oath and the signature should be witnessed by an official, such as a notary public.
Affidavit of Support	A document promising that the person who completes it will support an applicant financially in the U.S. Family and certain employment immigration cases require the I-864 Affidavit of Support, which is legally binding. All other cases use the I-134 Affidavit of Support
affidavit of support	Important form required which petitioner proves or agrees to reimburse the government if person being adjusted requires federal benefits within 5-10 years of adjusting or until person naturalizes
Affiliated	Associated or controlled by the same owner or authority.
Agent	In immigrant visa processing the applicant selects a person who receives all correspondence regarding the case and pays the immigrant visa application processing fee
Agricultural Worker	As a nonimmigrant class of admission, an alien coming temporarily to the United States to perform agricultural labor or services, as defined by the Secretary of Labor.
Alien	Any person not a citizen or national of the United States.
Allotment	The allocation of an immigrant number to a consular office or to USCIS. This number may be used for visa issuance or adjustment of status as described in the Operation of the Immigrant Numerical Control System.
Amerasian (Vietnam)	Immigrant visas are issued to Amerasians under Public Law 100-202 (Act of 12/22/87), which provides for the admission of aliens born in Vietnam after January 1, 1962, and before January 1, 1976, if the alien was fathered by a U.S. citizen. Spouses, children, and parents or guardians may accompany the alien.
Amerasian Act	Public Law 97-359 (Act of 10/22/82) provides for the immigration to the United States of certain Amerasian children. In order to qualify for benefits under this law, an alien must have been born in Cambodia, Korea,

	Laos, Thailand, or Vietnam after December 31, 1950, and before October 22, 1982, and have been fathered by a U.S. citizen.
AOS	Affidavit of Support, Form I-864. A document promising that the person who completes it will support an applicant financially in the U.S
Applicant (Visa)	A foreign citizen who is applying for a nonimmigrant or immigrant U.S. visa. The visa applicant may also be referred as a beneficiary for petition based visas
Application Support Centers	USCIS Offices fingerprint applicants for immigration benefits. Some USCIS applications, such as the Application for Naturalization or the Application to Register Permanent Residence or Adjust Status, require the USCIS to conduct a FBI fingerprint background check on the applicant. Most applicants that require a background check will be scheduled to appear at a specific Application Support Center (ASC).
Appointment Package	The letter and documents that tell an applicant of the date of the immigrant visa interview.
Apprehension	The arrest of a removable alien by U.S. Immigration and Customs Enforcement (ICE). Each apprehension of the same alien in a fiscal year is counted separately.
Approval Notice	A DHS, USCIS immigration form, Notice of Action, Form I-797 that says that USCIS has approved a petition, or request for extension of stay or change of status.
Arrival/departure	See i-94
Arrival-Departure Card	Also known as Form I-94, Arrival-Departure Record
Asylee	A person who cannot return to his home country because of a well-founded fear of persecution. An application for asylum is made in the U.S. to the DHS. Go to the USCIS website to learn more.
Attorney of Record	An attorney who has properly filed a Form G-28 in a particular case and is held responsible as an attorney for the respondent.
Beneficiaries	Aliens on whose behalf a U.S. citizen, legal permanent resident, or employer have filed a petition for such aliens to receive immigration benefits from the U.S. Citizenship and Immigration Services. Beneficiaries generally receive a lawful status as a result of

Copyright © 2011 – GreenCard123.Com by UNorth® – All Rights Reserved

	their relationship to a U.S. citizen, lawful permanent resident, or U.S. employer.
Beneficiary	An alien who is sponsored by a relative or a business, or has self-petitioned for an immigration benefit.
Beneficiary	An applicant for a visa as named in a petition from the DHS, USCIS.
BIA	An abbreviation for the Board of Immigration Appeals.
Biographical information form	See Ge-325A
Biometrics	Biologically unique information used to identify individuals
Board of Immigration Appeals	The part of the Executive Office for Immigration Review that is authorized to review most decisions of Immigration Judges and some types of decisions of Department of Homeland Security officers.
Bond	The amount of money set by the Department of Homeland Security or an Immigration Judge as a condition to release a person from detention for an Immigration Court hearing at a later date.
Bond Proceedings	An Immigration Court hearing on a request to determine a bond set by the Department of Homeland Security. Bond proceedings are separate from other Immigration Court proceedings.
Border Crosser	An alien resident of the United States reentering the country after an absence of less than six months in Canada or Mexico, or a nonresident alien entering the United States across the Canadian border for stays of no more than six months or across the Mexican border for stays of no more than 72 hours.
Business Nonimmigrant	An alien coming temporarily to the United States to engage in commercial transactions which do not involve gainful employment in the United States, i.e., engaged in international commerce on behalf of a foreign firm, not employed in the U.S. labor market, and receives no salary from U.S. sources.
Cancellation of Removal	A discretionary benefit adjusting an alien's status from that of deportable alien to one lawfully admitted for permanent residence. Application for cancellation of removal is made during the course of a hearing before an immigration judge.
Cancelled Without	A stamp an embassy or consulate puts on a visa when there is a mistake in

Prejudice	the visa or the visa is a duplicate visa (two of the same kind)
Case Number	The National Visa Center (NVC) gives each immigrant petition a case number. This number has three letters followed by ten digits (numbers)
Certificate of Citizenship	Identity document proving U.S. citizenship. Certificates of citizenship are issued to derivative citizens and to persons who acquired U.S. citizenship (see definitions for Acquired and Derivative Citizenship).
Certificate of Citizenship	A document issued by the DHS as proof that the person is a U.S. citizen by birth (when born abroad) or derivation (not from naturalization).
Certificate of Naturalization	A document issued by the DHS as proof that the person has become a U.S. citizen (naturalized) after immigration to the U.S.
Certificate of Translation	Any alien granted permanent resident status on a conditional basis (e.g., a spouse of a U.S. citizen; an immigrant investor), who is required to petition for the removal of the set conditions before the second anniversary of the approval of his or her conditional status.
Certified Decision	A decision certified to the AAO for review.
CFR	An abbreviation for the Code of Federal Regulations.
Change Status	Changing from one nonimmigrant visa status to another nonimmigrant visa status while a person is in the U.S. is permitted for some types of visas, if approved by USCIS.
Chargeability	In regards to the Visa Lottery, refers to the country that makes the visa candidate eligible to apply, either applicant's native country or his/her spouse, or parents country, if a Child under 21 and parents from eligible country
Charge/Chargeable	There are numerical limits on the number of immigrant visas that can be granted to aliens from any one foreign country.
Child	Generally, an unmarried person under 21 years of age who is: a child born in wedlock; a stepchild, provided that the child was under 18 years of age at the time that the marriage creating the stepchild relationship occurred; a legitimated child, provided that the child was legitimated while in the legal custody of the legitimating parent; a child born out of wedlock, when a

Copyright © 2011 - GreenCard123.Com by UNorth® - All Rights Reserved

	benefit is sought on the basis of its relationship with its mother, or to its father if the father has or had a bona fide relationship with the child; a child adopted while under 16 years of age who has resided since adoption in the legal custody of the adopting parents for at least 2 years; or an orphan, under 16 years of age, who has been adopted abroad by a U.S. citizen or has an immediate-relative visa petition submitted in his/her behalf and is coming to the United States for adoption by a U.S. citizen.	marriage	woman to enter into marriage without a civil or religious ceremony. It may not be recognized as a marriage for immigration purposes.
Child	Unmarried child under the age of 21 years. A child may be natural born, step or adopted. If the child is a stepchild, the marriage between the parent and the U.S. citizen must have occurred when the child was under the age of 18	Conditional residence (CR) visa	If you have been married for less than two years when your husband or wife (spouse) gets lawful permanent resident status (gets a green card), then your spouse gets residence on a conditional basis. After two years you and your spouse must apply together to the DHS to remove the condition to the residence. Learn about how to apply for a CR visa on our Immigrant Visa for a Spouse webpage.
Child	Unmarried individual under 21 years of age.	Conditional Resident	Any alien granted permanent resident status on a conditional basis (e.g., a spouse of a U.S. citizen; an immigrant investor), who is required to petition for the removal of the set conditions before the second anniversary of the approval of his or her conditional status
Civil Surgeon	A medically trained, licensed and experienced doctor practicing in the U.S. who is certified by USCIS (U.S. Citizenship and Immigration Service). These medical professionals receive U.S. immigration-focused training in order to provide examinations as required by the CDC (Center for Disease Control and Prevention) and USCIS. For medical examinations given overseas, please see Panel Physician. IMPORTANT: medical examinations will not be recognized if they are given by a doctor in the U.S. who is not a Civil Surgeon; please make sure that your appointment is with a Civil Surgeon or your results and documents will be invalid.	Country of -	Birth: The country in which a person is born. Chargeability: The independent country to which an immigrant entering under the preference system is accredited for purposes of numerical limitations. Citizenship: The country in which a person is born (and has not renounced or lost citizenship) or naturalized and to which that person owes allegiance and by which he or she is entitled to be protected. Former Allegiance: The previous country of citizenship of a naturalized U.S. citizen or of a person who derived U.S. citizenship. (Last) Residence: The country in which an alien habitually resided prior to entering the United States. Nationality: The country of a person's citizenship or country in which the person is deemed a national.
Code of Federal Regulations	The official interpretations of laws passed by Congress. These interpretations are known as "regulations." Regulations are first published in a government publication called the Federal Register. After publication in the Federal Register, regulations can be found in the Code of Federal Regulations (CFR). Most immigration regulations are in Title 8 CFR, Aliens and Nationality.	Crewman	A foreign national serving in a capacity required for normal operations and service on board a vessel or aircraft. Crewmen are admitted for twenty-nine days, with no extensions. Two categories of crewmen are defined in the INA: D1, departing from the United States with the vessel or aircraft on which he arrived or some other vessel or aircraft; and D2, departing from Guam with the vessel on which he arrived.
Code of Federal Regulations	The Code of Federal Regulations useful information on the laws regulating U.S. visa policy.		
Cohabit	To live together without a legal marriage ceremony.		
Common-law	An agreement between a man and		

Copyright © 2011 - GreenCard123.Com by UNorth® - All Rights Reserved

Cuban/Haitian Entrant	Status accorded 1) Cubans who entered illegally or were paroled into the United States between April 15, 1980, and October 10, 1980, and 2) Haitians who entered illegally or were paroled into the country before January 1, 1981. Cubans and Haitians meeting these criteria who have continuously resided in the United States since before January 1, 1982, and who were known to Immigration before that date, may adjust to permanent residence under a provision of the Immigration Control and Reform Act of 1986.	**Perjury**	true, to support his or her request or application. For example, a declaration may list the facts and then state: uI declare under penalty of perjury (under the laws of the United States of America) that the foregoing is true and correct." This statement should be followed by the date, signature, and printed name of the person signing.
Current/non-current	There are numerical limits on the number of immigrant visas that can be granted to aliens from any one foreign country. The limit is based on place of birth, not citizenship. Because of the numerical limits, this means there is a waiting time before the immigrant visa can be granted. The terms current/non-current refer to the priority date of a petition in preference immigrant visa cases in relationship to the immigrant cut-off date. If your priority date is before than the cut-off date according to the monthly Visa Bulletin, your case is current. This means your immigrant visa case can now be processed. However, if your priority date is later/comes after the cut-off date, you will need to wait longer, until your priority date is reached (becomes current). To find out whether a preference case is current, see the Visa Bulletin or telephone (202) 663-1541.	**Deferred Inspection**	See "Parolee"
		Denomination/Sect	A religious group or community.
		Department of State	Runs embassies and consulates which decide on immigrant and nonimmigrant visa . also runs passport office
		Department of Homeland Security (DHS)	DHS is comprised of three main organizations responsible for immigration policies, procedures, implementation and enforcement of U.S. laws, and more. These DHS organizations include United States Citizenship and Immigration Services (USCIS), Customs and Border Protection (CBP) and Immigration and Customs Enforcement (ICE). Together they provide the basic governmental framework for regulating the flow of visitors, workers and immigrants to the U.S. USCIS is responsible for the approval of all immigrant and nonimmigrant petitions, the authorization of permission to work in the U.S., the issuance of extensions of stay, change or adjustment of an applicant's status while the applicant is in the U.S, and more. CBP is responsible for admission of all travelers seeking entry into the U.S., and determining the length of authorized stay, if the traveler is admitted. Once in the U.S. the traveler falls under the jurisdiction of DHS. Visit the DHS website for more information.
Cut-off Date	The date that determines whether a preference immigrant visa applicant can be scheduled for an immigrant visa interview in any given month. The cut-off date is the priority date of the first applicant who could not get a visa interview for a given month. Applicants with a priority date earlier than the cut-off date can be scheduled. However, if your priority date is on or later than the cut-off date, you will need to wait longer, until your priority date is reached (becomes current). To find out whether a preference case is current, see the Visa Bulletin or telephone (202) 663-1541.	**Department of Labor**	A cabinet level unit/ministry of U.S. Government that has responsibility for labor issues. It has responsibility for deciding whether certain foreign workers can work in the U.S.
		Deportable Alien	An alien in and admitted to the United States subject to any grounds of removal specified in the Immigration and Nationality Act. This includes any alien illegally in the United States, regardless of whether the alien entered the country by fraud or misrepresentation or entered legally
Declaration under Penalty of	A statement by a person, in which the person states that the information is		

Copyright © 2011 - GreenCard123.Com by UNorth® - All Rights Reserved

	but subsequently violated the terms of his or her nonimmigrant classification or status.
Deportation	The formal removal of an alien from the United States when the alien has been found removable for violating the immigration laws. Deportation is ordered by an immigration judge without any punishment being imposed or contemplated. Prior to April 1997 deportation and exclusion were separate removal procedures. The Illegal Immigration Reform and Immigrant Responsibility Act of 1996 consolidated these procedures. After April 1, 1997, aliens in and admitted to the United States may be subject to removal based on deportability. Now called Removal, this function is managed by U.S. Immigration and Customs Enforcement.
Deportation	Occurs when a person is physically taken by DHS deportation officer to his or her native country,
Derivative Citizenship	Citizenship conveyed to children through the naturalization of parents or, under certain circumstances, to foreign-born children adopted by U.S. citizen parents, provided certain conditions are met.
Derivative Status	Getting a status (visa) through another applicant, as provided under immigration law for certain visa categories. For example, the spouse and children of an exchange visitor (J Visa holder), would be granted derivative status as a J-2 Visa holder. Derivative status is only possible if the principal applicant is issued a visa.
DHS	An abbreviation for the Department of Homeland Security.
DHS	Newly formed department responsible for government function related to security. Former INS has split into USCIS and ice
District	Geographic areas into which the United States and its territories are divided for the Immigration and Naturalization Service's field operations or one of three overseas offices located in Rome, Bangkok, and Mexico City. Each District Office, headed by a District Director, has a specified service area that may include part of a state, an entire state, or many states. District Offices are where most USCIS field staff are located. District Offices are responsible for

	providing certain immigration services and benefits to people resident in their service area, and for enforcing immigration laws in that jurisdiction. Certain applications are filed directly with District Offices, many kinds of interviews are conducted at these Offices, and USCIS staff is available to answer questions, provide forms, etc.
Diversity	A category of immigrants replacing the earlier categories for nationals of underrepresented countries and countries adversely "affected" by the Immigration and Nationality Act Amendments of 1965 (P.L. 89-236). The annual limit on diversity immigration was 40,000 during fiscal years 1992-94, under a transitional diversity program, and 55,000 beginning in fiscal year 1995, under a permanent diversity program.
Diversity visa	A green card lottery run by department of state I which 100000 people will be notified that they will be allowed to adjust status but only 50000 available
Diversity Visa Program	The Department of State has an annual lottery for immigration to the U.S. Up to 55,000 immigrants can enter the U.S. each year from countries with low rates of immigration to the U.S. See our information on the Diversity Visa Program.
Docket Control	The DHS mechanism for tracking the case status of potentially removable aliens.
Documentarily Qualified	The applicant has obtained all documents specified by the consular officer as sufficient to meet the formal visa application requirements, and necessary processing procedures of the consular office have been completed.
DOJ	An abbreviation for the United States Department of Justice.
DOL	U.S. Department of Labor. Hiring foreign workers for employment in the U.S. normally requires approval from several government agencies. First, employers must seek labor certification through the DOL. Once the application is certified (approved), the employer must petition the USCIS for approval of the petition before applying for a visa.
Domicile	Place where a person has his or her principal residence. The person must

Copyright © 2011 - GreenCard123.Com by UNorth® - All Rights Reserved

	intend to keep that residence for the foreseeable future. The sponsor of an immigrant must have domicile in the U.S. before the visa can be issued. This generally means that the sponsor must be living in the U.S. In certain circumstances, however one can be considered to have a domicile while living temporarily living overseas.
Duration of Status	In certain visa categories such as diplomats, students and exchange visitors, the alien may be admitted into the U.S. for as long as the person is still doing the activity for which the visa was issued, rather than being admitted until a specific departure dates. This is called admission for "duration of status". For students, the time during which a student is in a full course of study plus any authorized practical training, and following that, authorized time to depart the country, is duration of status. The length of time depends upon the course of study. For an undergraduate degree this is commonly four years (eight semesters). Normally the immigration officer gives a student permission to stay in the U.S. for "duration of status". Duration of Status (or D/S) is recorded on Form I-94, Arrival-Departure Record. The DHS U.S. immigration inspector at port-of-entry gives foreign visitors (all non-U.S. citizens) an Arrival-Departure Record, (a small white card) when they enter the U.S. Recorded on this card is the visa classification and the authorized period of stay in the U.S. This is either recorded as a date or the entry or D/S, meaning duration of status. The I-94 is a very important card to make sure you keep, because it shows the length of time you are permitted and authorized by the DHS to stay in the U.S. For more information visit the USCIS website
EAD	A photo identification card issued by the USCIS that evidences the holder's authorization to work in the us and obtain social security card
Educational and Cultural Affairs	The Bureau of Educational and Cultural Affairs (ECA) of the U.S. Department of State fosters mutual understanding between the people of the U.S. and the people of other countries to promote friendly, sympathetic, and peaceful relations. ECA administers a

	variety of exchange programs for non-U.S. secondary, undergraduate, graduate students and professionals, along with other duties. Visit the ECA Website
Embassy	Main office for the us government located in foreign country
Employer Sanctions	The employer sanctions provision of the Immigration Reform and Control Act of 1986 prohibits employers from hiring, recruiting, or referring for a fee aliens known to be unauthorized to work in the United States. Violators of the law are subject to a series of civil fines for violations or criminal penalties when there is a pattern or practice of violations.
EOIR	An abbreviation for the Executive Office for Immigration Review.
ESTA: Electronic System for Travel Authorization (ESTA)	is a free, automated system that determines the eligibility of visitors (nationals from 35 participating countries) to travel to the U.S. without a visa under the Visa Waiver Program (VWP). A valid ESTA approval is required for all VWP travel to the U.S. ESTA applications may be submitted at any time prior to travel, though it is recommended travelers apply when they begin preparing travel plans. To learn whether you may be able to travel on VWP, and therefore whether you need an ESTA authorization, see the Visa Waiver Program webpage on this website. For more information about ESTA and/or to apply, see the DHS, Custom and Border Protection's ESTA webpage
Exchange Visitor	An alien coming temporarily to the United States as a participant in a program approved by the Secretary of State for the purpose of teaching, instructing or lecturing, studying, observing, conducting research, consulting, demonstrating special skills, or receiving training.
Exchange Visitor	A foreign citizen coming to the U.S. to participate in a particular program in education, training, research, or other authorized exchange visitor program. See the Educational and Cultural Affairs Internet site and our Exchange Visitor page for more information.
Exchange Visitor Skills List	The Exchange Visitor Skills List (J Visas) is a list of fields of specialized knowledge and skills that are deemed necessary for the development of an exchange visitor's home country.

Copyright © 2011 - GreenCard123.Com by UNorth® - All Rights Reserved

	When you agree to participate in an Exchange Visitor Program, if your skill is on your country's Skills List you are subject to the two-year foreign residence (home-country physical presence) requirement, which requires you to return to your home country for two years at the end of your exchange visitor program, under U.S. law. Review the Exchange Visitor webpage to learn more.	**Federal Poverty Guidelines**	See Poverty Guidelines. The Department of Health and Human Services publishes a list every year giving the lowest income acceptable for a family of a particular size so that the family does not live in poverty. Consular officers use these figures in immigrant visa cases to determine whether a sponsor's income is sufficient to support a new immigrant, in accordance with U.S. immigration laws. Visit USCIS's Poverty Guidelines webpage for more information.
Exclusion	Prior to the Illegal Immigration Reform and Immigrant Responsibility Act of 1996, exclusion was the formal term for denial of an alien's entry into the United States. The decision to exclude an alien was made by an immigration judge after an exclusion hearing. Since April 1, 1997, the process of adjudicating inadmissibility may take place in either an expedited removal process or in removal proceedings before an immigration judge.	**Fiance(e):**	A person who plans or is contracted to marry another person. The foreign fiancé(e) of an American citizen may enter the U.S. on a K-1 visa to marry the American citizen. Visit our Fiancé(e) webpage to learn more.
		Fiancé(e)s of U.S. Citizen	A nonimmigrant alien coming to the United States to conclude a valid marriage with a U.S. citizen within ninety days after entry.
Exclusion	Occurs when a lawful permanent resident with a criminal record attemps to reenter the country and is not allowed to enter	**Field Offices**	Offices found in some Districts that serve a portion of the District's jurisdiction. A Field Office, headed by an Field Office Director, provides many services and enforcement functions. Their locations are determined, in part, to increase convenience to USCIS' customers.
Executive Office for Immigration Review	The part of the United States Department of Justice that is responsible for the Immigration Courts and the Board of Immigration Appeals.		
Family First Preference	A category of family immigration (F1) for unmarried sons and daughters of American citizens, and their children. Visit our Family Based Immigration webpage for more info.	**File number**	See A Number
		Files Control Office	An USCIS field office--either a district (including USCIS overseas offices) or a sub office of that district--where alien case files are maintained and controlled.
Family Fourth Preference	A category of family immigration (F4) for brothers and sisters of American citizens and their spouses and children. The American citizen must be 21 years of age or older before he/she can file the petition. Before 1992 this was known as fifth preference (P-5). Visit our Family Based Immigration webpage for more info.	**Filing receipt**	Small yellow cash register receipt attached to the receipt letter upon filing an adjustment case
		First Preference	A category of family immigration (F1) for unmarried sons and daughters of American citizens and their children. Visit our Family Based Immigration webpage for more info.
Family Second Preference	A category of family immigration (F2) for spouses, children and unmarried sons and daughters of lawful permanent residents. Visit our Family Based Immigration webpage for more info.	**Fiscal Year**	Currently, the twelve-month period beginning October 1 and ending September 30. Historically, until 1831 and from 1843-49, the twelve-month period ending September 30 of the respective year; from 1832-42 and 1850-67, ending December 31 of the respective year; from 1868-1976, ending June 30 of the respective year. The transition quarter (TQ) for 1976 covers the three-month period, July-September 1976.
Family Third Preference	A category of family immigration (F3) for married sons and daughters of American citizens and their spouses and children. Before 1992 this was known as fourth preference (P-4). Visit our Family Based Immigration webpage for more info.		
		Fiscal Year	The budget year for the U.S.

Copyright © 2011 – GreenCard123.Com by UNorth® – All Rights Reserved

	Government. It begins on October 1 and ends on September 30 of the following year.
FOIA	An abbreviation for the Freedom of Information Act.
Foia	Important law allowing anyone to obtain copy of his or her file held at a governmental agency, such as uscis
Following to Join	A type of derivative visa status when the family member gets a visa after the principal applicant.
Foreign Affairs Manual (9 FAM)	Foreign Affairs Manual Chapter 41 relates to nonimmigrant visas. Chapter 42 covers immigrant visas. 9 FAM Chapter 40 relates to visa ineligibilities and waivers. Go to our site to review the FAM relating to visas.
Foreign Government Official	As a nonimmigrant class of admission, an alien coming temporarily to the United States who has been accredited by a foreign government to function as an ambassador, public minister, career diplomatic or consular officer, other accredited official, or an attendant, servant or personal employee of an accredited official, and all above aliens' spouses and unmarried minor (or dependent) children.
Foreign Information Media Representative	As a nonimmigrant class of admission, an alien coming temporarily to the United States as a bona fide representative of foreign press, radio, film, or other foreign information media and the alien's spouse and unmarried minor (or dependent) children.
Foreign State of Chargeability	The independent country to which an immigrant entering under the preference system is accredited. No more than 7 percent of the family-sponsored and employment-based visas may be issued to natives of any one independent country in a fiscal year. No one dependency of any independent country may receive more than 2 percent of the family-sponsored and employment-based visas issued. Since these limits are based on visa issuance rather than entries into the United States, and immigrant visas are valid for 6 months, there is not total correspondence between these two occurrences. Chargeability is usually determined by country of birth. Exceptions are made to prevent the separation of family members when the limitation for the country of birth has been met.

Fourth Preference	A category of family immigration (F4) for brothers and sisters of American citizens and their spouses and children. The American citizen must be 21 years of age or older before he/she can file a petition. Before 1992 this was known as fifth preference (P-5). Visit our Family Based Immigration webpage for more info.
Full and Final Adoption	A legal adoption in which the child receives all the rights of a natural born, legitimate child. For more adoptions information visit our Adoptions website.
g-325a	Detailed biographic information form that is required with an adjustment of status application and other petitions. One of the copies is sent to the embassy in the native country and another is sent to the ICA to perform record checks. Required for all adjustment applications 14 years or older
General Naturalization Provisions	The basic requirements for naturalization that every applicant must meet, unless a member of a special class. General provisions require an applicant to be at least 18 years of age and a lawful permanent resident with five years of continuous residence in the United States, have been physically present in the country for half that period, and establish good moral character for at least that period.
Geographic Area of Chargeability	Any one of five regions--Africa, East Asia, Latin America and the Caribbean, Near East and South Asia, and the former Soviet Union and Eastern Europe--into which the world is divided for the initial admission of refugees to the United States. Annual consultations between the Executive Branch and the Congress determine the ceiling on the number of refugees who can be admitted to the United States from each area. Beginning in fiscal year 1987, an unallocated reserve was incorporated into the admission ceilings.
Green card	A wallet-sized card showing that the person is a lawful permanent resident (immigrant) in the U.S. It is also known as a permanent resident card (PRC), an alien registration receipt card and I-551. It was formerly green in color. For more information visit the USCIS website.

Copyright © 2011 - GreenCard123.Com by UNorth® - All Rights Reserved

Green Card holder	Lawful permanent resident
Green Card number	See a number
Green Card stamp	Temporary stamp placed by USCIS officer into a passport signifying his or her adjustment of status
Hemispheric Ceilings	Statutory limits on immigration to the United States in effect from 1968 to October 1978. Mandated by the Immigration and Nationality Act Amendments of 1965, the ceiling on immigration from the Eastern Hemisphere was set at 170,000, with a per-country limit of 20,000. Immigration from the Western Hemisphere was held to 120,000, without a per-country limit until January 1, 1977. The Western Hemisphere was then made subject to a 20,000 per country limit. Effective October 1978, the separate hemisphere limits were abolished in favor of a worldwide limit.
Homeless	Persons from countries that do not have an American Embassy or Consulate where they can apply for immigrant visas are "homeless". For example, the U.S. Government does not have an embassy in Iran. Residents of Iran are "homeless" for visa purposes.
Household income	The income used to determine whether a sponsor meets the minimum income requirements under Section 213A of the Immigration and Nationality Act (INA) for some immigrant visa cases.
i-364	Affidavit of support
I-551 (Green Card):	Permanent residence card or alien registration receipt card or "green card." See Lawful Permanent Resident.
i-797	A letter by USCIS/Consulate informing the applicant of the receipt of application or approval of the application
i-864	Affidavit of support
i-94	Small white card stapled into ones passport upon admission to the US on a non immigrant visa. It contains the date of expiration of the non immigrant visa
I-94(W)	The I-94 Arrival/Departure Record fort nonimmigrant travelers or I-94W (Green) for Visa Waiver Program travelers. When you are admitted the CBP officer at the U.S. port of entry will stamp your passport and issue a completed Form I-94 or I-94W to you, which denotes how long you are legally authorized to stay within the U.S. Visit the CBP website to learn more.
ICE	An abbreviation for the U.S. Immigration and Customs Enforcement, a part of the Department of Homeland Security.
Illegal alien	One who is in the us out of status or who entered without inspection
Immediate Relative	Spouse, widow(er) and unmarried children under the age of 21 of an American citizen. A parent is an immediate relative if the American citizen is 21 years of age or older. There are no numerical limits to immigration of immediate relatives.
Immediate relative	Spouse parent child of us citizen. Adopted children must have been adopted before age of 16 and step children before age of 18
Immediate Relatives	Certain immigrants who because of their close relationship to U.S. citizens are exempt from the numerical limitations imposed on immigration to the United States. Immediate relatives are: spouses of citizens, children (under 21 years of age and unmarried) of citizens, and parents of citizens 21 years of age or older.
Immigrant	See "Permanent Resident Alien"
Immigrant visa	A visa for a person who plans to live indefinitely and permanently in the U.S. Visit our Immigrant Visa section of this website.
Immigration Act of 1990	Public Law 101-649 (Act of November 29, 1990), which increased the limits on legal immigration to the United States, revised all grounds for exclusion and deportation, authorized temporary protected status to aliens of designated countries, revised and established new nonimmigrant admission categories, revised and extended the Visa Waiver Pilot Program, and revised naturalization authority and requirements.
Immigration and Nationality Act	The Act (INA), which, along with other immigration laws, treaties, and conventions of the United States, relates to the immigration, temporary admission, naturalization, and removal of aliens.
Immigration and Nationality Act (INA):	American immigration law. The Immigration and Nationality Act, or INA, was created in 1952, Public Law No. 82-414. The INA has been

Copyright © 2011 - GreenCard123.Com by UNorth® - All Rights Reserved

Immigration and Naturalization Service (INS):	A branch of the Department of Justice that formerly existed and had responsibility for immigration and naturalization. INS was renamed and became part of DHS on March 1, 2003. To learn more, go to the DHS website.
Immigration Judge	An attorney appointed by the Attorney General to act as an administrative judge within the Executive Office for Immigration Review. They are qualified to conduct specified classes of proceedings, including removal proceedings.
Immigration Marriage Fraud Amendments of 1986	Public Law 99-639 (Act of 11/10/86), which was passed in order to deter immigration-related marriage fraud. Its major provision stipulates that aliens deriving their immigrant status based on a marriage of less than two years are conditional immigrants. To remove their conditional status the immigrants must apply at an U.S. Citizenship and Immigration Services office during the 90-day period before their second-year anniversary of receiving conditional status. If the aliens cannot show that the marriage through which the status was obtained was and is a valid one, their conditional immigrant status may be terminated and they may become deportable.
Immigration Reform and Control Act of 1986 (IRCA)	Public Law 99-603 (Act of 11/6/86), which was passed in order to control and deter illegal immigration to the United States. Its major provisions stipulate legalization of undocumented aliens who had been continuously unlawfully present since 1982, legalization of certain agricultural workers, sanctions for employers who knowingly hire undocumented workers, and increased enforcement at U.S. borders.
In status	It's important to understand the concept of immigration status and the consequences of violating that status. Being aware of the requirements and possible consequences will make it more likely that you can avoid problems with maintaining your status. Every visa is issued for a particular purpose and for a specific class of visitor. Each visa classification has a set of requirements that the visa holder must follow and maintain. Those who follow the requirements maintain their status and ensure their

	ability to remain in the U.S. Those who do not follow the requirements violate their status and are considered "out of status". For more information see "Out of Status" below. In Status means you are in compliance with the requirements of your visa type under immigration law. For example, you are a foreign student who entered the U.S. on a student visa. If you are a full time student and pursuing your course of study, and are not engaged in unauthorized employment, you are "in status". If you work full time in your uncle's convenience store and do not study, you are "out of status". See the DHS, USCIS website Extension of Stay and Change of Status.
INA	See "Immigration and Nationality Act"
INA	See Immigration and Nationality Act.
Inadmissible	An alien seeking admission at a port of entry who does not meet the criteria in the INA for admission. The alien may be placed in removal proceedings or, under certain circumstances, allowed to withdraw his or her application for admission.
Inadmissible	Any one of a number of grounds such as criminal acts or medical conditions that cause an alien not to be admitted to the US
Industrial Trainee	See "Temporary Worker"
Ineligible/Ineligibility	Immigration law says that certain conditions and actions prevent a person from entering the U.S. These conditions and activities are called ineligibilities, and the applicant is ineligible for (cannot get) a visa. Examples are selling drugs, active tuberculosis, being a terrorist, and using fraud to get a visa. Read our information on the Classes of Aliens Ineligible to Receive Visas to learn more.
Infopass	An online appointment made through the USCIS website to speak to an immigration information officer regarding the status of a pending case or to take certain nations in regards to it
INS	An abbreviation of the name for the Immigration and Naturalization Service offices. The INS was abolished and its functions placed under three agencies – U.S. Citizenship and Immigration Services (USCIS), ICE and CBP – within the newly created DHS.
Ins	As of march 01, 2003 ins does not

Copyright © 2011 - GreenCard123.Com by UNorth® - All Rights Reserved

	exist. USCIS , ice
Inspection	To be inspected by an immigration officer at an airport or border to on a ship. The officer will check to see that all documents are in order. The office may admit, send the alien back or refer the alien to deferred admission
International Representative	As a nonimmigrant class of admission, an alien coming temporarily to the United States as a principal or other accredited representative of a foreign government (whether officially recognized or not recognized by the United States) to an international organization, an international organization officer or employee, and all above aliens' spouses and unmarried minor (or dependent) children.
Intracompany Trainee	An alien, employed for at least one continuous year out of the last three by an international firm or corporation, who seeks to enter the United States temporarily in order to continue to work for the same employer, or a subsidiary or affiliate, in a capacity that is primarily managerial, executive, or involves specialized knowledge, and the alien's spouse and minor unmarried children.
IRCA	See "Immigration Reform and Control Act of 1986 (IRCA)"
IV	Immigrant Visa
Joint Sponsor	A person who accepts legal responsibility for supporting an immigrant with an I-864 Affidavit of Support along with the sponsor. The joint sponsor must be at least 18 years of age, an American citizen or lawful permanent resident and have a domicile in the U.S. The joint sponsor and his/her household must have the 125 percent income requirement by itself for the immigrant that he/she sponsors. Visit our NVC section on Joint Sponsors for more information.
Jurisdiction	Authority to apply the law in a given territory or region. For example, the INS district office in the area where a person lives has jurisdiction or authority to decide on a fiancé(e) petition.
Kentucky Consular Center (KCC):	A U.S. Department of State facility located in Williamsburg, Kentucky. It gives domestic (U.S.) support to the worldwide operations of the Bureau of Consular Affairs Visa Office. It manages the Diversity Visa (DV) Program.
Labor Certification	Requirement for U.S. employers seeking to employ certain persons whose immigration to the United States is based on job skills or nonimmigrant temporary workers coming to perform services for which qualified authorized workers are unavailable in the United States. Labor certification is issued by the Secretary of Labor and contains attestations by U.S. employers as to the numbers of U.S. workers available to undertake the employment sought by an applicant, and the effect of the alien's employment on the wages and working conditions of U.S. workers similarly employed. Determination of labor availability in the United States is made at the time of a visa application and at the location where the applicant wishes to work.
Labor Certification	The initial stage of the process by which certain foreign workers get permission to work in the U.S. The employer is responsible for getting the labor certification from the Department of Labor. In general the process works to make sure that the work of foreign workers in the U.S. will not adversely affect job opportunities, wages and working conditions of U.S. workers.
Labor Condition Application (LCA):	A request to the Department of Labor for a foreign worker to work in the U.S.
Lawful Permanent Resident (LPR)	Any person not a citizen of the United States who is residing the in the U.S. under legally recognized and lawfully recorded permanent residence as an immigrant. Also known as "Permanent Resident Alien," "Resident Alien Permit Holder," and "Green Card Holder."
Lawful Permanent Resident (LPR):	A person who has immigrated legally but is not an American citizen. This person has been admitted to the U.S. as an immigrant and has a Permanent Resident Card, Form I-551 (formerly called Alien Registration Card, also known as green card). It is a wallet-sized card showing that the person is a lawful permanent resident (immigrant) in the U.S. Learn more about Lawful Permanent Residents, including how to replace or renew a Permanent Resident Card, on the USCIS Website. Learn about requirements for entry into the U.S. on the CBP website. This person may also be called a legal permanent resident, a green card

Copyright © 2011 - GreenCard123.Com by UNorth® - All Rights Reserved

	holder, a permanent resident alien, a legal permanent resident alien (LPRA) and resident alien permit holder.
Lawful Permanent Resident Alien (LPRA):	Lawful permanent resident.
Lawful permanent resident lpr	The most correct term for someone who has adjusted status to immigrant visa
Laws (Immigration and visa related laws)	The Code of Federal Regulations useful information on the laws regulating U.S. visa policy.
Lay Worker	A person who works in a religious organization but is not a member of the formal clergy.
LEA	See local educational agency.
Legalization Dependents	A maximum of 55,000 visas were issued to spouses and children of aliens legalized under the provisions of the Immigration Reform and Control Act of 1986 in each of fiscal years 1992-94.
Legalized Aliens	Certain illegal aliens who were eligible to apply for temporary resident status under the legalization provision of the Immigration Reform and Control Act of 1986. To be eligible, aliens must have continuously resided in the United States in an unlawful status since January 1, 1982, not be excludable, and have entered the United States either 1) illegally before January 1, 1982, or 2) as temporary visitors before January 1, 1982, with their authorized stay expiring before that date or with the Government's knowledge of their unlawful status before that date. Legalization consists of two stages--temporary and then permanent residency. In order to adjust to permanent status aliens must have had continuous residence in the United States, be admissible as an immigrant, and demonstrate at least a minimal understanding and knowledge of the English language and U.S. history and government.
Legitimated	Most countries have legal procedures for natural fathers of children born out of wedlock to acknowledge their children. A legitimated child from any country has two legal parents and cannot qualify as an orphan unless:
Legitimation	The legal process which a natural father can use to acknowledge legally his children who were born out of wedlock (outside of marriage). A

	legitimated child can be a "child" under immigration law under these conditions: • the legitimation took place according to the law of the child's residence or the father's residence; • the father proved (established) that he is the child's natural father; • the child was under the age of 18; and • The child was in the legal custody of the father who legitimated the child when the legal process of legitimating took place.
LIFE	An abbreviation for Legal Immigration and Family Equity Act.
LIFE Act	Legal Immigration Family Equity (LIFE) Act and amendments. This act of Congress allows foreign spouses of American citizens, the children of those foreign spouses, and spouses and children of certain lawful permanent residents (LPR) to come to the U.S. to complete the processing for their permanent residence. This Act became effective on December 21, 2000.
Local Educational Agency	School or school district. Also called LEA. This term is used for deciding tuition charges for secondary school students in F-1 visa status.
Lose status	To stay in the U.S. longer than the period of time which DHS gave to a person when he/she entered the U.S., or to fail to meet the requirements or violate the terms of the visa classification. The person becomes "out of status". For example, you entered the U.S. on a student visa to study at a university. You work at your uncle's convenience store without authorization, and do not study. You have lost status. You are out of status.
Lottery	See diversity visa program
Lottery	Diversity visa
LPR	An abbreviation for lawful permanent resident.
LPR or LPRA	See lawful permanent resident (LPR)
Machine Readable Passport (MRP):	A passport which has biographic information entered on the data page according to international specifications. A machine readable passport is required to travel with a visa on the Visa Waiver Program. See the Visa Waiver Program (VWP) to learn more about the requirements.
Machine Readable Visa	A visa that contains biometric information about the passport

Copyright © 2011 - GreenCard123.Com by UNorth® - All Rights Reserved

(MRV):	holder. A visa that immigration officers read with special machines when the applicants enter the U.S. It gives biographic information about the passport holder and tells the DHS information on the type of visa. It is also called MRV.	**National Visa Center (NVC):**	A Department of State facility located in Portsmouth, New Hampshire. It supports the worldwide operations of the Bureau of Consular Affairs Visa Office. The NVC processes immigrant visa petitions from the DHS for people who will apply for their immigrant visas at embassies and consulates abroad. It also collects fees associated with immigrant visa processing. Go to the NVC webpage for more information.
Maintain status	To follow the requirements of the visa status and comply with any limitations on duration of stay.		
Means-tested Public Benefits	Assistance from a government unit. Benefits include food stamps, Medicaid, Supplemental Security Income, Temporary Assistance for Needy Families, and State Child Health Insurance Program.	**Nationality**	Citizenship of the person (applying or in question)
		Native	A person born in a particular country is a native of that country.
Medical and Legal Parolee	See "Parolee"	**NATO Official**	As a nonimmigrant class of admission, an alien coming temporarily to the United States as a member of the armed forces or as a civilian employed by the armed forces on assignment with a foreign government signatory to NATO (North Atlantic Treaty Organization), and the alien's spouse and unmarried minor (or dependent) children.
Medical Waiver	A medical waiver permits an immigration applicant to be allowed into, or remain in the United States despite having a health condition identified as grounds of inadmissibility. Terms and conditions can be applied to a medical waiver on a case by case basis.		
Migrant	A person who leaves his/her country of origin to seek residence in another country.	**Naturalization**	The conferring, by any means, of citizenship upon a person after birth.
Missionary Work	Work performed for a religious organization to spread the faith (religion) and advance the principles and doctrines of the religion. Such work may include religious instruction, help for the elderly and needy and proselytizing.	**Naturalization**	A citizen who acquires nationality of a country after birth. That is, the person did not become a citizen by birth, but by a legal procedure. See the USCIS website for more information.
		Naturalization	Process where a green card holder becomes us citizen
Motion	Any type of written request, normally to the immigration court but also to a USCIS office or service center	**Naturalization Application**	The form used by a lawful permanent resident to apply for U.S. citizenship. The application is filed with U.S. Citizenship and Immigration Services at the Service Center with jurisdiction over the applicant's place of residence.
MRV	See Machine Readable Visa		
NACARA	Nicaraguan Adjustment and Central American Relief Act		
NAFTA	North American Free-Trade Agreement.	**Nonimmigrant**	An alien who seeks temporary entry to the United States for a specific purpose. The alien must have a permanent residence abroad (for most classes of admission) and qualify for the nonimmigrant classification sought. The nonimmigrant classifications include: foreign government officials, visitors for business and for pleasure, aliens in transit through the United States, treaty traders and investors, students, international representatives, temporary workers and trainees, representatives of foreign information media, exchange visitors, fiancé(e)s of U.S. citizens, intracompany
Name check	One of the four security checks run before adjusting any application.,. information is queries from FBI's record system.		
National	A person owing permanent allegiance to a state.		
National Interest Waiver	This is for physicians and doctors who work in an area without adequate health care workers or who work in Veterans Affairs' facilities. These physicians and doctors can file immigrant visa petitions for themselves without first applying for a labor certification.		

Copyright © 2011 – GreenCard123.Com by UNorth® – All Rights Reserved

	transferees, NATO officials, religious workers, and some others. Most nonimmigrants can be accompanied or joined by spouses and unmarried minor (or dependent) children.
Nonimmigrant Visa (NIV):	A U.S. visa allows the bearer, a foreign citizen, to apply to enter the U.S. temporarily for a specific purpose. Nonimmigrant visas are primarily classified according to the principal purpose of travel. With few exceptions, while in the U.S., nonimmigrants are restricted to the activity or reason for which their visa was issued. Examples of persons who may receive nonimmigrant visas are tourists, student, diplomats and temporary workers. For more information, see Temporary Visitors to the U.S.
Non preference Category	Nonpreference visas were available to qualified applicants not entitled to a visa under the preferences until the category was eliminated by the Immigration Act of 1990. Nonpreference visas for persons not entitled to the other preferences had not been available since September 1978 because of high demand in the preference categories. An additional 5,000 nonpreference visas were available in each of fiscal years 1987 and 1988 under a provision of the Immigration Reform and Control Act of 1986. This program was extended into 1989, 1990, and 1991 with 15,000 visas issued each year. Aliens born in countries from which immigration was adversely affected by the Immigration and Nationality Act Amendments of 1965 (Public Law 89-236) were eligible for the special nonpreference visas.
North American Free Trade Agreement (NAFTA)	Public Law 103-182 (Act of 12/8/93), superseded the United States-Canada Free-Trade Agreement as of 1/1/94. It continues the special, reciprocal trading relationship between the United States and Canada (see United States-Canada Free-Trade Agreement), and establishes a similar relationship with Mexico.
Notice of Action	A DHS, USCIS immigration form, Notice of Action, Form I-797 that says that USCIS has received a petition you submitted, taken action, approved a petition or denied a petition.
NSEERS	National Security Entry-Exit Registration System also known as

	Special Registration, was put in place after September 11, 2001, to keep track of those entering and leaving our country in order to safeguard U.S. citizens and America's borders. Learn more on the Immigration and Customs Enforcement website.
Numerical Limit, Exempt from	Those aliens accorded lawful permanent residence who are exempt from the provisions of the flexible numerical limit of 675,000 set by the Immigration Act of 1990. Exempt categories include immediate relatives of U.S. citizens, refugees, asylees (limited to 10,000 per year by section 209(b) of the Immigration and Nationality Act), Amerasians, aliens adjusted under the legalization provisions of the Immigration Reform and Control Act of 1986, and certain parolees from the former Soviet Union and Indochina.
Nursing Relief Act of 1989	Public Law 101-238 (Act of 12/18/89), provides for the adjustment to permanent resident status of certain nonimmigrants who as of September 1, 1989, had H-1 nonimmigrant status as registered nurses; who had been employed in that capacity for at least 3 years; and whose continued nursing employment meets certain labor certification requirements.
NVC	See National Visa Center
Occupation	For an alien entering the United States or adjusting without a labor certification, occupation refers to the employment held in the country of last legal residence or in the United States. For an alien with a labor certification, occupation is the employment for which certification has been issued.
Orphan	The Immigration and Nationality Act provides a definition of an orphan for the purposes of immigration to the United States.
Orphan	A child who has no parents because of death, disappearance, desertion or abandonment of the parents. A child may also be considered an orphan if the child has an unwed mother, or a single living parent who cannot care for the child and has released him/her irrevocably (permanently) for adoption and emigration. Adoptive parents must make sure that a child meets the legal definition of an "orphan" before adopting a child from another country. For more information visit our

Copyright © 2011 - GreenCard123.Com by UNorth® - All Rights Reserved

	Adoptions website.
Orphan Petition	Form I-600
Out of status	A U.S. visa allows the bearer to apply for entry to the U.S. in a certain classification, for a specific purpose. For example, student (F), visitor (B), temporary worker (H). Every visa is issued for a particular purpose and for a specific class of visitor. Each visa classification has a set of requirements that the visa holder must follow and maintain. When you arrive in the U.S., a DHS CBP inspector determines whether you will be admitted, length of stay and conditions of stay in, the U.S. When admitted you are given a Form I-94 (Arrival/Departure Record), which tells you when you must leave the U.S. The date granted on the I-94 card at the airport governs how long you may stay in the U.S. If you do not follow the requirements, you stay longer than that date, or you engage in activities not permitted for your particular type of visa, you violate your status and are considered be "out of status". It is important to understand the concept of immigration status and the consequences of violating that status. Failure to maintain status can result in arrest, and violators may be required to leave the U.S. Violation of status also can affect the prospect of readmission to the U.S. for a period of time, by making you ineligible for a visa. Most people who violate the terms of their status are barred from lawfully returning to the U.S. for years. See our Visa Expiration Date page for more information.
Out of Wedlock	A child born of parents who were not legally married to each other at that time.
Overstay	An "Overstay" occurs when a visitor stays longer than permitted as shown on his/her Arrival/Departure (I-94) card. A violation of the CBP defined length of admission may make you ineligible for a visa in the future. See Out of status.
Panama Canal Act Immigrants	Three categories of special immigrants established by Public Law 96-70 (Act of 9/27/79): 1) certain former employees of the Panama Canal Company or Canal Zone Government, their spouses and accompanying children; 2) certain former employees of the U.S. Government in the Panama Canal

	Zone who are Panamanian nationals, their spouses and children; and 3) certain former employees of the Panama Canal Company or Canal Zone Government on April 1, 1979, their spouses and children. The Act provides for admission of a maximum of 15,000 immigrants, at a rate of no more than 5,000 each year.
Panel Physician	A medically trained, licensed and experienced doctor practicing overseas who is appointed by the local U.S. Embassy or Consulate. These medical professionals receive U.S. immigration-focused training in order to provide examinations as required by the CDC (Center for Disease Control and Prevention) and USCIS (U.S. Citizenship and Immigration Services). For medical examinations given in the U.S., please see "Civil Surgeon."
Panel Physician	U.S. Embassies and Consulates which issue immigrant visas have selected certain doctors to do the medical examinations for immigrant visa applicants. To view their medical documents please visit our Medical Examination webpage to find your local Panel Physician.
Parolee	A parolee is an alien, appearing to be inadmissible to the inspecting officer, allowed into the United States for urgent humanitarian reasons or when that alien's entry is determined to be for significant public benefit. Parole does not constitute a formal admission to the United States and confers temporary status only, requiring parolees to leave when the conditions supporting their parole cease to exist. Types of parolees include:
Per Country Limit	The maximum number of family-sponsored and employment-based preference visas that can be issued to citizens of any country in a fiscal year. The limits are calculated each fiscal year depending on the total number of family-sponsored and employment-based visas available. No more than 7 percent of the visas may be issued to natives of any one independent country in a fiscal year; no more than 2 percent may issued to any one dependency of any independent country. The per-country limit does not indicate, however, that a country is entitled to the maximum number of visas each year, just that it cannot

Copyright © 2011 - GreenCard123.Com by UNorth® - All Rights Reserved

	receive more than that number. Because of the combined workings of the preference system and per-country limits, most countries do not reach this level of visa issuance.
Permanent Resident	Any person not a citizen of the United States who is residing in the U.S. under legally recognized and lawfully recorded permanent residence as an immigrant. Also known as "Permanent Resident Alien", "Lawful Permanent Resident," "Resident Alien Permit Holder," and "Green Card Holder."
Permanent Resident (correctly called Lawful Permanent Resident (LPR))	A person who has immigrated legally, admitted to the U.S. by DHS and has a Permanent Resident Card, Form I-551 (formerly called Alien Registration Card, also known as green card. Form-551 is a wallet-sized card documenting that person is a lawful permanent resident (immigrant) in the U.S. Learn more about Lawful Permanent Residents, including how to replace or renew a Permanent Resident Card, on the USCIS Website. Learn about requirements for entry into the U.S. on the CBP Website. The Permanent Resident Card,, issued by DHS is not a visa, although some people incorrectly may think so. LPR's may also be called a legal permanent resident, green card holder, a permanent resident alien, a legal permanent resident alien (LPRA) and resident alien permit holder. An LPR is not an American citizen.
Permanent Resident Alien	An alien admitted to the United States as a lawful permanent resident. Permanent residents are also commonly referred to as immigrants; however, the Immigration and Nationality Act (INA) broadly defines an immigrant as any alien in the United States, except one legally admitted under specific nonimmigrant categories (INA section 101(a)(15)). An illegal alien who entered the United States without inspection, for example, would be strictly defined as an immigrant under the INA but is not a permanent resident alien. Lawful permanent residents are legally accorded the privilege of residing permanently in the United States. They may be issued immigrant visas by the Department of State overseas or adjusted to permanent resident status by U.S. Citizenship and Immigration Services in the United States.

Petitioner	A person who files an immigration petition or application.
Physical Presence	The place where a person is actually, physically located.
Polygamy	Having more than one husband or wife at the same time. Polygamy is illegal under American law.
Port of Entry	Any location in the United States or its territories that is designated as a point of entry for aliens and U.S. citizens. All district and files control offices are also considered ports, since they become locations of entry for aliens adjusting to immigrant status.
Port of Entry	Place (often an airport) where a person requests admission to the U.S. by the DHS, CBP officer. Learn more on the CBP website.
Post	U.S. Embassy, Consulate or other diplomatic mission abroad. Not all U.S. Embassies, Consulates and missions are visa-issuing posts. Visit a lost of U.S. Embassies, Consulates, and Missions
Poverty Guidelines	The Department of Health and Human Services publishes a list every year giving the lowest income acceptable for a family of a particular size so that the family does not live in poverty. Consular officers use these figures in immigrant visa cases to determine whether a sponsor's income is sufficient to support a new immigrant, in accordance with U.S. immigration laws. Go to the Federal Poverty Guidelines to learn more.
Practitioner	A person who is authorized to file immigration petitions or applications with USCIS on behalf of aliens.
Precedent Decision	A published decision of the BIA or the AAO that is binding on all USCIS officers in the administration of the Immigration and Nationality Act (INA).
Preference Immigration	A system for determining which and when people can immigrate to the U.S. within the limits of immigration set by Congress. In family immigration preference is based on the status of the petitioner (American citizen or lawful permanent resident) and his/her relationship to the applicant. Visit our Family Based Immigration webpage for more info. In employment immigration it is based on the qualifications of the applicant and labor needs in the U.S.Visit our Employment-based Visas webpage for more info.

Copyright © 2011 - GreenCard123.Com by UNorth® - All Rights Reserved

Preference System (Immigration Act of 1990)	The nine categories since fiscal year 1992 among which the family-sponsored and employment-based immigrant preference visas are distributed. The family-sponsored preferences are: 1) unmarried sons and daughters of U.S. citizens; 2) spouses, children, and unmarried sons and daughters of permanent resident aliens; 3) married sons and daughters of U.S. citizens; 4) brothers and sisters of U.S. citizens. The employment-based preferences are: 1) priority workers (persons of extraordinary ability, outstanding professors and researchers, and certain multinational executives and managers); 2) professionals with advanced degrees or aliens with exceptional ability; 3) skilled workers, professionals (without advanced degrees), and needed unskilled workers; 4) special immigrants; and 5) employment creation immigrants (investors).
Preference System (prior to fiscal year 1992)	The six categories among which 270,000 immigrant visa numbers were distributed each year during the period 1981-91. This preference system was amended by the Immigration Act of 1990, effective fiscal year 1992. (see Preference System - Immigration Act of 1990). The six categories were: 1) unmarried sons and daughters (over 21 years of age) of U.S. citizens (20 percent); 2) spouses and unmarried sons and daughters of aliens lawfully admitted for permanent residence (26 percent); 3) members of the professions or persons of exceptional ability in the sciences and arts (10 percent); 4) married sons and daughters of U.S. citizens (10 percent); 5) brothers and sisters of U.S. citizens over 21 years of age (24 percent); and 6) needed skilled or unskilled workers (10 percent). A nonpreference category, historically open to immigrants not entitled to a visa number under one of the six preferences just listed, had no numbers available beginning in September 1978.
Pre-inspection	Complete immigration inspection of airport passengers before departure from a foreign country. No further immigration inspection is required upon arrival in the United States other than submission of Form I-94 for nonimmigrant aliens.
Principal Alien	The alien who applies for immigrant status and from whom another alien may derive lawful status under immigration law or regulations (usually spouses and minor unmarried children).
Principal Applicant	The person named in the petition. For example, an American citizen may file a petition for his married daughter to immigrate to the U.S. His daughter will be the principal applicant, and her family members will get visas from her position. They will get derivative status. Or a company may file a petition for a worker. The worker is the principal applicant. Family members get derivative status.
Priority Date	In the USCIS Immigrant visa petition application process, the priority date is the date the petition was filed. If the alien relative has a priority date on or before the date listed in the visa bulletin, then he or she is currently eligible for a visa.
Priority Date	The priority date decides a person's turn to apply for an immigrant visa. In family immigration the priority date is the date when the petition was filed at a DHS, office or submitted to an Embassy or Consulate abroad. In employment immigration the priority date may be the date the labor certification application was received by the Department of Labor (DOL).
Public Charge	Refers to becoming dependent upon the government for the expenses of living (food, shelter, clothing, etc.). Following U.S. immigration law, an applicant is ineligible for a visa if he/she will be a public charge. For more information about Public Charge see the USCIS website.
Qualifying date	The date which the Visa Office of the Department of State uses the qualifying date to determine when to send the Instruction Package to an immigrant visa applicant. The Instruction Package tells the applicant what documents need to be prepared for the immigrant visa application.
Rank Order Number	The number that Kentucky Consular Center gives to the entries of DV Program (lottery) as the computer selects them. The first entries chosen have the lowest numbers. The Visa Office of the Department of State gives winning entries a chance to apply

Copyright © 2011 – GreenCard123.Com by UNorth® – All Rights Reserved

	for immigration according to their rank order number for their region. Visit our DV Program webpage for more information on the Diversity Visa Lottery Program.
Receipt Notice	A DHS, USCIS form Notice of Action, I-797, which says that the DHS has received a petition.
Record of Proceedings	The official file containing documents relating to an alien's case.
Re-entry Permit	A travel document that the DHS issues to lawful permanent residents (LPR's) who want to stay outside of the U.S. for more than one year and less than two years. LPR's who cannot get a passport from their country of nationality can also apply for a re-entry permit. You can put visas for foreign countries in a re-entry permit.
Refugee	Any person who is outside his or her country of nationality who is unable or unwilling to return to that country because of persecution or a well-founded fear of persecution. Persecution or the fear thereof must be based on the alien's race, religion, nationality, membership in a particular social group, or political opinion. People with no nationality must generally be outside their country of last habitual residence to qualify as a refugee. Refugees are subject to ceilings by geographic area set annually by the President in consultation with Congress and are eligible to adjust to lawful permanent resident status after one year of continuous presence in the United States.
Refugee	A person who has a well-founded fear of persecution if he/she should return to his/her home country. He/she applies to come to the United States in another country and enters the U.S. as a refugee. See the DHS, USCIS website Refugee information to learn more.
Refugee	One who is in the US having been granted refugee status
Refugee Approvals	The number of refugees approved for admission to the United States during a fiscal year.
Refugee Arrivals	The number of refugees admitted to the United States through ports of entry during a fiscal year.
Refugee Authorized Admissions	The maximum number of refugees allowed to enter the United States in a given fiscal year. As set forth in the Refugee Act of 1980 (Public Law 96-

	212) the President determines the annual figure after consultations with Congress.
Refugee-Parolee	A qualified applicant for conditional entry, between February 1970 and April 1980, whose application for admission to the United States could not be approved because of inadequate numbers of seventh preference visas. As a result, the applicant was paroled into the United States under the parole authority granted to the Secretary of Homeland Security.
Regional Offices	The three USCIS Regional Offices that supervise the work of USCIS Districts. The Regional Directors report to the Associate Director for Domestic Operations in USCIS Headquarters, Washington, DC. The three Regional Offices are located in (Eastern Region) Burlington, VT, (Central Region) Dallas, TX, and (Western Region) Laguna Nigel, CA. A fourth Regional Office (Southeastern Region) is planned for Orlando, FL.
Registry Date	Aliens who have continuously resided in the United States since January 1, 1972, are of good moral character, and are not inadmissible, are eligible to adjust to legal permanent resident status under the registry provision. Before the Immigration Reform and Control Act of 1986 amended the date, aliens had to have been in the country continuously since June 30, 1948, to qualify.
Removal	The expulsion of an alien from the United States. This expulsion may be based on grounds of inadmissibility or deportability.
Required Departure	See "Voluntary Departure"
Resettlement	Permanent relocation of refugees in a place outside their country of origin to allow them to establish residence and become productive members of society there. Refugee resettlement is accomplished with the direct assistance of private voluntary agencies working with the Department of Health and Human Services Office of Refugee Resettlement.
Resident Alien	Applies to non-U.S. citizens currently residing in the United States. The term is applied in three different manners; please see Permanent Resident, Conditional Resident, and Returning

Copyright © 2011 - GreenCard123.Com by UNorth® - All Rights Reserved

	Resident
Retrogression	Sometimes a case that is current one month will not be current the next month. This occurs when the annual numerical limit has been reached. This usually happens near the end of a fiscal year (October 1 to September 30 of the next year). When the new fiscal year begins, the Visa Office gets a new supply of visa numbers and usually brings back the cut-off dates to where they were before retrogression.
Returning Resident	Any Lawful Permanent Resident who has been outside the United States and is returning to the U.S. Also defined as a "special immigrant." If outside of the U.S. for more than 180 days, must apply for readmission to the U.S. If outside of the U.S. for more than one year and is returning to his or her permanent residence in the United States, usually must have a re-entry documentation from USCIS or an immigrant visa from the Department of State.
Returning Residents	Lawful permanent residents who want to return to the U.S. after staying abroad more than one year or beyond the expiration of their re-entry permits. For more information, visit our Returning Resident webpage
Revalidation or Renewal of a Visa	Nonimmigrant visa applicants who currently have a visa, and are seeking renewal or revalidation of their visa for future travel to the U.S. must apply abroad, generally in their country of residence. The exception is renewal or revalidation of A, G, and NATO diplomatic and official visas (except A-3, G-5 and NATO-7), which continue to be processed in Washington and at the U.S. Mission to the United Nations in New York. See Visa Renewal to learn more.
Revocation of a Visa	Cancellation of a visa. The visa is no longer good (valid) for travel to the U.S.
ROP	An abbreviation for Record of Proceedings.
Safe Haven	Temporary refuge given to migrants who have fled their countries of origin to seek protection or relief from persecution or other hardships, until they can return to their countries safely or, if necessary until they can obtain permanent relief from the conditions they fled.
SAW	See Special Agricultural Worker

Schedule "A" Occupations	The Department of Labor (DOL) has given the DHS, authority to approve labor certifications for these occupations. These occupations are physical therapists, professional nurses and people of exceptional ability in the sciences or arts.
Second Preference	A category of family immigration (F2) for spouses, children and unmarried sons and daughters of lawful permanent residents. Visit our Family Based Immigration webpage for more info.
Section 213A	A section of the Immigration and Nationality Act (INA) which establishes that sponsors have a legal duty to support immigrants they want to bring (sponsor) to the U.S. They must complete Form I-864 Affidavit of Support.
Service Centers	Four offices established to handle the filing, data entry, and adjudication of certain applications for immigration services and benefits. The applications are mailed to USCIS Service Centers -- Service Centers are not staffed to receive walk-in applications or questions.
Sibling	Brother or sister.
Skills List	The Exchange Visitor Skills List (J Visas) is a list of fields of specialized knowledge and skills that are deemed necessary for the development of an exchange visitor's home country. When you agree to participate in an Exchange Visitor Program, if your skill is on your country's Skills List you are subject to the two-year foreign residence (home-country physical presence) requirement, which requires you to return to your home country for two years at the end of your exchange visitor program, under U.S. law. Review the Exchange Visitor webpage to learn more
Son/daughter	In immigration law a child becomes a son or daughter when he/she turns 21 or marries. A son or daughter must have once met the definition of a child in immigration law.
Special Agricultural Worker	Farm workers in perishable products who worked for a specified period of time and were able to adjust status to lawful permanent resident according to the Immigration Reform and Control Act of 1986
Special Agricultural	Aliens who performed labor in perishable agricultural commodities

Copyright © 2011 - GreenCard123.Com by UNorth® - All Rights Reserved

Workers (SAW)	for a specified period of time and were admitted for temporary and then permanent residence under a provision of the Immigration Reform and Control Act of 1986. Up to 350,000 aliens who worked at least 90 days in each of the 3 years preceding May 1, 1986 were eligible for Group I temporary resident status. Eligible aliens who qualified under this requirement but applied after the 350,000 limit was met and aliens who performed labor in perishable agricultural commodities for at least 90 days during the year ending May 1, 1986 were eligible for Group II temporary resident status. Adjustment to permanent resident status is essentially automatic for both groups; however, aliens in Group I were eligible on December 1, 1989 and those in Group II were eligible one year later on December 1, 1990.
Special Immigrant	A special category of immigrant visas (E-4) for persons who lost their citizenship by marriage; persons who lost citizenship by serving in foreign armed forces; certain foreign medical school graduates; Panama Canal immigrants; and certain others. Visit our Employment-based Visas webpage for more information
Special Immigrants	Certain categories of immigrants who were exempt from numerical limitation before fiscal year 1992 and subject to limitation under the employment-based fourth preference beginning in 1992; persons who lost citizenship by marriage; persons who lost citizenship by serving in foreign armed forces; ministers of religion and other religious workers, their spouses and children; certain employees and former employees of the U.S. Government abroad, their spouses and children; Panama Canal Act immigrants; certain foreign medical school graduates, their spouses and children; certain retired employees of international organizations, their spouses and children; juvenile court dependents; and certain aliens serving in the U.S. Armed Forces, their spouses and children.
Special Naturalization Provisions	Provisions covering special classes of persons whom may be naturalized even though they do not meet all the general requirements for

	naturalization. Such special provisions allow: 1) wives or husbands of U.S. citizens to file for naturalization after three years of lawful permanent residence instead of the prescribed five years; 2) a surviving spouse of a U.S. citizen who served in the armed forces to file his or her naturalization application in any district instead of where he/she resides; and 3) children of U.S. citizen parents to be naturalized without meeting certain requirements or taking the oath, if too young to understand the meaning. Other classes of persons who may qualify for special consideration are former U.S. citizens, servicemen, seamen, and employees of organizations promoting U.S. interests abroad.
Sponsor	There are many ways to sponsor an alien. The term "sponsor" in the immigration sense, often means to bring to the United States or "petition for". If you would like to sponsor, or petition for, a relative, please read the information entitled "Immigration Through a Family Member" If you would like to sponsor, or petition for, an employee, please see the instructions entitled "How Do I Get Immigrant Status Based on Employment?" If you would like to sponsor, or petition for, an overseas orphan, please refer to the information entitled "How do I bring an orphan to the United States to live?"
Sponsor	1) A person who fills out and submits an immigration visa petition. Another name for sponsor is petitioner, OR 2) a person who completes an affidavit of support (I-864) for an immigrant visa applicant.
Sponsored Immigrant	An immigrant who has had an affidavit of support filed for him/her.
Spouse	Legally married husband or wife. A co-habiting partner does not qualify as a spouse for immigration purposes. A common-law husband or wife may or may not qualify as a spouse for immigration purposes, depending on the laws of the country where the relationship occurs
State Workforce Agency	The agency or bureau in each State that deals with employment and labor issues. For the address of workforce agency in each State go to the U.S.

Copyright © 2011 - GreenCard123.Com by UNorth® - All Rights Reserved

	Department of Labor, Foreign Labor Certification site.		6 to 18 months and may be extended depending on the situation. Removal proceedings are suspended against aliens while they are in Temporary Protected Status.
Stateless	Having no nationality.		
Stepchild	A spouse's child from a previous marriage or other relationship. In order for a stepchild to be able to immigrate as a "child," the marriage creating the stepchild/stepparent relationship must have happened before the stepchild was 18 years of age.	**Temporary Resident**	See "Nonimmigrant"
		Temporary Worker	An alien coming to the United States to work for a temporary period of time. The Immigration Reform and Control Act of 1986 and the Immigration Act of 1990, as well as other legislation, revised existing classes and created new classes of nonimmigrant admission. Nonimmigrant temporary worker classes of admission are as follows:
Stowaway	An alien coming to the United States surreptitiously on an airplane or vessel without legal status of admission. Such an alien is subject to denial of formal admission and return to the point of embarkation by the transportation carrier.		
Student	As a nonimmigrant class of admission, an alien coming temporarily to the United States to pursue a full course of study in an approved program in either an academic (college, university, seminary, conservatory, academic high school, elementary school, other institution, or language training program) or a vocational or other recognized nonacademic institution.	**Temporary Worker**	A foreign worker who will work in the U.S. for a limited period of time. Some visas classes for temporary workers are H, L, O, P, Q and R. If you are seeking to come to the U.S. for employment as a temporary worker in the U.S. (H, L, O, P, and Q visas), your prospective employer must file a petition with the DHS, USCIS. This petition must be approved by USCIS before you can apply for a visa. Select temporary workers to visit the USCIS website and learn more. Select temporary worker visas to go to the Department of State website to learn more, and review information about NAFTA workers (TN visa) and treaty traders/investors (E visas).
Subject to the Numerical Limit	Categories of legal immigrants subject to annual limits under the provisions of the flexible numerical limit of 675,000 set by the Immigration Act of 1990. The largest categories are: family-sponsored preferences; employment-based preferences; and diversity immigrants.		
Surviving Parent	A child's living parent when the child's other parent is dead, and the living parent has not remarried.		
SWA	See State Workforce Agency	**Termination of a Case**	If the applicant fails to reply to the inquiry correspondence sent by their embassy or consulate, termination of their visa application will begin. The embassy or consulate will first send a Follow-up Letter and Instruction Package to the applicant. If the applicant does not answer within one year, a termination letter is sent. At this point the applicant has one more year to activate the immigrant visa case. If there is no answer in one year, the case is terminated. You can stop termination of a case by notifying the embassy or consulate before the prescribed time period has lapsed, that the applicant does not want the case to be closed (terminated).
Tax-exempt	A condition of the law in which an organization or people in some kinds of work do not have to pay taxes which regular citizens or businesses must pay. Religious organizations are often tax-exempt		
Temporary Protected Status (TPS)	Establishes a legislative basis for allowing a group of persons temporary refuge in the United States. Under a provision of the Immigration Act of 1990, the Secretary of Homeland Security may designate nationals of a foreign state to be eligible for TPS with a finding that conditions in that country pose a danger to personal safety due to ongoing armed conflict or an environmental disaster. Grants of TPS are initially made for periods of		
		Third Country National	Someone who is not an American and not a citizen of the country in which you are applying for a visa. Suppose you are a Kenyan visiting Mexico. If you apply for a visa to visit the U.S.

Copyright © 2011 – GreenCard123.Com by UNorth® – All Rights Reserved

Third Preference	while you are in Mexico, we will consider you a third country national. A category of family immigration (F3) for married sons and daughters of American citizens and their spouses and children. Before 1992 this was known as fourth preference (P-4). Visit our Family Based Immigration webpage for more info.
Transit Alien	An alien in immediate and continuous transit through the United States, with or without a visa, including, 1) aliens who qualify as persons entitled to pass in transit to and from the United Nations Headquarters District and foreign countries and 2) foreign government officials and their spouses and unmarried minor (or dependent) children in transit.
Transit Without Visa (TWOV)	A transit alien traveling without a nonimmigrant visa under section 233 of the INA. An alien admitted under agreements with a transportation line, which guarantees his immediate and continuous passage to a foreign destination.
Treaty Trader or Investor	As a nonimmigrant class of admission, an alien coming to the United States, under the provisions of a treaty of commerce and navigation between the United States and the foreign state of such alien, to carry on substantial trade or to direct the operations of an enterprise in which he/she has invested a substantial amount of capital, and the alien's spouse and unmarried minor children.
Two Year Home-Country Physical Presence Requirement	This refers to (J) exchange visitors who are required to return to your home country for two years at the end of your exchange visitor program, under U.S. immigration law. To learn more review the Exchange Visitor webpage.
Underrepresented Countries, Natives of	The Immigration Amendments of 1988, Public Law 101-658 (Act of 11/5/88) allowed for 10,000 visas to be issued to natives of underrepresented countries in each of fiscal years 1990 and 1991. Under-represented countries are defined as countries that received less than 25 percent of the maximum allowed under the country limitations (20,000 for independent countries and 5,000 for dependencies) in fiscal year 1988.
United States - Canada Free-Trade Agreement	Public Law 100-449 (Act of 9/28/88) established a special, reciprocal trading relationship between the United States and Canada. It provided two new classes of nonimmigrant admission for temporary visitors to the United States-Canadian citizen business persons and their spouses and unmarried minor children. Entry is facilitated for visitors seeking classification as visitors for business, treaty traders or investors, intracompany transferees, or other business people engaging in activities at a professional level. Such visitors are not required to obtain nonimmigrant visas, prior petitions, labor certifications, or prior approval but must satisfy the inspecting officer they are seeking entry to engage in activities at a professional level and that they are so qualified. The United States-Canada Free-Trade Agreement was superseded by the North American Free-Trade Agreement (NAFTA) as of 1/1/94.
Upgrade a petition	If you naturalize (become an American citizen) you may ask the to change the petitions you filed for family members when you were a lawful permanent resident (LPR) from one category to another. This is called upgrading. For example, a petition for a spouse will be changed/upgraded from F2 to IR1. That is, the petition changes from a preference category with numerical limits to an immediate relative category without numerical limits. The applicant no longer has to wait for her/his priority date to be reached.
USCIS	An abbreviation for U.S. Citizenship and Immigration Services, a part of the Department of Homeland Security.
Visa	A U.S. visa allows the bearer to apply for entry to the U.S. in a certain classification (e.g. student (F), visitor (B), temporary worker (H)). A visa does not grant the bearer the right to enter the United States. The Department of State (DOS) is responsible for visa adjudication at U.S. Embassies and Consulates outside of the U.S. The Department of Homeland Security (DHS), Bureau of Customs and Border Protection (BCBP) immigration inspectors determine admission into, length of stay and conditions of stay in, the U.S. at a port of entry. The information on a nonimmigrant visa only relates to when an individual may apply for entry into the U.S. DHS

Copyright © 2011 - GreenCard123.Com by UNorth® - All Rights Reserved

	immigration inspectors will record the terms of your admission on your Arrival/Departure Record (I-94 white or I-94W green) and in your passport.
Visa	A citizen of a foreign country, wishing to enter the U.S., generally must first obtain a visa, either a nonimmigrant visa for temporary stay, or an immigrant visa for permanent residence. Visa applicants will need to apply overseas, at the U.S. Embassy or Consulate, generally in their country of permanent residence. The type of visa you must have is defined by immigration law, and relates to the purpose of your travel. A visa allows a foreign citizen to travel to the U.S. port-of entry, and request permission of the U.S. immigration inspector to enter the U.S. Issuance of a visa does not guarantee entry to the U.S. The CBP Officer at the port-of-entry determines whether you can be admitted and decides how long you can stay for any particular visit. Visit our What Is A Visa? webpage for more information.
Visa	Refers to one of the nonimmigrant temporary visas of which most common is the tourist b-2 visa
Visa bulletin	Monthly newsletter by department of state available online or via mail which indicates categories of the visa currently available
Visa Expiration Date	The visa expiration date is shown on the visa. This means the visa is valid, or can be used from the date it is issued until the date it expires, for travel for the same purpose, when the visa is issued for multiple entries. This time period from the visa issuance date to visa expiration date as shown on the visa, is called visa validity. If you travel frequently as a tourist for example, with a multiple entry visa, you do not have to apply for a new visa each time you want to travel to the U.S. As an example of travel for the same purpose, if you have a visitor visa, it cannot be used to enter at a later time to study in the U.S. The visa validity is the length of time you are permitted to travel to a port-of-entry in the U.S. to request permission of the U.S. immigration inspector to permit you to enter the U.S. The visa does not guarantee entry to the U.S. The Expiration Date for the visa should not

	be confused with the authorized length of your stay in the U.S., given to you by the U.S. immigration inspector at port-of-entry, on the Arrival-Departure Record, Form I-94, or I-94W for the Visa Waiver Program. The visa expiration date has nothing to do with the authorized length of your stay in the U.S. for any given visit.
Visa Numbers	Congress establishes the amount of immigration each year. Immigration for immediate relatives is unlimited; however, preference categories are limited. To distribute the visas fairly among all categories of immigration, the Visa Office in the Department of State distributes the visas by providing visa numbers according to preference and priority date. To learn more on how the numbers are created each month review our Operation of the Immigrant Numerical Control System webpage.
Visa Validity	This generally means the visa is valid, or can be used from the date it is issued until the date it expires, for travel for the same purpose for visas, when the visa is issued for multiple entries. The visa expiration date is shown on the visa. Depending on the alien's nationality, visas can be issued for any number of entries, from as little as one entry to as many as multiple (unlimited) entries, for the same purpose of travel. If you travel frequently as a tourist for example, with a multiple entry visa, you do not have to apply for a new visa each time you want to travel to the U.S. As an example of travel for the same purpose, if you have a visitor visa, it cannot be used to enter at a later time to study in the U.S. The visa validity is the length of time you are permitted to travel to a port-of-entry in the U.S. to request permission of the U.S. immigration inspector to permit you to enter the U.S. The visa does not guarantee entry to the U.S. The Expiration Date for the visa should not be confused with the authorized length of your stay in the U.S., given to you by the U.S. immigration inspector at port-of-entry, on the Arrival-Departure Record, Form I-94, or I-94W for the Visa Waiver Program. The visa expiration date has nothing to do with the authorized length of your stay in

Copyright © 2011 - GreenCard123.Com by UNorth® - All Rights Reserved

	the U.S. for any given visit.		hearing before an immigration judge or an expedited removal.
Visa Waiver Program	Allows citizens of certain selected countries, traveling temporarily to the United States under the nonimmigrant admission classes of visitors for pleasure and visitors for business, to enter the United States without obtaining nonimmigrant visas. Admission is for no more than 90 days. The program was instituted by the Immigration Reform and Control Act of 1986 (entries began 7/1/88). Under the Guam Visa Waiver Program, certain visitors from designated countries may visit Guam only for up to 15 days without first having to obtain nonimmigrant visitor visas.	**Work authorization**	If you are not a citizen or a lawful permanent resident, you may need to apply for an Employment Authorization Document to prove you may work in the U.S. To learn more visit USCIS's webpage.
		Work permit	Employment authorization document
Visa Waiver Program (VWP)	Citizens of participating countries meeting the Visa Waiver Program requirements to may be allowed to enter the U.S. as visitors for pleasure or business without first getting a visa. Visitors can stay only 90 days and cannot extend their stay. Go to our information on the Visa Waiver Program to learn more.		
Voluntary Departure	The departure of an alien from the United States without an order of removal. The departure may or may not have been preceded by a hearing before an immigration judge. An alien allowed to voluntarily depart concedes removability but does not have a bar to seeking admission at a port-of-entry at any time. Failure to depart within the time granted results in a fine and a ten-year bar to several forms of relief from deportation.		
Voluntary Service Program	An organized project that a religious or nonprofit charitable organization does to provide help to the poor or needy or to further a religious or charitable cause. Participants may be eligible for B visas.		
Waiver of Ineligibility	In immigration law certain foreign nationals are ineligible for visas to enter the U.S. for medical, criminal, security or other conditions and activities. Some applicants for visas are able to apply for permission to enter the U.S. despite the ineligibility. The applicant must apply for permission to enter the U.S. (waiver). See Classes of Aliens Ineligible to Receive Visas for more information.		
Withdrawal	An arriving alien's voluntary retraction of an application for admission to the United States in lieu of a removal		

Copyright © 2011 - GreenCard123.Com by UNorth® - All Rights Reserved

Index

Copyright © 2011 - GreenCard123.Com by UNorth® - All Rights Reserved

D

E

F

G

H

I

Copyright © 2011 - GreenCard123.Com by UNorth® - All Rights Reserved

Copyright © 2011 - GreenCard123.Com by UNorth® - All Rights Reserved

Copyright © 2011 - GreenCard123.Com by UNorth® - All Rights Reserved